O'Briens
wine · beer · spirits

Exclusive importers of 350
award winning wines from
60 wineries worldwide

www.obrienswines.ie

The Best of Wine in Ireland 2007

© A. & A. Farmar 2006
© Articles by the named contributors 2006

All rights reserved. No text may be reproduced in any medium or storage system without permission from the publishers or else under the terms of any licence permitting limited copying issued by the Irish Copyright Licensing Agency. The database of which this book is an emanation is copyright of A. & A. Farmar Ltd.

British Library Cataloguing in Publication Data
A CIP catalogue record for this book is available from the British Library

ISBN(10) 1-899047-61-1
ISBN(13) 978-1-899047-61-1

Published by
A. & A. Farmar
78 Ranelagh Village, Dublin 6
Ireland
Tel (01) 496 3625 Fax (01) 497 0107
afarmar@iol.ie

Editorial director: Anna Farmar

Production director: Tony Farmar

Contributions by Niamh Boylan, Pat Carroll, Katherine Farmar, Kevin Summons-Walsh, John Wilson

Cover design by Brosna Press
Typesetting by Bookworks
Printed and bound by ColourBooks

The Best of Wine in Ireland

2007

Edited by
John Wilson

A. & A. Farmar

Contents

Reference section

Indexes

Publishers' foreword

Welcome to the twelfth annual edition of *The Best of Wine in Ireland*.

Since we started this project twelve years ago there have been enormous changes in the Irish wine market. Among these changes are a deepening of the range and quality of wines available in Ireland, and a matching change in the number of people interested in wine. A comparison of the 1996 *Best of Wine in Ireland* with the current edition will show how regular improvements in the book have echoed these changes. (We have a few copies left of most editions if anyone would like to complete their set.)

This year's edition is edited once again by John Wilson who was involved at every stage from the selection of wines to the lively introductions to the countries. We are grateful for the calm, enthusiasm and authority he has once again brought to the task. This year Pat Carroll once again brought her unique combination of wine knowledge and copy-editing skills to the great improvement of the book.

It would not be possible to produce *The Best of Wine in Ireland*, year after year, without the generous support we receive from the wine trade. We would like to thank especially the distributors who submit samples and more-or-less patiently respond to our requests for further information. Denis Byrne of the Wicklow Arms of Delgany stored and looked after the wines for us while the initial tasting was in progress. A special thanks once again to Mitchells who loaned us their splendid first floor rooms for the star tastings.

We would also like to thank the tasters who give so freely of their time and experience to evaluate the wines.

We are always happy to hear from new distributors of interesting wines. If you would like to participate in the next edition, please contact us in Spring 2007.

Anna and Tony Farmar
October 2006

A mouth-watering feast of wines

Welcome to the twelfth annual edition of *The Best of Wine in Ireland*. For over a decade we have picked for your enjoyment the very best wines available on the Irish market. I have been involved in most editions, initially as a member of the tasting panel, and more recently as editor. Working on the book offers a fantastic opportunity to see how the wine market has developed in Ireland, and to track changing tastes over a period of remarkable growth in interest, knowledge and consumption of wine in this country.

For this edition, I tasted over 2,000 wines from 72 importers, a mammoth task that took most of the summer. This year, the number of wines worth a place in the book has crept up to 727 compared to the 540 wines that featured in last year's edition. This increase is largely due to the importers being more canny in submitting wines, selecting only those that they truly believe are the best in their stable. I am delighted with this, and believe that this year's selection is stronger than ever.

Here is a mouth-watering feast of wines, including a great many that are new to the market. A major innovation this year is the inclusion of stockists for most of the wines (some of course are so new to the market that stockists cannot yet be listed). Many of you in the past have suggested this; it is only possible now with the improved databases of the importers. I wish to thank the importers for their help and assistance, willingly supplying samples of their wines. Without them there would be no guide. I hope that they will sell lots more wine as a result.

The award winners in this edition are outstanding wines in their field, worthy of the accolade. I know I shall return to them many times throughout the coming year. Although no particular style won out this year, I do believe that each wine is individually great, and stands out from its peers. I hope that you agree. On the other hand, you should not ignore the other wines. The wines in this book won their places after a strict selection process; they are all worth going out of your way to buy. I hope that this edition adds in some way to your enjoyment of what I think is the world's greatest beverage.

Happy drinking!

John Wilson

Importer of the Year

The Importer of the Year is the one whose wines, as selected for the book, have scored the highest average overall mark. This year the clear winner is the Wicklow Wine Co. whose wines scored consistently highly across the board. Previous winners of the award include Comans, Findlaters, Karwigs, O'Briens and Tyrrell and Co.

The Wicklow Wine Co.

Over the last decade, as the wine business has grown exponentially, many of the old traditions have died out. These days most wine companies are driven by accountants and marketing departments interested solely in volume and margin. The smaller individual producers can find it difficult to find importers willing to take the time and effort to sell their lesser-known, but often far more interesting, wines. It is vital that we support those smaller specialist companies driven by people with a real passion for wine.

I had the pleasure of working with the two people behind the Wicklow Wine Co., Ben Mason and Michael Anderson, for several years, and know them better than most. They are driven by a real love of wine, and take a purist pleasure in seeking out the best and the different, rather than taking the easy option.

Each has his own obsession in life. Ben has sourced an exciting, eclectic range of wine from two countries—Portugal and Germany. Portugal is represented by the wonderful table wines and ports of Niepoort, the great value wines of Quinta de Cabriz, and many others besides. From Germany, the Wicklow Wine Co. offers the thrilling, full-bodied, dry Rieslings of Georg Breuer and Bassermann-Jordan, alongside the exquisitely delicate Mosels of Richter.

Michael spent a number of years working in France, and knows the people, the language and culture well. His side of the business lies in the less well-trodden paths of France, often offering some staggering bargains. The list includes Domaine Tunel and Domaine Martin, and the varietals of the Ardèche; one of the great producers of the Languedoc, Domaine d'Aupilhac, and a host of wines from the South West, including this year's award-winning Château Court-Les-Mûts.

This only scratches the surface of what is on offer from the Wicklow Wine Co. At times, Ben and Michael must drive their accountant mad, bringing in small parcels from all over Europe. A trip to their small shop in Wicklow is always a real pleasure, one I do not make nearly often enough these days. There is usually some wine open, usually 'something interesting' that one of the two has unearthed on a trip abroad. If you don't live near the town of Wicklow, they also distribute their wines to a number of similar specialist shops dotted round the country. In a world that is becoming smaller, where everything is becoming more similar, theirs are the sort of wines that are worth going the distance to find.

Michael Anderson (left) and Ben Mason at the Wicklow Wine Co.

The Wicklow Wine Co., Main Street, Wicklow.
Tel (0404) 66767 Email wicklowwineco@eircom.net

Wines of the year

White Wine of the Year

Grosset Polish Hill Riesling 2005
Clare Valley, Australia

Liberty Wines €26.49

I had the pleasure of meeting Jeffrey Grosset for a second time when he visited Ireland earlier this year. He has a quiet, modest demeanour, which masks the intense, determined side of his character. Make no mistake, Grosset has one aim in life—to make great wine in his own uncompromising style. All of his wines are excellent (look out for Gaia, his red wine), but his reputation has been made on Riesling, and on Polish Hill Riesling in particular. It is undoubtedly one of the great Rieslings of the world, a wine that shows a delicious austerity in its youth, but with the ability to age for years.

Polish Hill is in the Clare Valley, a historic area north of Adelaide in South Australia. Clare Valley Riesling has a unique style, the result of cooler breezes coming in off the gulfs to the west and a higher altitude. The alcohol is lower, the fruit crisp and elegant, often with a mineral streak. It is not always the most crowd-pleasing style, and a mile away from the big, rich Australian wines we know so well. Jeffrey Grosset is confident about the future. 'We can afford to ignore the UK writers and Robert Parker too. After a hundred and fifty years we know what we can do, and what we can't do; we can offer vintage variety and typicity.' The Polish Hill vineyard is one of the coolest in the valley, sited on less generous shale soils that stress the vine and reduce berry size. It was originally owned by a Pole, Joseph Niemitz, in 1857, who was then joined by many of his countrymen.

Grosset is not from a winemaking family, but early on he shared his parents' interest in wine. At the age of 16, he attended agricultural college and went on to Roseworthy College. He began making wine at the age of 21. Riesling, says Grosset, 'is the variety that best expresses where it comes from'. His Watervale Riesling is more generous, more forward, with a broader palate, but still held in rein by mouth-watering lime acidity.

Jeffrey Grosset

Those of you still convinced that Australia makes only big, brash white wines should be forced to try last year's award-winning white, Tyrrell's Vat 1 Hunter Valley Semillon, alongside this wine. Both are complex, restrained, world-class wines that sit quite comfortably among the world's great white wines.

This is the 25th vintage of Polish Hill Riesling, a worthy way to celebrate one of Australia's great wines. It is a wine of wonderful purity and austerity, lean, but with subtle floral nuances, great concentration of flavour and huge length. It is drinking beautifully now, a wine that will thrill the Riesling aficionado; but it will certainly develop further over the next decade. I, for one, intend buying a case, and would strongly suggest that you do likewise.

Tasting note:
Brilliant, cool Riesling. The nose is lightly aromatic, the palate still very tight, with a strong mineral streak, along with intense crunchy green-apple fruit. It is austere, but not short of fruit, with finely etched acidity. The impression is of an incredibly restrained, elegant wine with a huge follow-through. Drink now or hold up to a decade.

Available from: Le Caveau, Kilkenny

The Best of Wine in Ireland 2007

Red Wine of the Year

Muga Selección Especial Rioja Reserva 2001
Rioja, Spain

Comans €24.95

This year, Rioja triumphs again, winning Red Wine of the Year. Last year it was Bodegas Alvaro Palacios, this year Bodegas Muga. While Palacios would be seen by many as one of the leaders of the modern style of Rioja, and Muga exponents of old-style wines, both share a determination to produce the finest wine possible.

Rioja is the best-known wine region of Spain. In this country, we drink large quantities of its wine. One of the few wines released on the market already aged and ready to drink, most Rioja is a blend of two to four different Spanish grape varieties. Traditionally, Tempranillo provided the elegance, Garnacha the power, Graciano the staying power, and Mazuelo a peppery, slightly robust touch. These days, Tempranillo plays the leading role in most quality Rioja.

La Rioja Alta

Bodegas Muga is situated in La Rioja Alta, the highest and coolest part of Rioja, noted for its fine and elegant wines. This is one of the best estates in Rioja, family-owned since its foundation in 1932 by Isaac Muga and his wife Aurora Caño. Everything here is done by hand, with meticulous attention paid to detail at every stage. Muga has 70 hectares of vines and its own cooperage to ensure the highest-quality oak. It is one of the last bodegas to fine the wines with egg whites. Tradition is everything here, and the company has a reputation for making the very finest 'old-style' Riojas; these are wines that are given lengthy ageing in oak barriques prior to bottling. The Muga Prado Enea Gran Reserva 1996, featured elsewhere in this book, is a textbook example.

In recent years, most companies have begun producing a 'modern'-style Rioja, aged for a shorter period in oak barrels and in bottle prior to release. The Selección Especial straddles the two ideas; it is aged for almost three years in new oak, and has the potential to mature and develop further in bottle. However, it has the softness and approachability of the old style.

The vineyards used for Selección Especial are at a higher altitude, with 35-year-old vines. The wine is made from 70 per cent Tempranillo, 20 per cent Garnacha and 10 per cent Mazuelo and Graciano. The wine is aged for 30 months in new oak barriques, 80 per cent French. It is a fine wine in the true sense, rich in flavour but complex, elegant and perfectly balanced in the mouth. It will please both traditionalists and modernists, a

Jorge Muga

wine that is dangerously easy to drink. Being relatively low in tannin, it should prove a perfect all-rounder with a wide variety of foods, particularly meat and cheese dishes. It is a worthy winner, a wine that is already a firm favourite in this country.

Tasting note:
This has everything; elegance combined with real concentration in the developing blackcurrant and cherry fruits, hints of vanilla spice and a lovely long-drawn-out finish with some peppery dry tannins. Try it with plain roast lamb.

Available from: Callans, Dundalk; Jus de Vine, Portmarnock; McHughs, Kilbarrack & Malahide Road; The Mill Wine Cellar, Maynooth; Next Door, Enfield; Terrys, Limerick

The Best of Wine in Ireland 2007

Sparkling Wine of the Year

Joseph Perrier Cuvée Royale Brut Champagne 1996
Champagne, France

Comans €41.86

This is the first time that the same wine has won a Wine of the Year award on two occasions. Not only that, but it was just pipped at the post last year. This time around, it clearly beat all rivals at the star tasting.

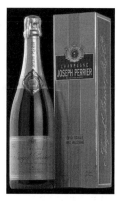

Joseph Perrier is one of the smaller champagne houses, owned by the same family since its inception in 1825. The current proprietor is Jean-Claude Fourman. It is not one of the glitzy, heavily branded names that you will come across in glossy magazines; nor does it always receive its fair share of coverage from wine journalists. However, it regularly carries off prizes for its excellent non-vintage Brut, as well as the vintage. The price is also worth noting—considerably less than many of the entry-level non-vintage champagnes of other, better-known companies. I would argue that it is a real bargain.

The 1996 vintage was excellent in Champagne, one noted for its outstanding structure and acidity, which have allowed the best wines to age wonderfully. This is a champagne for the true connoisseur, a complex wine that is maturing beautifully, but with plenty of time left. It is beginning to show wonderful, rich, biscuity flavours with hints of honey and mushroom, all held together perfectly by a firm backbone of acidity. Joseph Perrier considers this its best vintage since 1950. It is made from a blend of wines from 15 *grand cru* vineyards (the best quality in Champagne) 50 per cent Chardonnay, 45 per cent Pinot Noir and a tiny percentage of Pinot Meunier. It was aged in the cellars for four years before disgorgement.

Tasting note:
Delicately fruity and toasty nose. Serious power, however, on the palate, with a melange of honey, pears and apples. Lovely balance of acidity with fruit—the rich centre palate carries through to a finish that shows finesse and a creamy elegance.

Available from: Cheers, Bray; Corks, Terenure; O'Dwyers, Navan; O'Neills, SCR; Uncorked, D16; Wine Deli, Waterford

Dessert Wine of the Year

Château Court-les-Mûts Saussignac 2001
South West France

Wicklow Wine €16.96 per half-bottle

Why is it that so many wine-drinkers, reared on sweet fizzy drinks and addicted to the dessert trolley and chocolate, turn up their noses at dessert wines? These are some of the great treasures of the wine world, wines that work well with most desserts, but also a great many savoury dishes. I frequently prefer a glass of something sticky to a dessert.

This is the first French dessert wine to receive the award since its inception four years ago, a surprise to me, as they produce some of the great sweet wines of the world. If you enjoy balanced sweet wines, wines with a refreshing edge, rather than masses of residual sugar, there are two areas to seek out. One is the Loire Valley, the other South West France. Not only are the wines excellent, but often they are ridiculously cheap.

Pierre-Jean Sadoux

Saussignac is a relatively new *appellation contrôlée*, created only in 1982. It lies between the vineyards of Monbazillac and those of Bordeaux in South West France. Château Court-les-Mûts is the property of Pierre-Jean Sadoux. It was bought by his father when he returned from Algeria in 1960. Pierre-Jean joined in the early 1970s, having completed his degree in oenology at Bordeaux University. Today, in turn, his own son, Pierre-Vincent, is learning the ropes. They now have 14 people working on the estate, which has 70 hectares under vine. The property also produces dry white and red wines under the Bergerac appellation.

Court-les-Mûts Saussignac is made from 100 per cent Sémillon, with an average age of over fifty years. In most years, there are three *tris*, or passes, made through the vineyards over the period of a month. This enables pickers to select only those grapes that have been affected by noble rot, a curious and much-sought-after botrytis that concentrates the flavours and richness of the grapes. In order to allow the development of noble rot, growers must wait until mid-October, and pick well into November, with all the attendant risks. The wine is fermented in 100 per cent new French oak barriques, and is aged for a further 18 months prior to bottling.

The Court-les-Mûts has developed significantly over the last year, when it was dominated by fresh pear and apricot fruits; now it has added a distinct barley sugar and spice character, with some orange too, whilst still retaining a delicious freshness. It works very nicely with desserts, foie gras, blue cheese, or just by itself.

Tasting note:
Rich marzipan and barley sugar aromas; intense barley sugar and almonds given real life by some tangy orange-peel acidity and a wonderfully clean finish. Beautifully balanced dessert wine. A superb, mature wine and a worthy winner of this year's award.

Available from: Corkscrew, D2; Fallon & Byrne, D2; French Flair, Tralee; Hand Made Wines, Lismore, Co. Waterford; Harvest, Galway; Jus de Vine, Portmarnock; Listons, D2; Louis Albrouze, D2; Michael's Wines, Mount Merrion; Mitchells, Kildare Street & Glasthule; Morton's, Ranelagh; On the Grapevine, Dalkey; Power & Smullen, Lucan; Probus Wines, Oughterard; Red Island, Skerries; Redmonds, Ranelagh; Wicklow Wine Co.

Old World White Wine of the Year

Château des Rontets Clos Varambon Pouilly-Fuissé 2003

Burgundy, France

Searsons €23

Pouilly-Fuissé lies in Mâcon, in the larger, southern part of Burgundy. It is a region that produces a great many excellent wines, often at very reasonable prices. Here the growing season lasts longer, and the resulting wines are often richer than their counterparts further north. But 2003, that scorching hot summer in France, caused great difficulties in Burgundy, especially in Mâcon. Many of the wines are clumsy and over-alcoholic. Yet Château des Rontets succeeded in producing an award-winning wine, rich but refreshing, and with the all-important acidity to provide real balance.

The key may lie in the estate's location. I quote an email sent to me by Searson's wine buyer Kate Barrett:

> Absolutely the coldest vineyard I have ever visited but with amazing views, on the top of the hill above the village, a beautiful old house but in need of repair, nothing flash, doing it all slowly with any extra cash going into the cellar. I have just always loved the incredible purity of fruit but also really good integration, and felt that it was weighing in well and outclassing many other bigger names.

Claire Gazeau and Fabio Montrasi

The estate has been in the hands of the Gazeau-Varambon family since 1850, but until recently all the grapes were sold off to *négociants*. It was only with the arrival of architect Claire Gazeau from Paris and her Italian husband that things began to change. Slowly they began to renovate the chais and the château, and to improve the quality of the grapes. All the vines lie in a single plot surrounding the château, on the top of a hill known as Les Rontets, near the village of Fuissé, overlooking the famous rock of Solutré. A small parcel of vines dates back to 1910; the rest were planted between 1950 and 1960. The vineyard is organically farmed, and is awaiting full certification. The wine is fermented in old oak casks, without the addition of sugar or acid, using indigenous yeasts.

Fifteen years ago, Pouilly-Fuissé was an often-abused name, making overpriced, inferior wines. Since then, we have seen a number of top-class estates setting themselves apart from the pack, producing excellent wines of real quality. Château des Rontets is clearly one of these.

Tasting note:
Honeyed, rich nose; complex, taut, youthful green fruits. It has plenty of new oak, but excellent length, and some very well-defined lime and toasted nut flavours.

Available from: O'Driscolls, Cahirciveen; Red Island, Skerries; Searsons, Monkstown

New World Red Wine of the Year

Felton Road Pinot Noir 2004
Central Otago, New Zealand

WineKnows €38

This is not the first time Felton Road has won an award; their excellent Riesling was Best New World White two years ago. But it is Pinot Noir that made the reputation of Felton Road, a wine that is known and revered throughout the wine world. Englishman Nigel Greening was one such fan; so much so that he purchased his own vineyard in Central Otago, determined to make a similar wine. On his arrival, he discovered the winery was for sale, and promptly bought it.

Central Otago has been the rising star of New Zealand for the last decade. In a country that has had difficulty ripening red grapes fully, it has proved the perfect location to grow that most difficult and fussy variety, Pinot Noir. Central Otago is the only wine-producing region in New Zealand to have a continental climate, with its bitterly cold winters, and a long growing season with cool nights—not unlike Burgundy, the Kiwis figured, and how right they were. Along with Martinborough, also in New Zealand, and Oregon in the US, this is one of the few places outside Burgundy that has succeeded with this variety. The trademark Central Otago Pinot has perfectly ripe cherry and bramble fruit, with a delicious piquancy, and a streak of refreshing acidity.

Blair Walter, Felton Road winemaker (left) and Nigel Greening, Felton Road owner

In less than two decades, Felton Road has established itself as one of the great boutique wineries. However, Nigel Greening still retains a refreshing honesty and modesty. Talk to him for two minutes, and you will realise that this man is a Pinot nut, a man who tastes widely and frequently. I came across him at a burgundy press tasting in London earlier this year. The sole problem with his winery is one of quantity; all their wines sell out very rapidly each year, and Ireland receives only a small allocation. If you are interested in trying one of the world's great Pinots, I suggest that you do it sooner rather than later!

Tasting note:

Very fragrant perfumed aromas, with some elegant red fruits; this is very good—refined, smooth redcurrants, cherries and black-berries in a juicy, quite concentrated wine, with well-judged new oak. A delicious wine that is a joy to drink.

Available from: Connoisseur Wines, Dundalk; Fallon & Byrne, Dublin 2; Jus de Vine, Portmarnock; Le Caveau, Kilkenny; On the Grapevine, Booterstown and Dalkey

White Wine of the Year for under €20

Springfield Estate Life from Stone Sauvignon Blanc 2005

Robertson, South Africa

Papillon €18.50

Every wine-producing region needs someone to push the boundaries and try something new. Springfield Estate in Robertson is one such winery. Abrie Bruwer is the winemaker, an intelligent, thoughtful man who does not wish to make the standard, commercial style of wine; his sister, the irrepressible Jeanette, sells the stuff. Together they form a formidable team, responsible for some of South Africa's most interesting wines; there are three reds, all Cabernet-based, two Chardonnays and two Sauvignons.

Abrie Bruwer is constantly experimenting, using natural yeasts, bottling his wines unfined and unfiltered, even making Tokaji-style sweet wines in his cellar. Occasionally it all goes wrong, but Bruwer would prefer this to consistent mediocrity. But usually it all goes right, and the wines are brilliant; individual, hand-crafted wines full of character that stand out from the crowd.

Robertson is a strange place for Sauvignon to find a home. It is very hot and dry, conditions usually better suited to big reds. But there are several things that make Robertson perfect for white wine, and Sauvignon in particular. There is the limestone-quartz soil, with its ability to drain excess rain but retain moisture at the same time—it is great for horses too, the other main occupation in the Robertson Valley. Although temperatures are high during the day, they drop rapidly at night, as the south-east winds come in from the Atlantic 100 kilometres away. This fluctuation in temperature (which also occurs in Marlborough, New Zealand's premier Sauvignon district) is ideal for creating the aromatic qualities present in all great Sauvignon. Life from Stone is certainly not short of aromatics; it is an intensely lively, crisp wine with the finest of green fruits, citrus peel and classic Sauvignon aromas of gooseberries and peas.

Tasting note:
Very aromatic nose—peas and honeysuckle; intense fruits on the palate too, with delicate, very ripe pea pods and elderflowers, finishing dry; very light, very well made, and no lack of flavour. One to thrill the Sauvignon aficionado.

Available from: Bin No. 9, Goatstown; Cellars, Naas Road; Corkscrew, D2; Grape Escape, Lucan; O'Briens; Redmonds, Ranelagh

The Best of Wine in Ireland 2007

Red Wine of the Year for under €20

Torbreck Woodcutter's Shiraz 2004
Barossa Valley, Australia

O'Briens €15.49

I was delighted to see this wine win through. It is textbook Barossa Shiraz, rich and powerful, but not over-ripe. For my money, it is one of the best-value Aussie wines on the market. It is also made by a brilliant winemaker, Dave Powell. Powell worked for five years with the legendary Barossa winemaker Robert O'Callaghan before setting up his own operation. This is an old milking shed, with the most basic of equipment, and an Irish-style cottage out the back as the visitor centre. Wines are made in open-top fermenters, and Powell buys in hand-picked grapes from some of the oldest vineyards in the Barossa. All the wines are vineyard-specific, and many are very expensive—collectors' items in the US and Australia.

The Woodcutter's Shiraz is a reference to Powell's time working in the forests of Scotland. It is big and bold, but all perfectly in balance. Try it with grills, barbecues or hearty casseroles.

Dave Powell

Tasting note:
Big, rich, intense wine filled with soft, overripe berries and figs—big, beautiful, full-on wine with lush, sweet fruit.

Available from: O'Briens

Best Value White Wine of the Year

M&S Mineralstein Riesling Deutscher Tafelwein 2005

Rhein-Mosel, Germany

Marks & Spencer €9.99

Here's an experiment for you to try: the next time you have friends around for a drink, casually serve them a glass of this wonderful wine without telling them what it is. I guarantee you they will like it. Mention that it is a German Riesling and they will wrinkle their noses. A great many people, especially those over forty, equate German Riesling with sweet Liebfraumilch. Strange really, as Liebfraumilch contains no Riesling, and a great many German Rieslings are dry.

New World Riesling, from New Zealand in particular, has become very fashionable recently. The Germans owe them a debt of gratitude. They should also thank the forward-thinking buyers at Marks & Spencer for dreaming up this wine and being able to sell it at such an incredibly cheap price. It is from vines selected by Gerd Stepp and Matthias Gaul, an unusual blend of Riesling from two areas: the Mosel for delicacy and the warmer Rheinpfalz for richness. Put together, they make for a wonderful, fresh, crisp, dry (well, just off-dry) wine with delicious pear and apple fruits. It is the sort of wine that you will need to stock up on. It is a brilliant all-rounder, a party wine, an aperitif, or with most fish and seafood.

Gerd Stepp

Tasting note:
Delicious, fresh, crisp green-apple fruit set off by some racy acidity—summery, delightful—how could anyone fail to like it?

Available from: Marks & Spencer

GOLDEN KAAN
A TOUCH OF LUXURY

Adventure, breathtaking nature, a touch of luxury.
That is South Africa, that is GOLDEN KAAN.
Enjoy this excellent wine in four different varietals!

www.goldenkaan.com

Ninguén
MOUNTAIN VINEYARD

ONLY FROM THE BEST TERROIR
CAN THE FINEST WINE BE CRAFTED

The Best of Wine in Ireland 2007

Best Value Red Wine of the Year

Golden Kaan Shiraz 2003
Western Cape, South Africa

Greenhills €8.99

Each year I wonder will we come across a sufficient number of decent, reasonably-priced wines to include in *The Best of Wine in Ireland*. Each year I am pleasantly surprised that a large number succeed in winning places against much more expensive competition. This year, half a dozen reds were in contention for Best Value Red, including a new vintage of last year's winner, the Cono Sur Pinot Noir from Chile. However, after a number of tastings it was the Golden Kaan Shiraz that stood out. The Golden Kaan range is the result of a joint venture between German giant Racke and KWV, an equally large South African wine producer. So far, the range has sold over ten million bottles worldwide, which in itself does not guarantee anything. However, the Shiraz is a very nicely crafted wine. Soft, ripe and easy, with plenty of spice, just enough structure, and no drying tannins on the finish, it is a great all-purpose, easy-drinking wine that is unlikely to offend, and will very definitely please most palates.

The grapes are gathered from warm-climate areas around Paarl, to the north of Stellenbosch. The wine is aged in American oak to give it that warm, spicy richness and softness on the palate. Chief winemaker Sterik de Wet obviously knows how to put together a very decent glass of drinkable wine, and we should all be grateful for that.

Tasting note:
Warm, ripe, inviting strawberries and smooth damsons, with lightly spicy oak in a nicely rounded, supple wine. A great all rounder to please everyone; ideal with most meat and cheese dishes.

Available from: Eurospar; Mace; SPAR; SPAR Express

Views and issues

'CONNOISSEUR, n. A specialist who knows everything about something and nothing about anything else. An old wine-bibber having been smashed in a railway collision, some wine was poured on his lips to revive him. "Pauillac, 1873," he murmured, and died.'

Ambrose Bierce
The Devil's Dictionary

Problems in France Pat Carroll

The French wine industry is in crisis. Not all of it—the top tier is doing very well—but the middle-ranking and bottom tiers are struggling in many areas. Competition, especially from the New World, has left French winemakers with vast quantities of wine that they cannot sell. At the moment, subsidies pay for surplus wine to be distilled and turned into industrial alcohol, but new EU proposals aim to end this funding and grub up vineyards in an effort to 'encourage uncompetitive producers to leave the sector'.

Wine consumption in France is falling, Australia and Chile have knocked France into the number three slot in Ireland, and French wine producers in the south are protesting in the streets. The demonstrations are led by CRAV (Regional Committee for Viticultural Action), which is demanding financial support from the government. The producers' situation is serious, with many bankruptcies and falling land prices. In the Languedoc, wine producers' unions have predicted that 30–50 per cent of their wineries could close over the next few years.

The worst-affected areas have seen violent direct action: €2 million worth of damage to the French railway system in the south; a bomb thrown through a call centre window near Montpellier; a Bordeaux *négociant*'s office raided and thousands of hectolitres of wine destroyed; attacks on tankers carrying Italian and Spanish wine. Protests and subsidies are responses to a crisis, but, in the long term, French winemakers will have to deal with the market forces that created the situation. There is no problem with the best wines. Prices for top bordeaux keep rising and have reached stratospheric levels with the superb 2005 vintage, with increases of up to 300 per cent. Everyone wants *premier cru* burgundy and *cru classé* bordeaux, but when it comes to buying wine in the €6–12 price bracket, many consumers choose New World wines in preference to French. Why? Because they find the wines more approachable and easier to understand, with a grape variety named on the label and extra information on the back—back labels are still far too rare on French bottles. New World wines are often sealed with a screwcap instead of a cork, minimising the risk of spoilage. French wines are also complicated, with over 400 *appellations contrôlées* (ACs), which consumers can find intimidating—it's so much easier to go for Chilean Merlot or Australian Chardonnay. If your current favourite isn't on the shelf, there are plenty of other brands to choose from.

But the French are fighting back. It is an understatement to say that French winemakers are constrained by regulations, for example on labelling, but this is about to change. The government has accepted a report recommending clarification of the way AC wines are named and an end to the ban on naming grape varieties. This would allow grapes such as 'Merlot' or 'Cabernet Sauvignon' to appear in large letters on the front label, with 'AC Bordeaux' in smaller print. Oak chips and staves will also be permitted in the production of AC wines instead of expensive oak barrels, which will reduce costs. It will also become legal to use artificial means to reduce alcohol in wine, which could help the depressed home market, where drink-drive laws have led to a fall in consumption.

Will it be enough? One way forward is for the French to imitate the New World and produce more branded wines, which are much more cost-effective to market than a range of wines from hamlets all over France. A difficulty for French producers is that wines sourced from different regions and blended into one brand are not entitled to AC status. French producers find the idea of branded wines slightly distasteful, preferring to make wine closely associated with a local area (or *terroir*), but the signs are that this could change.

One factor in France's favour is that global wine consumption is rising. Despite the drop to third place in market share here, French wine imports into Ireland fell only slightly in 2005, as Irish per capita consumption continues to increase. Relaxing the labelling regulations will help the marketing initiatives of French marketing organisations such as Sopexa and will make French wines more accessible to the consumer. Whether these changes will be enough to stimulate sales in the depressed sectors remains to be seen.

Top ten sherries *Kevin Summons-Walsh*

Sherry is the most misunderstood, unfashionable, under-rated and under-priced wine style in the world. The word 'style' is used carefully, as sherries can be anything from light, very dry and crisp, to full bodied and nutty, even sweet. Why should *The Best of Wine in Ireland* bang on about such a dinosaur of a wine? The answer is obvious to anyone who has tried a good quality sherry—the trouble is that most people have not.

Choosing ten top sherries may seem a difficult task for some—and it is, but not for the difficulty of dredging up ten drinkable wines. There are so many high-quality, thoroughly enjoyable sherries available in Ireland today that the difficulties arise in cutting the list of chosen wines down to ten. One could literally stroll into Mitchell's, for example, and select any ten from the superb Lustau range—pick these as your top ten and you won't be disappointed.

This is a personal choice of sherries enjoyed over the last year, in no particular order. So, to quote Maria von Trapp, 'these are a few of my favourite drinks'.

Herederos de Argüeso 'San Leon' Manzanilla
€8 (37.5 cl)

Aromas transport you to the seaside—ozone, salty sea air. This is full bodied for a manzanilla, bone dry and salty, with almond and prawn flavours, and a very long finish. With its full-on taste, this is a mouth-watering aperitif. Manzanilla does not get any better.

Approach Trade

Lustau 'Jarana' Solera Reserva Fino
€10 (37.5 cl)

Having a subdued green olive nose, this is a dry, mouth-filling, full-bodied style of fino. It's crisp, with minerally green and black olive flavours, also nutty. This has a meaty olive finish, and is so very moreish. Big and bold.

Mitchell & Son

Tesco Finest Dry Oloroso
€10

It's nuts all the way on the nose, with toffee added in. This is full, rich and dry with a caramelly, walnutty flavour and an excellent finish. It's also incredible value for money—where else in the wine world can you find such high-quality wine, matured in the winery for at least three years, and at under a tenner?

Tesco

Barbadillo 'Principe' Amontillado

€36

A very almondy and coconut nose is followed by soft, round, smooth, salty, nutty toffee—there's a lot going on. Here you can definitely taste flavours of both fino and oloroso; by definition, this is how amontillado should taste! A classic of its style.

Berry Brothers & Rudd

Lustau 'Peninsula' Solera Reserva Palo Cortado

€13 (37.5 cl)

This has a fantastic, subtle nose of cold tea, creamy toffee and prunes, also brazil nut—quite complex. It's soft, full bodied, very dry with zappy acidity and caramel/toffee tastes. Very approachable, and has a delicate, long fruit and nut finish—wine for contemplation. The rarest type of sherry, and always good.

Mitchell & Son

Sanchez Romate 'Cardenal Cisneros' Pedro Ximénez

€26

Thick, heavy, black, decadently sweet—this vinous equivalent of Christmas pudding is a dessert in itself. Aromas and flavours of raisins, cream, fruitcake, rum and banoffi all vie for your attention; the length of finish is amazing. The only sweet sherry chosen, and simply perfect as a nightcap.

Findlater Grants

Gonzalez Byass 'Tio Pepe' Fino

€13

Yes, the old favourite makes an appearance on the list, as the archetypal fino. Simply because so much of this is produced, the consistency is always there. It has a very green olive nose, and it's mouth-wateringly dry. Zingy acidity complements the meaty olive flavours and almondy finish. Definitely should be a constant fixture in every fridge.

Barry Fitzwilliam Maxxium

Lustau ' Emperatriz Eugenia' Very Rare Oloroso

€18 (37.5 cl)

This has a deep amber colour, with a large, dark primrose rim indicating great age—at least twenty years in this case (Very Rare is a special designation). The oh-so-smooth nose is of walnuts, coconut, caramel, muscovado sugar, and all things brown and nice. On the palate it's bone dry, full bodied, with brazil nut, boudoir biscuit, brown sugar, burnt sugar—many flavours at once. Caramel and hazelnuts linger on your palate for fully three minutes. This is simply outstanding quality wine. Enjoy.

Mitchell & Son

Herederos de Argüeso Amontillado
€16

Now here's a sherry for aficionados. After an austere, salty, very mature nose the full-on, uncompromising salt and lemon flavours with honeyed toffee in the background provide a great example of old-fashioned, aged amontillado. Warning—this full-on style is not for the novice, but it certainly has the wow factor.

Approach Trade

Lustau Single Cask Almacenista Vides Palo Cortado
€42

Single cask sherries are the equivalent of a winemaker's top cuvee—la crème de la crème. As well as the usual brazil nut and toffee there are fruity olive oil aromas. It's so soft, round, and balanced with mouth-filling flavours—hazelnuts, caramel, vanilla, fruity coconut, meaty black olives. Complex, and the finish is quite amazing; you can't tell when the wine has been swallowed, the aftertaste is so strong and lasting.

Mitchell & Son

A simple plea to finish—please try a decent sherry !

Stickies and sweeties *Niamh Boylan*

The most misunderstood category of wines must surely be sweet wines. 'Heavens, no, never touch them' is a frequent response when offering someone a glass of dessert wine. BUT, there's sweet and sweeter, so let's de-mystify and look at some of these wonderful wines and how they can be enjoyed with food.

Sweet wine is produced all over the world in many different ways with varying degrees of sweetness. So, if your penchant is for something light and elegant with a subtle sweetness, or perhaps a full-on nectar and honeyed delight you'll find a style to excite your palate. France and Germany, Italy and Hungary have centuries-long traditions of producing sumptuous sweeties. In the New World, Australia and South Africa tend to lead the pack with their unique stickies, and Canada with its brilliant ice wine is a surprise member of the sweet brigade.

There are two general styles of sweet wine—the first where grapes are picked when over-ripe or when the bunches have been attacked by a friendly fungus called 'botrytis' or Noble Rot. Noble Rot is a term sometimes seen on New World wine labels. Its effect is to concentrate the sugars in the grapes resulting in a really delicious juice. The second category is one where the juice is fortified with grape spirit during fermentation resulting in a very rich sweet liquor with increased alcohol level.

Sweet wines have great eye appeal displaying a glorious range of colours, from the most delicate baby pink (Muscat de Rivasaltes), to rich straw gold (Sauternes and Barsac), and on to the intense polish of glowing amber (Tokaji and Vin Santo) and the deep tawny brick red of Banjuls).

When choosing a sweet wine remember to pick one which is sweeter than your dessert, otherwise the wine will taste sour. Acidity is an all-important element, bringing balance to any dessert wine—too little and the wine will taste flabby and yukky in the mouth. A surprising feature of sweet wine is that some can be drunk and enjoyed with savoury as well as sweet dishes. So—what to have with what, that is the question. The following suggestions are some of my own favourites, well tested by my love for sweet wine.

Let's deal with the lighter, less unctuous styles first and then move up the scale to the sumptuous (and usually expensive) special occasion styles. One of the lightest of all sweeties is grapey flavoured Asti. In Italy every other restaurant serves a little glass of Asti with that lovely wibbley-wobbley Panna Cotta dessert. It's also pretty good with Pavlova and icecream.

Southern France offers a wonderful variety of dessert wines, with ripe peach and orange blossom aromas. Jurançon is one of the most interesting, produced solely from the Petit Manseng grape. Lively floral and apricot flavours, lifted with fresh lemony acidity, make for a delicious wine well suited to fruit salads or blue cheese. Monbazillac is made from the same grapes as Sauternes, but is much lighter in style and also a good foil for fruit desserts. On the savoury front it can make an interesting match with Chinese dishes. The Golden Rule with wine, sweet included, is 'light wine with light delicate dishes and richer more unctuous styles with strongly flavoured foods.'

Germany and Austria have a long tradition of beautifully balanced sweeties, wines of great elegance and finesse and in many cases surprisingly low alcohol. The top category Beerenauslese and Trocken-beerenauslese are decadently sweet and nectar like. On the savoury front, German Riesling Auslese is pretty good with pork and duck as the acidity helps counteract the rich fatty meat. It is also good with onion quiche and simple poached fruit.

Australian stickies can be quite sensational—wonderful on their own but stunning with the right pudding. There are some gorgeous Rieslings and Semillons to choose from, perfect with caramel cream or sticky toffee pudding. California produces some fabulous exotic Muscat delights which are heavenly with pecan pie and chocolate- or orange-flavoured mousses.

Some of the most delicious and least known sweet wines come from the Anjou region of France. Produced from the Chenin Blanc grape these luscious lovelies have great aging potential. Look for Quarts de Chaume and Coteaux du Layon and enjoy with frangipane and fruit tarts, or with a mature blue cheese—fantastic! Muscat de Beaumes-de-Venise is also super with fruit tarts and crumbles and divine with summer pudding. Pink and posh.

Not all dessert wines are produced from white grapes. There are many gorgeous examples such as Banyuls from Southern France and the little known Brachetto, a sparkling red from Piedmont. It's a frisky, frivolous style with delightful flavours of fresh crushed strawberries—fancy an icecream anyone? Banyuls is altogether more serious and is one of the few wines which goes brilliantly with rich chocolate and mocha desserts. Maury is very similar—full of luscious moist treacley flavours. It has a particular affinity with dried fruit—think mince pies and Christmas pudding or perhaps that lovely Italian ice-cream dessert, Cassata.

Two wines with a very ancient and historic tradition are Tokaji from Hungary and Italy's Vin Santo. These should, of course, be served lightly chilled. Tart up a bread and butter pudding with a little glass of Tokaji, or perhaps one of the many yummy Aussie late-harvest Semillons. Vin Santo is not just for dipping your biscotti into, Tiramisu is even more sinful with a small glass. Vin Santo is also magic with sticky pudding.

And now to wines at the pinnacle of the sugar scale, famous, fabulous and utterly divine! Sauternes and Barsac are the ultimate expression of the most truly sweet and exotically flavoured of all dessert wines. Three grape varieties feature—Semillon, Sauvignon Blanc and Muscadelle. What makes these wines unique is the way the grapes are affected by botrytis. It imparts a complex, highly perfumed honeyed character to the wine, resulting in many layers of flavour. One of the greatest of food and wine matches is that of foie gras and Sauternes. How decadent is that! For another bit of magic try Sauternes with some ripe blue cheese (preferably Roquefort). But a fine Sauternes is very special and really deserves to be savoured very slowly, on its own, lingering over each ambrosial sip.

If after all these suggestions you still can't decide what to eat, just pour a glass, sit back and enjoy. Many sweet wines are bottles in 37.5 cl or 50 cl sizes and sit quite happily in the fridge for a few days, so you can have lots of little treats. The lighter styles are perfect as aperitif wines—a sophisticated alternative to Kir. Check out the chapter on sweet wines and you'll find a super selection to tantalise your taste buds.

Organic and biodynamic wines *Pat Carroll*

Organic wine

According to the EU regulations that govern so much of our lives, there is no such thing as organic wine. The European standard is for 'organically grown grapes', which are used to make wine that is loosely termed 'organic wine'. Strictly speaking, 'organic wine' is 'wine produced from organically grown grapes'—the term that appears on labels.

Organic growers do not use synthetic fertilisers, fungicides, herbicides or insecticides. Instead, they use natural fertilisers such as compost, manure and plants with fertilising abilities to nourish the soil to make it 'alive'. Most organic vineyards have herbs, grass and plants growing between the vines, to encourage biodiversity and make 'green manure' to keep the soil healthy. Organic principles extend beyond the vines to the whole vineyard ecosystem, where plant and animal diversity is encouraged.

Some counter-measures against pests and diseases are permitted. Sulphur and Bordeaux mixture (a spray composed of copper sulphate, lime and water) are used to protect vines from mildew. Spraying copper, which persists in the soil, seems a questionable practice for organic producers to follow, but it is permitted and the residues do not leach through to the wine if sufficient time is allowed between spraying and harvest. Albet i Noya, the Spanish organic producer, is experimenting with herbal preparations as a substitute for copper.

Canopy management techniques, which involve cutting back leaves to allow light and air to the vines, can be a substitute for fungicides. Natural predators are encouraged in the vineyard to eradicate pests: for example, ladybirds can be introduced to prey on red spider mites. Pheromones are used to attract destructive pests into sticky traps or to create sexual confusion, whereby grape berry moths, for example, find it hard to track down females among the profusion of pheromones in the vineyard, which prevents mating and keeps vines free from their berry- and leaf-eating caterpillar offspring.

In the winery, organic producers follow guidelines set by their local certification bodies. Rules vary between countries, but the organic approach is to apply eco-friendly principles and keep intervention in the winery to a minimum.

Producers in cooler northern Europe are allowed to chaptal-ise (add sugar—preferably organic—to increase alcohol levels in cooler years); those in the warmer Mediterranean countries can acidify using tartaric acid. Only natural, non-GM yeasts are allowed. Sulphur dioxide (E220), which is used in many foods as a preservative, is permitted in Europe at levels about a third less than conventional wines.

Not all organic growers declare themselves as such on their labels. The reasons are varied: they don't want to deal with all the form-filling required by the certifying authori-ties; they don't wish to be associated with the image of organic wines; or they want to keep their options open in case something drastic happens to the vines so that they can revert to spraying.

Well-known organic producers include Domaine Wein-bach and Domaine Eugène Meyer (Alsace); Fetzer's Bonterra range (California); Planeta (Italy); Perrin (Rhône); and Albet i Noya and Mas Igneus (Spain). Château de Beaucastel in the Rhône, Mas de Daumas Gassac and Domaine de Trévallon in the south of France and Ernst Loosen in Germany follow organic principles but don't apply for certification.

Biodynamic wine
Biodynamics takes the holistic concept a stage further than organics, and strives to create a balanced ecosystem that extends beyond the vineyard. It is based on the teachings of Rudolf Steiner (1861–1925), an Austrian who founded the philosophy of Anthroposophy, which tried to connect human spirituality with the spiritual nature of the universe, or cosmos. Proponents of Biodynamic theory argue that all the forces of the earth, sun, moon and stars should be harnessed to promote optimum growth and health in plants. It sees the cosmos as one interrelated whole. Growers following the system believe that the four elements of plant growth—root, leaf, flower and fruit—each relate to a particular phase of the moon. They rely on a Biodynamic sowing and planting calendar to decide when to carry out certain tasks. For example, grapes should be picked and wine bottled on a 'fruit day'. Marks & Spencer now holds its wine tastings on fruit days (when the moon is in front of fire signs Aries, Leo or Sagittarius), believing that the wines 'show' better on these days.

Homeopathic preparations made from yarrow, camomile, nettle, dandelion, oak, horsetail or valerian are sprayed on vines, soil or compost. No artificial or chemical treatments are allowed. Two preparations—ground quartz and cows' dung—are placed in cows' horns and buried during the winter. The somewhat sinister-sounding practice of spraying a solution of burned pests' bodies ('pest ashing') around the vineyard apparently discourages relatives of the cremated insects or animals from returning. The use of sulphur or Bordeaux mixture, the anti-mildew sprays allowed on organic vineyards, is permitted. As with organics, there is no Europe-wide certifying body. Demeter, the main certifying authority, regulates Biodynamic growers through member organisations in different countries. Standards for Biodynamic winemaking follow more or less the same principles as organic, with minimum intervention and lower sulphur dioxide levels than conventional wines.

Even those who are sceptical about the principles underlying Biodynamics (including some Biodynamics practitioners) are impressed by the quality of the wines the system produces. Some high-profile producers farm according to Biodynamic principles, among them Olivier Humbrecht of Domaine Zind Humbrecht (Alsace); Anne-Claude Leflaive of Domaine Leflaive and Lalou Bize-Leroy of Domaine Leroy (Burgundy); Nicolas Joly of Clos de la Coulée de Serrant in Savennières, Noël Pinguet of Domaine Huet in Vouvray and

Didier Dagueneau in Pouilly-Fumé (Loire); Michel Chapoutier (Rhône) (some wines); and Gérard Gauby of Domaine Gauby and Robert Eden of Comte Cathare (south of France). In the New World, producers include Millton Vineyards in New Zealand and Viñedos Emiliana Orgánicos in Chile. All these producers have found that using Bio-dynamic methods has given them fantastic wines, while sustaining the soil and preserving the environment.

Are these wines suitable for vegetarians or vegans?
Organic and Biodynamic wines are not necessarily suitable for vegetarians or vegans. Although the grapes contain no animal products (provided the aforementioned 'pest ashes' have been washed off), egg whites or isinglass made from fish swim bladders can be used to clarify ('fine') the wine. Wines fined with bentonite, a clay substance, are suitable for vegetarians and vegans. This will often be indicated on the label. Vegetarians and vegans could have a problem with Biodynamic preparations made using cows' horns. Manure is used liberally in both organic and Biodynamic vineyards, as it is in organic vegetable production, which could create difficulties for people who do not wish to exploit animals.

What are the benefits?
With organic or Biodynamic wines you are guaranteed a wholesome product (apart from a little sulphur dioxide in most cases) and the satisfaction of knowing that you are contributing to sustainable, environmentally friendly viti-culture. Organic and Biodynamic producers use smaller amounts of sulphur than conventional producers, which can be helpful for people with certain sensitivities.

How will I know which ones to try?
Organic and Biodynamic wines are just like all other wines in one important respect: their quality depends on the skill of the winemaker. The wines chosen for this book (indicated by **Organic**) have been independently tasted and assessed as the best on the market. If you haven't tried these wines, now is the time to do so. Standards have risen dramatically over the last few years and there has been an increase in the number of serious producers who have decided to follow organic/Biodynamic principles.

Where can I buy these wines?
Most importers have one or two organic/Biodynamic wines, but the main specialists are Mary Pawle Wines and Vendemia (see Distributors for contact details). The Irish market for organic wines is increasing, but not in line with demand for organic meat, fruit and vegetables, perhaps

because consumers are less aware of the heavy use of chemical sprays—herbicides, insecticides, fungicides—in conventional vineyards.

I am grateful to Mary Pawle and Urs Tobler for their help with research.

Sources
Hilary Wright, *The Great Organic Wine Guide* (Piatkus, London, 2000)
Monty Waldin, *Biodynamic Wines* (Mitchell Beazley, London, 2004)

Organic and biodynamic wines recommended in this guide

Wine name	Vintage	Colour	Price band	Page
Alain Chabanon Campredon Coteaux du Languedoc	2004	Red	€15–€18	103
Albet y Noya Col.leccio Penedès	1999	Red	€18–€22	175
Borghi IGT Pinot Grigio della Venezie	2005	White	€12–€15	118
Colli della Murgia Selvato IGT Puglia	2003	Red	€12–€15	125
Cullen Sauvignon Blanc Semillon	2004	White	€22–€30	14
Dom. Le Clos de Caveau Vacqueyras	2003	Red	€15–€18	89
Fetzer Bonterra Vineyards Chardonnay	2004	White	€15–€18	182
Jacques Frelin Caylus VdP des Côtes de Gascogne	2004	White	€9–€12	110
Jean Bousquet Malbec	2005	Red	€12–€15	4
La Coccinelle de la Grolet Côtes de Bourg	2003	Red	€9–€12	58
La Luna del Rospo Gil Storni Monferrato	2003	Red	€22–€30	132
Laibach The Ladybird	2004	Red	€18–€22	163
Le Moulin des Nonnes Cuvée Inés Minervois	2003	Red	€9–€12	100
Le Moulin des Nonnes Cuvée Inés Minervois	2004	White	€9–€12	96
Miguel Torres Tormenta Cabernet Sauvignon Reserva	2004	Red	€12–€15	44
Osoti Rioja Crianza	2003	Red	€12–€15	173
Parvus Privat Cabernet Rosé Alella	2005	Rosé	€12–€15	180
Rovero Rouve Barbera d'Asti Superiore	2000	Red	€22–€30	133
7 Days Malbec	2005	Red	Under €9	2

Tasters' choices

Every year we invite members of the tasters' panel to let their hair down and share recent special wine experiences with us. There is no limit—anything goes, from an exquisite 1945 Bordeaux to a Retsina enjoyed on a beach with that special someone. The only rule is that members of the trade may not enthuse about wines they themselves import.

Niamh Boylan
Charpentier Champagne Brut Prestige nv
Champagne, France €34.95

Like a famous grande dame from Champagne, I need no excuse to drink it. A real favourite this year is the Brut Prestige from a family domaine run by Jackie Charpentier. This is stylish stuff with a wonderful creamy palate—lots of fresh citrus flavours and hints of nutty bread with a fine yeasty richness. This certainly has the ability to match food—how about kedgeree or fish cakes, or the ultimate wine and food pairing, oysters? Super.
Wines Direct

Allegrini La Poja IGT Veronese 2001
Veneto, Italy €45–50

The ancient La Grola vineyard on a high plateau in the Veneto is the source of this amazing wine. La Poja is named after a small site in the La Grola, which grows quality Corvina grapes. From this wild and beautiful terrain comes a stunningly original wine from the Valpolicella Classico area. A wonderful nose entices the senses in a long seductive play. Rich, figgy, prune and cherry chocolate liqueur flavours are wrapped with a big tannic backbone and great acidity. This is a seriously big wine (14.3 per cent), so enjoy it with roast red meats and game. For a truly decadent experience, order a white truffle risotto and La Poja (in Italy of course). Well, it's just a thought.
Liberty Wines

Mount Horrocks Watervale Semillon 2003
Clare Valley, Australia €22

Not the most fashionable of grapes, Semillon is capable of producing some of the greatest classic wines. The feisty Stephanie Toole owns the Mount Horrocks boutique winery and here Semillon from the Watervale vineyard in the Clare Valley is an absolute smasher. The grapes are all hand-picked and the resulting wine shows great intensity of flavour and elegance. It's a rich, sumptuous style with a lush palate of ripe, honeyed quince and greengage fruit, lovely light toasty notes from French oak, and perfect tangy acidity. Definitely a foodie wine, it was just great with roast guinea fowl. I loved the long, silky finish—very, very classy.

Liberty Wines

Pat Carroll
Dom. Le Moulin des Nonnes Cuvée Inés Minervois Blanc 2004
South of France €10.99

I tasted this wine at one of the Best of Wine tastings and I thought it was brilliant—I also discovered it had the added benefit of lasting for several days in the fridge without losing flavour. Made from Roussanne, Grenache Blanc and Muscat Blanc à Petits Grains, it has concentrated fruitiness with spice and honey flavours. It's also organic, so it ticks that box as well. Great quality at this price.

Woodford Bourne

Produttori del Barbaresco Rio Sordo Barbaresco Riserva 1999
Piedmont, Italy €30–35

This year I went to northern Italy on a wine trip, and I can thoroughly recommend it as a place to visit. Apart from the wine, there are ancient towns and villages round every corner and wonderful food at great prices. One of the highlights of our trip was the visit to Produttori del Barbaresco, the rather prosaically named co-op that produces excellent Barbaresco. Before 1894, the Nebbiolo grapes grown in the region went into Barolo wines (just next door). It took the foresight of Domizio Cavazza, an Alba oenologist, to create the co-op, which today produces some of the best Barbaresco around. The wines are very drinkable, with an elegance and balance that make them superb with food. Their slight earthiness suits them well to game and truffle dishes (especially risotto), but they are pretty versatile in the food stakes. Made in the traditional way, the wine spends three years in huge old oak casks, followed by eight months in bottle, but the cherry-type fruit survives and flourishes, gaining extra dimensions of truffles and prunes. Although this wine isn't available in Ireland, Karwig imports other Barbarescos from the Produttori, all of which can be highly recommended.

Bisol Prosecco di Valdobbiadene Superiore di Cartizze nv
Veneto, Italy €32

I'm staying in northern Italy with my sparkling wine. Prosecco is a delightful sparkler, with soft flavours and low alcohol—only 11–11.5 per cent. Bisol is one of the top producers. Unusually for Prosecco, the Bisol family owns 50 hectares of vineyards, which gives it control over the whole winemaking process from vineyard to bottle. The Cartizze is a cru, taken from the stony, humid Cartizze hill, where grapes ripen slowly and achieve greater complexity. This certainly comes through in the wine, which is very full-flavoured for a Prosecco, with excellent acidity, rich grape/apple fruit and even a biscuity touch.
Searsons

Laurence Faller
Dom. Pierre Morey Le Montrachet 1985
Burgundy, France

Among my recent tastings, this Montrachet made a great impression on all the tasters. It combined richness with subtle elegance, showing concentrated and defined flavours of pear, honey and minerals, high extract, intensity and freshness. It was kindly brought by a friend and went perfectly with a fine lobster simply served with a touch of melted salted butter.

Ch. de Beaucastel Hommage à Jacques Perrin Châteauneuf-du-Pape 1990
Rhône, France

Black-ruby colour, generous, concentrated with deep flavours of cedar, spices and leather. Still young and a bit rough at the edges on its own, but perfect with the lamb dish we paired it with.

Boutari Moschofilero 2004
Peloponnese, Greece

Imagine a taverna on a beach in a Greek island at sunset. With superb grilled fish, my beloved one and I enjoyed this Moschofilero (white wine made from an ancient variety grown high in the Peloponnese). It was delicious, fresh, intensely aromatic (flowers, melon), with very good body and balance as well as a long finish.

Anne Mullin

Chateau Trimoulet St Emilion Grand Cru Classe 2000
Bordeaux, France €29.99

When it comes to red wine, I cannot resist the classics and this is one of the truly classic, elegant wines of St Emilion from the superb 2000 vintage. Aged in 100% new oak for 18 to 20 months. There are wonderful aromas of spicy warm bramble fruits and hints of vanilla and cedar wood. This well known St Emilion  has good savoury flavours, is full bodied with layers and layers of complex flavours and laden with ripe, luscious blackcurrant berries. It is rich, ripe and robust and beautifully balanced with a long, delicious finish and great length.

A superb wine, drinking beautifully now, soft, elegant and velvety and yet capable of ageing for years to come. One of the beauties of a St Emilion wine is that it is always very approachable while it is young yet has great ageing potential.

Findlater Grants

Marco D'Oro Valdo Prosecco di Valdobbiadene nv
Veneto, Italy €18.99

On a trip to Tuscany this summer I had the pleasure of tasting this sparkling wine, and imagine my delight when I returned and discovered it is now available in Ireland .
It is dry, crisp and so refreshing on the palate with lots of fresh, ripe, juicy melon and pear flavours and a hint of nutty almonds, yet with a long, smooth finish. Delicious to drink as an aperitif on a warm summer day or ideal with light summer dishes.

The Veneto Region in Northern Italy is the home of Prosecco, made from the grape by the same name and produced according to the Italian method of secondary fermentation which always produces a really fresh appealing fizz.

Febvre

Domaine Gillet Emilian Macon Village 2001
Burgundy, France €22.99

Nowadays good white burgundy is beyond the reach of the average wine drinker and is reserved for those extra special occasions. This wine, however, is a top-class burgundy at an affordable price. It is made with super-ripe Chardonnay grapes to achieve a purity of fruit flavours which is reflected in the wine.

There are attractive aromas of tangerine peel with a hint of spice, vanilla and butter. There is lovely refreshing acidity and excellent weight of ripe, buttery fruits with just a hint of new oak on the palate. It is a complex wine, well made, elegant and stylish with a warm, lingering finish. Despite being such a big bold wine it still has great freshness.

So if you thought you didn't like Chardonnay, try this classy wine, almost a pedigree, full of breeding and style–burgundy at its best.

Wines Direct

Kevin Summons-Walsh

Telmo Rodriguez Basa Rueda 2005
Castilla-León, Spain €11.95

This is a wine that simply makes your mouth come alive. Green, nettly, fresh, herbaceous pea pod aromas leap from the glass—you'd be forgiven for thinking it was a New World Sauvignon Blanc. It has zingy, zappy acidity with flavours of lime, lemon and a touch of kiwi fruit. There are also mangetout and pea tastes and a bitter twist. It's crisp and refreshing, with a long lemon zest finish. Verdejo, an underrated Spanish grape, is used to make this wine, with 5 per cent Sauvignon Blanc in the blend. Delicious summer drinking, or as an aperitif.

Approach Trade

Dom. Mazurd Cuvée Mazurka Côtes du Rhône 1999
Rhône, France €19

Now, this is not your usual Côtes du Rhône. M Mazurd makes a range of basic wines, but he likes to age his top wines for years in old oak barrels. The current vintage on the shelves is 1999, and it's interesting to see how such a humble appellation can develop. The colour is pale, almost tawny, with a broad brown rim. The smoky, oaky aromas are the first to excite the nose; these are followed by underlying perfumed rosehip. It's very dry at first on the palate—you think all the fruit has dried out, then WHAM!, in come redcurrant, rosehip and more smoky flavours. It's complex, and has a finish that can be measured in minutes. This is serious, quirky Côtes du Rhône that is simply perfect with a spicy, medium-bodied Havana cigar.

Barry Fitzwilliam Maxxium

Setanta Wines Cuchulain Shiraz 2003
Adelaide Hills, Australia €20

This is a rarity—an understated Australian. The aromas are of damson and liquorice; quite concentrated and fruity. Dense, ripe, fruity flavours of plum and black cherry follow, and lead to a lingering finish. However, this is not just your typical Oz fruit bomb; though it's drinking well now, this wine is just a baby. Although big, it's beautifully in balance, and this bodes well for its future development. This is a must for buying a case and putting it away in a quiet corner, then cracking open a bottle every six months to check its progress—and I haven't even mentioned the Irish connection or the eye-catching labelling.

Inis Wines

David Whelehan
Château Latour 1961
Bordeaux, France

Many wines have yielded very favourable and lasting impressions of tasting excellence. As I rack my brains as to what has been the greatest wine-tasting pleasure for me, images of cellars, crusty bread, runny cheeses and old Rhône, burgundy and bordeaux vintages spring to mind. As the filtering process continues, my greatest memories clearly relate to the great wines of Bordeaux and more specifically the wines of Pauillac. Possibly the most silence-inducing wine was that of the great Château Latour 1961 bought by my father for a few pounds very early on in his wine career and thankfully shared with his family at home in a very unfussy way over supper. Categorically, this wine was extraordinary and evoked an endless trail of adjectives . . . the lasting impression being the purity of black fruit. The wine clearly demonstrated how superb a great Pauillac can be and to date no other region's wines have surpassed the greatest of this AC.

John Wilson
Muscadet
Loire Valley, France

This summer, we had a short holiday in Brittany, my wife having discovered that it produced no wine. No wine, no visits, she correctly assumed. Having just tasted 2,000-odd wines for this book, my palate was a little jaded anyway. I tried out a few ciders, but also bought some Muscadet in the local supermarket. I went for the most expensive—€3–3.65 a bottle. Muscadet was the trendy drink twenty years ago. Since then, over-production and changing tastes have seen sales plummet in Ireland. However, over the last few years the regulations have been tightened up and there are some fantastic wines now on the market. With a bowl of lightly boiled prawns (bought still wriggling at the market), garlicky mayonnaise, good French bread and a green salad, my Muscadet was unbelievably good—fresh, lemony, lightly fruity, with a leesy touch and a crisp, dry finish. Eating al fresco, it all made for one of those memorable holiday experiences.

La Iña fino sherry

Jerez, Spain €15

Earlier this year I was fortunate enough to be invited to Vinoble, a dessert and fortified wine fair held every two years in the wonderful setting of the Alcazar in Jerez. I adore both sherry and sweet wines, so I was a very happy camper! The first night I met up with some Danish friends and headed off for a late dinner. In a busy tapas bar on the square, we ordered a variety of fishy things—octopus, squid, prawns and hake fried with cumin—along with a bottle of La Iña fino. The sherry was brilliant—chilled, light, zesty, crisp and dry, the perfect match for the seafood.

Later, several bottles of La Iña later, we ordered some of the amazing Spanish jamon, along with some cheese. We then moved on to the Lustau Vides palo cortado, one of the great treats of the sherry world, dry and intensely nutty. It was a perfect start to a fantastic week—sipping sherry, standing by upturned barrels, chatting to old friends, and watching the vibrant nightlife of Jerez well into the small hours on a balmy warm night.

Dom. des Roches Neuves Terres Chaudes Saumur-Champigny 2004

Loire Valley, France €24.99

I am part of that small minority that loves the red wines of the Loire Valley. This far north, Cabernet Franc, a much-underrated grape variety, needs good exposure and the right soil to get full ripeness. But when it does, you get this fine-edged, just-ripe wine with perfectly defined, crisp red summer fruits, allied to a lightly herbaceous touch. The wines are never heavy, never overly alcoholic. For me, there is no wine that can touch it. This wine is an absolutely brilliant example of what I mean—concentration, intensity and purity of fruit in an elegant, thrilling wine. Drink now or keep two to five years.

Febvre

The wines

The wines are listed in order of country/region, colour (red or white), price band, then by name. There are separate chapters for sparkling (including Champagne) and dessert wines. If you can't find the wine you are looking for try the index. The price bands are guidelines only. All of the wines in this book are ready to drink now (October 2006), and for the next 12 months. Some will improve further over time and this is mentioned in the tasting note.

Argentina

Argentina is at last beginning to realise the potential we knew was there for the last decade. There have always been some great wines around; but then there have also been a number of clumsy, over-alcoholic, over-oaked (and over here) wines too. Others had excessive green tannins, a result of ripening too quickly in the hot Mendoza sun.

But, over the last year or so, I have come across a number of very special, inexpensive wines that prove that Argentina is beginning to fulfil its promise of the 1990s. Equally exciting is the fact that there are some different grape varieties; certainly there are good Cabernets and Chardonnays, but I have a feeling that it may be with Syrah, Malbec, and Viognier (and possibly Tannat and Cabernet Franc too) that Argentina achieves its real potential.

Most of the wines listed below are from Mendoza, the heart of the Argentine wine industry, responsible for 90% of the country's wine. In addition, there are several wines from Cafayate, an area worth keeping an eye out for—there are wines with real elegance being made here. Hopefully we will soon see wines from other regions, including the far south of the country, where, once again, there is huge potential.

Volume is not a problem in Argentina and, with exports priced in US dollars, we can look forward to some very well-priced wines over the next few years.

White

Under €9

Callia Viognier 2005   **Special Value!**

Light, very tasty apricot and mild pineapple fruit in a tangy, easy-drinking wine—simple but delicious.

O'Briens

Price Under €9
Region San Juan
Grape Viognier
Alc/vol 13%

O'Briens

€12–€15

Lagarde Classic Viognier 2005

Delicious, full, rich Viognier with all the correct components and much more; luscious apricots and nectarines with a bitter edge, a nicely creamy palate, and good persistence.

Price	€12–€15
Region	Mendoza
Grape	Viognier
Alc/vol	14.5%

Bowes

Bin 9; Gaffney's, Tipperary; Kelly's Wine Vault; Kinnegar Wines; Morton's of Ranelagh; UnWined

Tittarelli Classic Reserve Torrontés 2005

Not the most flamboyant Torrontés, but an attractive, easy-drinking wine with rich pineapple and tropical fruits, and a very decent, long, dry finish.

Price	€12–€15
Region	Mendoza
Grape	Torrontés
Alc/vol	13.5%

Bowes

Cana; Deveneys; Donnybrook Fair; Fallon & Byrne; Gaffneys, Tipperary; Morton's of Ranelagh; Unwined

€18–€22

★ Lagarde Classic Semillon 2005

A lovely golden colour. Rich, clean, beautifully defined yellow fruit with a smooth texture and tangy grapefruit finish. Try it with grilled black sole or a plain roast chicken.

Price	€18–€22
Region	Mendoza
Grape	Semillon
Alc/vol	13%

Bowes

Fallon & Byrne; Friendship Wines, Limerick; Gaffneys, Tipperary

Red

Under €9

7 Days Malbec 2005   Organic Special Value!

Light, easy, sweet and fruity—just tails off a little, but this is very good supple wine.

Price	Under €9
Region	Famatina Valley
Grape	Malbec
Alc/vol	13.5%

Koala Wines

Cheers: Bray, Shankill; Get Fresh, Deansgrange; Londis, Trading Post, Galway; Next Door, Waterford; Shannon Knights, Shannon; SuperValu: Churchtown, Clane, Clifden, Kells, Wicklow

Quara Malbec 2004

Special Value!

A smooth mouthful of sweet plum fruit with a peppery edge; soft on the finish. Good easy drinking.

Molloy Liquor Stores

Price	Under €9
Region	Cafayate
Grape	Malbec
Alc/vol	13.5%

Newgate

Quara Tannat 2004

Special Value!

Soft, ripe red fruits—strawberries and plums—with a distinct spicy, herby, peppery element. Very attractive wine.

Molloy Liquor Stores

Price	Under €9
Region	Cafayate
Grape	Tannat
Alc/vol	13.5%

Newgate

€9–€12

Finca Flichman Reserva Oak Aged Cabernet Sauvignon 2005

Special Value!

Rich, textured, oaky, sweetish, soft Cabernet—plenty of stuffing and swish, smooth length. Improves with every sip.

Kelly's Wine Vault, Clontarf; Londis; Next Door, Arklow; JJ O'Driscoll, Cork; SPAR, Dungarvan; SuperValu, Aston Quay

Price	€9–€12
Region	Mendoza
Grape	Cab Sauv
Alc/vol	14.5%

Kelly & Co.

Michel Torino Malbec 2004

Special Value!

Very pleasant, clean, solid, quite elegant damsons and loganberries with a satisfying, rounded finish. Ready to drink now.

Bailys of Howth; Coopers, Limerick; Gibneys; Harvest; Londis; Mace/Vivo

Price	€9–€12
Region	Cafayate
Grape	Malbec
Alc/vol	13.5%

Classic Drinks

Pascual Toso Cabernet Sauvignon 2004

Special Value!

Rich, very satisfying wine stuffed with dark forest fruits; some good spicy tannins on the finish.

Cana Off-licence, Mullingar; Donnybrook Fair; Greenacres, Wexford; Joyces, Salthill; Jus de Vine, Portmarnock; O'Donovans, Cork; Red Island Wines, Skerries; Redmonds, Ranelagh; Sweeneys, Glasnevin

Price	€9–€12
Region	Mendoza
Grape	Cab Sauv
Alc/vol	13.5%

Vineyard Galway

Terrazas de los Andes Malbec 2004

Good, concentrated, rounded loganberries and plums finishing on a dry note. Well-made wine in a very full-bodied style.

Price €9–€12
Region Mendoza
Grape Malbec
Alc/vol 14%

Dillons

Tesco; Lynchs, Glanmire; Next Door, Blessington; C & T Supermarket, Skerries; The Mill Wine Cellar, Maynooth; Londis Kinvara; Londis Tarmonbarry; Corner House, Westport

Tittarelli Italian line Sangiovese 2003

Light, very elegant mocha and coffee, with some dark cherries on the finish. Very interesting, a pleasant drink and quite convincing.

Price €9–€12
Region Mendoza
Grape Sangiovese
Alc/vol 13.5%

Bowes

Cana; Donnybrook Fair; Friendship Wines, Limerick; UnWined; Wicklow Wine Co.

€12–€15

Altos Los Hormigos Malbec 2005

Big, youthful, pure loganberry fruit with an attractive rasping note and some clean tannins on the finish. Lovely, full-bodied, concentrated, savoury wine.

Price €12–€15
Region Mendoza
Grape Malbec
Alc/vol 13.9%

Liberty Wines

Fallon & Byrne; Le Caveau; O'Briens; Red Island, Skerries; Redmonds; simplywines.ie

Crios de Susana Balbo 2004

Very good-value, rich, ripe, pure dark fruits, smooth and velvety with very good length. This is stylish, full-bodied wine.

Wines Direct

Price €12–€15
Region Mendoza
Grape Malbec
Alc/vol 14%

Wines Direct

Jean Bousquet Malbec 2005   **Organic**

Rounded, ripe, sweet fruits, four-square, some tobacco, concentrated with a solid tannic structure.

Mannings Emporium, Cork; O'Donovans, Cork; Quay Co-op, Cork

Price €12–€15
Region Tupungato, Mendoza
Grape Malbec
Alc/vol 14%

Mary Pawle

Xama Che Cabernet Sauvignon 2003

Pleasant, rounded, mature cassis with a spicy edge and soft tannins on the finish. Well-made wine with a bit of oomph.

Price	€12–€15
Region	Mendoza
Grape	Cab Sauv
Alc/vol	14%

Gaffneys, Tipperary; Friendship Wines, Limerick

Bowes

€15–€18

★ Famiglia Bianchi Malbec 2002

Big, concentrated, firm but ripe loganberries with a piquant, long, dry tail—this is very stylish wine that calls out for a steak.

Price	€15–€18
Region	San Rafael
Grape	Malbec
Alc/vol	14%

Bowes

Celtic Whiskey; Donybrook Fair; Friendship Wines, Limerick

★ Terrazas de los Andes Malbec Reserva 2003

A mega-mouthful of concentrated dark fruits, plenty of tannin too, but smooth, concentrated and classy.

Price	€15–€18
Region	Mendoza
Grape	Malbec
Alc/vol	14%

Lynch's Off Licence, Glanmire; Redmond of Ranelagh; McCabes, Blackrock/Foxrock; Simply Delicious Foxrock; Martha's Vineyard Rathfarnham; The Drinks Store, D7; Eurospar, Dalkey; Rushes SPAR, Stillorgan; Eurospar, Naas

Dillons

€18–€22

Trapiche Viña Pedro Gonzalez Malbec 2003

A huge mouthful of sultry, soft, ripe dark fruits overlaid with sweet coconut spice and coffee, with a rounded, smooth finish.

Price	€18–€22
Region	Mendoza
Grape	Malbec
Alc/vol	14.5%

Carvills, Camden St; Cheers, Bray; Higgins, Clonskeagh; Shiels, Dorset St

Comans

All of the wines in this book are ready to drink now (October 2006), and for the next 12 months. Some will improve further over time and this is mentioned in the tasting note.

€22–€30

★★ Luigi Bosca Gala 1 2003

A huge wine, but one that has real
class and structure; the nose is very
peppery, with loganberry fruit; the
palate is tight, with taut, cool dark
fruits, plenty of perfectly integrated
drying tannins, a savoury touch, huge
concentration and great length.

Macs, Limerick; Redmonds, Ranelagh; Searsons, Monkstown

Price	€22–€30
Region	Mendoza
Grape	Malbec/Petit Verdot/Tannat
Alc/vol	14.5%

Searsons

★ Luigi Bosca Gala 2 2003

Big, forward, leathery nose with an
animal touch; explosive, intense,
swish ripe cassis sprinkled with spice,
but with a lovely structure too; this is
excellent, classy, meaty stuff.

McCabes, Blackrock; Patrick Stewart; Searsons, Monkstown

Price	€22–€30
Region	Mendoza
Grape	Cab Sauv/ Cab Franc/Merlot
Alc/vol	14.5%

Searsons

€30–€40

★ Terrazas de los Andes Afincado Malbec 2003

Big, ripe fruit aromas;
huge levels of ripe
cassis and raspberries
with abundant dark
chocolate on a very
long finish.

*The Dew Drop Athboy; The Mill
Wine Cellar, Maynooth; Next Door,
Blessingtown; Egans Drogheda*

Price	€30–€40
Region	Mendoza
Grape	Malbec
Alc/vol	14%

Dillons

Australia

In this country, we love Australian wines; they vie with those from Chile as our most popular tipple. It seems we cannot get enough of those upfront, ripe fruit flavours. Nothing wrong with that either; to the new wine consumer, French wines were difficult to understand, and equally difficult to drink with their dry tannins and lighter fruit. Australia has always specialised in consistent, accessible wines that offer real value for money. This is still pretty much the case, although some argue that the big brands are not as good as they used to be.

The Australian wine industry has always been incredibly dynamic and market-driven, expanding and adapting to meet international demand. In recent years, production has grown massively, but demand has not necessarily followed suit. This year and last, many growers have simply left their grapes to rot on the vines, unable to obtain an economically viable price.

However, I believe that the key to getting more pleasure from Australian wine is to learn a little about the terroir. The concept may be French, indicating wines with a sense of place, but Australia has a host of different climates, micro-climates and soils—we are talking about an area the size of Europe. It is not surprising that the country produces a huge range of wines. The great majority of inexpensive Australian wines come from a couple of vast, irrigated vineyards, designed to produce volume above all else. Move up a euro or two, and the leap in quality is quite amazing.

There are delicate, elegant white and red wines, medium-bodied wines with unique flavours, as well as the full-throttle powerful wines from the warmer regions. We should not forget the world-class sweet wines, nor the excellent sparkling wines. All in all, Australia has a lot to offer. We list over one hundred entries, wines with real character and style. I would urge you to go out and experiment a little.

White

€9–€12

d'Arenberg The Stump Jump Riesling Sauvignon Marsanne 2005

Special Value!

Fresh, fruity, rounded and ripe with delicious pure melon and juicy pear fruit. A great all-rounder, especially for parties or as an aperitif.

Price	€9–€12
Region	McLaren Vale
Grape	Riesling/Sauv Blanc/ Marsanne
Alc/vol	13.5%

SuperValu, Raheny and Killester; Jus de Vine, Portmarnock; The Vintry, Rathgar; Uncorked, Rathfarnham; Lonergans, Clonmel, Wine Centre, Kilkenny; Florries Fine Wines, Iramore; Öld Štand, Mullingar; Mortons, Galway; Grenhams, Ballinasloe; Fahys, Ballina; Diceys, Ballyshannon

Taserra

Grant Burge Barossa Vines Sauvignon Blanc 2005

A very different kind of Sauvignon, but very enjoyable—rich but refreshing orange-peel zestiness with a toffee note. Certainly no lack of character.

Price	€9–€12
Region	Barossa Valley
Grape	Sauv Blanc
Alc/vol	13.5%

Oddbins

Oddbins

Houghton Pemberton Chardonnay 2001

Special Value!

Yummy, toasty, nutty nose. Peach and tropical fruit on the palate with well-judged acidity and oak. Very flavoursome finish.

Price	€9–€12
Region	Western Australia
Grape	Chardonnay
Alc/vol	14%

Allied Drinks

Tahbilk Marsanne 2004

Special Value!

Light, clean lemons and cool pear fruits, with a mineral-charged dry finish and a very subtle hint of honey. Delicious wine with lovely purity of fruit.

Price	€9–€12
Region	Victoria
Grape	Marsanne
Alc/vol	12.5%

Comans

The McGuigan Gold Sauvignon 2005

Light, fresh, cool green fruits with some limes; more mineral-driven than upfront fruit, but attractive, easy-drinking Sauvignon.

Price	€9–€12
Region	Adelaide Hills
Grape	Sauv Blanc
Alc/vol	13%

Tesco

€12–€15

Alkoomi Sauvignon Blanc 2005

A good, well-made Sauvignon, quite lean and fresh, with a light grassiness and some lean lime flavours—one of the best Aussie Sauvignons at this price.

Wines Direct

Price **€12–€15**
Region **Western Australia**
Grape **Sauv Blanc**
Alc/vol **12.5%**

Wines Direct

Basilisk McPherson Marsanne Viognier 2004

Traces of vanilla pod on the apricot nose. Not a trace of sweeness on the palate, which is full of ripe apricot fruit with a herby background. Full-bodied, quite high in alcohol, with enough acidity to keep it fresh, this is a satisfying mouthful with good flavour.

Price **€12–€15**
Region **Victoria**
Grape **Marsanne/Viognier**
Alc/vol **13%**

O'Briens

d'Arenberg The Olive Grove Chardonnay 2005

Pure, rich, very ripe red-apple fruit in an exuberant, big, sweetly concentrated tasty wine. This would go down beautifully with some prawns.

Langans, Kiltimagh, Mayo; Jus de Vine, Portmarnock; O'Brien's Off Licence; Fitzgeralds, Macroom; Salthill Liquor Store, Galway; Terrys Wine Shop, Limerick;McCabes Blackrock, The Gables Foxrock, The Vintry, Rathgar; Uncorked Rathfarnham; Florries Fine Wines, Tramore

Price **€12–€15**
Region **McLaren Vale**
Grape **Chardonnay**
Alc/vol **14.5%**

Taserra

> **How to use this book**
> The wines are listed in order of country/region, colour (red or white), price band, then by name. There are separate chapters for sparkling (including Champagne) and dessert wines. If you can't find the wine you are looking for try the index. The price bands are guidelines only. All of the wines in this book are ready to drink now (October 2006), and for the next 12 months. Some will improve further over time and this is mentioned in the tasting note.

McWilliams Hanwood Estate Riesling 2005

This is lovely fresh wine with a hint of sherbet and loads of fresh green apples and zingy lime zest; excellent length.

Price	€12–€15
Region	SE Australia
Grape	Riesling
Alc/vol	12.5%

Cheers Delgany; Chester Beatty OL, Ashford; Corkscrew, D2; Donnybrook Fair; Fallon & Byrne, D2; Grape Escape, Lucan; Jus de Vine, Portmarnock; Kellys, Clontarf; Macs, Limerick; Marthas Vineyard, Rathfarnham; McCabes; O'Donovans, Cork; On The Grapevine Dalkey & Booterstown; Red Island Wine Co., Skerries; Thomas Martins, Fairview; Thomas Woodberrys, Galway; World Wide Wines, Waterford

Cassidys

Peter Lehmann Eden Valley Riesling 2004

Aussie Riesling as it should be—delicious, lemony, tangy, green-apple fruits, with a lively, crisp, dry finish. Great by itself or with fish.

Price	€12–€15
Region	Eden Valley
Grape	Riesling
Alc/vol	12%

Donnybrook Fair; O'Donovans, Cork; O'Neills, SCR; Redmonds, Ranelagh; The Lord Mayor, Swords; Uncorked, Rathfarnham

Comans

€15–€18

★ d'Arenberg The Hermit Crab Viognier Marsanne 2004

Powerful, rich nose, leading on to a full-on, luscious palate of ripe peaches, apricots and tropical fruits—delicious, full-bodied white wine.

Price	€15–€18
Region	McLaren Vale
Grape	Viognier/Marsanne
Alc/vol	14.5%

O'Sullivan Old Wines, Blarney; Mill Wine Centre, Maynooth; The Vintry, Rathgar; O'Briens, Sandymount; Jus de Vine, Portmarnock; McCabes Blackrock, Uncorked, Rathfarnham; The Gables, Foxrock

Taserra

★ Evans & Tate Margaret River Chardonnay 2004

Elegant, lightly textured, smooth lanolin and pears with some pine-apple; complex, very enjoyable Chardonnay that seduces gently.

Price	€15–€18
Region	Margaret River
Grape	Chardonnay
Alc/vol	14%

O'Neills, SCR; Molloys of Clonsilla; On the Grapevine, Dalkey; SPAR, Ballycullen; Uncorked, Rathfarnham

Comans

★ Hanenhof Barossa Valley Viognier 2005

This is lovely ripe wine with classy, juicy, soft fruits spread out across the creamy palate. There is a floral note and some honey too, with a delicious mellow finish.

Price	€15–€18
Region	Barossa Valley
Grape	Viognier
Alc/vol	14.5%

Eugene's, Kenmare; Karwigs; Redmonds, Ranelagh

Karwigs

MadFish Unwooded Chardonnay 2005

Fresh and crisp with a heart of green fruit with a subtle creaminess, finishing on a zippy note.

Claudio's; Guys, Clifden; Mill Wine Cellar, Maynooth

Price €15–€18
Region Western Australia
Grape Chardonnay
Alc/vol 13%

Nicholson

Ninth Island Chardonnay 2003

Subtly textured, with concentrated green-apple fruit and light lanolin on a lingering finish. This grows on you with every sip—a great food wine.

Donnybrook Fair; McCabes; Sweeneys; Selected independent retailers

Price €15–€18
Region Tasmania
Grape Chardonnay
Alc/vol 13.5%

Gleesons

Penfolds Thomas Hyland Chardonnay 2005

Classic New World Chardonnay with a touch of style—lightly oaked, nicely textured melons and ripe fruit with a spicy touch and a soft, easy finish.

Coopers Off Licence, Tipperary; Drink Store, Dublin; Gables, Foxrock; Halpins Fine Wines; Joyce, Athenry and Knocknacarra; McCabe's; O'Donovan's, Douglas; Strand, Fairview; Sweeney Wines, Glasnevin; Vesey Arms

Price €15–€18
Region South Australia
Grape Chardonnay
Alc/vol 13.5%

Findlater Grants

Pikes Clare Valley Riesling 2005

Lemon and lime zest on the nose follow through on to a clean, very light palate with some green apples.

Claudio's; Kellys of Clontarf

Price €15–€18
Region Clare Valley
Grape Riesling
Alc/vol 12%

Nicholson

Taltarni Lalla Gully 2004

Lean, clean and mouth-puckering dry minerals, with light green apples and a crisp, dry finish. Zesty, fresh wine that will certainly wake your tastebuds up. Try it with seafood.

Drink Store, Manor Street; Morton's, Galway; Searsons, Monkstown

Price €15–€18
Region Tasmania
Grape Riesling
Alc/vol 13%

Searsons

Tamar Ridge Riesling 2002

Very deep colour, with a developed nose of light kerosene and honey; fully mature, crisp, honeyed yellow fruits, dry on the finish. One for the true Riesling aficionado.

Price	€15–€18
Region	Tasmania
Grape	Riesling
Alc/vol	13%

Ampersand Wines

Goose Off-Licence, Drumcondra; Grape Escape, Lucan; McCambridge's, Galway; Sweeneys, Glasnevin

★★ Tamar Ridge The Devil's Corner Unwooded Chardonnay 2001

Quite a deep green colour; crisp, minerally green fruits with a lovely herby touch, showing some development, but good length, and oak-free and dry! New World Chablis?

Price	€15–€18
Region	Tasmania
Grape	Chardonnay
Alc/vol	13%

Ampersand Wines

Jus de Vine; McCambridges, Galway; Mortons, Ranelagh; World Wide Wines, Waterford

★ Tim Adams Clare Valley Semillon 2004

Straw colour with green highlights Striking honey/apricot nose. The palate is fully dry, with soft depth of fruit with herby/mineral overtones, good integrated acidity and a long, fruity finish. Very well put together and food-friendly. Will improve for a further five years.

Price	€15–€18
Region	Clare Valley
Grape	Semillon
Alc/vol	12%

Tesco

★ Torbreck Woodcutter's Semillon 2003

Delicious aromas with subtle nuances of bonbons, pineapple and honey. No sweetness on the full-flavoured, well-structured palate, which abounds in rich baked apples, toast and hazelnuts. Rounded in the mouth without too much acidity, but with a long, creamy, textured finish.

Price	€15–€18
Region	Barossa Valley
Grape	Semillon
Alc/vol	14%

O'Briens

€18–€22

Millbrook Viognier 2004

Pleasing nose of apricots and flowers. Delicious palate of firm apricot/apple flavours with a gentle creaminess that makes the wine very easy to drink. Acidity is medium, but this would do very nicely as a standalone sipping wine.

Claudio's, George's St Arcade; Grape Escape, Lucan; McHugh's, Kilbarrack and Malahide; Morton's, Galway and Ranelagh; Nectar Wines, Sandyford Village; Red Island Wines, Skerries

Price **€18–€22**
Region **Western Australia**
Grape **Viognier**
Alc/vol 14.5%

Nectar Wines

★ Mount Horrocks Watervale Clare Valley Riesling 2005

A delicious, nervy young Riesling, with nicely rounded pure apple fruit, a streak of crisp citrus, and a long, dry finish. Excellent now, but will certainly develop for years to come.

Donnybrook Fair; Fallon & Byrne

Price **€18–€22**
Region **Clare Valley**
Grape **Riesling**
Alc/vol 13%

Liberty Wines

★★ Peter Lehmann The Barossa Reserve Riesling 2000

Developed, rich honey and toasty elements add complexity to the crisp lime fruit. This is one for Riesling lovers. A lovely, rounded, mellow mouth-feel, and an incredible finish. Wonderful wine—a real treat.

Jus de Vine, Portmarnock; O'Donovans, Cork; The Vintry, Rathgar; Shiels, Dorset St; Uncorked, Rathfarnham

Price **€18–€22**
Region **Eden Valley**
Grape **Riesling**
Alc/vol 12%

Comans

Setanta Emer Chardonnay 2004

From the lean and clean school— light, elegant lanolin and new oak merge with clean green-apple fruit in an elegant wine that is showing some pleasing development.

Bunch of Grapes, Clonee; Coach House, Ballinteer; Connoisseur, Dundalk; Donnybrook Fair; Foodhall, Portlaoise; Jus de Vine; Mill, Maynooth; Red Island, Skerries; Silver Granite; Thomas's, Foxrock

Price **€18–€22**
Region **Adelaide Hills**
Grape **Chardonnay**
Alc/vol 13.5%

Inis Wines

★ The Colonial Estate L'Expatrie Barossa Semillon 2003

This has some very wacky flavours—a delineated palate of waxy yellow apples, high acidity, light enough alcohol and a burnt toastiness on the finish. A wine with real character, and one that I can see developing further.

Price €18–€22
Region Barossa Valley
Grape Semillon/Riesling

Gilbeys

€22–€30

★ Cullen Sauvignon Blanc Semillon 2004   Organic

This is a real cut above the rest: concentrated, aromatic Sauvignon, with a broad-textured melon palate, given extra complexity by some subtle vanilla notes; excellent wine with everything singing in harmony. It will improve further.

Price €22–€30
Region Margaret River
Grape Sauv Blanc/ Semillon
Alc/vol 14%

Liberty Wines

Fallon & Byrne; Jus de Vine

Grosset Polish Hill Riesling 2005

NEW WORLD WHITE WINE OF THE YEAR

Brilliant, cool Riesling. The nose is lightly aromatic, the palate still very tight, with a strong mineral streak, along with intense crunchy green-apple fruit. It is austere, but not short of fruit, with finely etched acidity. The impression is of an incredibly restrained, elegant wine with a huge follow-through. Drink now or hold up to a decade.

Price €22–€30
Region Clare Valley
Grape Riesling
Alc/vol 13%

Liberty Wines

Le Caveau, Kilkenny

> *Where to buy the wine*
> If your local retailer does not stock a particular wine, contact the distributor named in italic after the tasting note who will be pleased to give you details of the nearest stockist.

★ Shadowfax Chardonnay 2004

This is very good wine—a light toastiness, some rich lemon zestiness, good concentration and developing apple fruits; classy and long, ending on a persistent dry note.

Price	€22–€30
Region	Victoria
Grape	Chardonnay
Alc/vol	13.5%

Berry Bros & Rudd

Berry Bros & Rudd

€30–€40

★★ Tyrrell's Vat 1 Hunter Semillon 1999

Last year's winner may have moved on a vintage, but it is still very much on song. Very fresh, floral, lemon-scented aromas give way to a silky, smooth, light mouthful of tangy citrus, a touch of honey and toast and a great, lingering finish.

Price	€30–€40
Region	Hunter Valley
Grape	Semillon
Alc/vol	10.5%

Barry Fitzwilliam Maxxium

Londis; Morton's of Ranelagh

★ Tyrrell's Vat 47 Hunter Chardonnay 2001

Deep colour; oaky, buttery nose; rich, soft, oaky, quite delicate and elegant with a toastiness, lovely lime and lemon flavours and super citrus length.

Price	€30–€40
Region	Hunter Valley
Grape	Chardonnay
Alc/vol	12.5%

Barry Fitzwilliam Maxxium

Morton's of Ranelagh

Red

€9–€12

d'Arenberg The Stump Jump Grenache Shiraz Mourvèdre 2004

Special Value!

Ripe strawberries and liquorice in a supple, nicely savoury wine.

Mill Wine Centre, Maynooth; Lilac Wine Shop, Fairview; Fresh Supermarket, D7; The Vintry, Rathgar; Bradys, Shankhill; Hollands, Bray; Wicklow Wine Co.; Lynchs, Tullamore; Gaffneys, Nenagh; Terrys, Wine Shop, Limerick; Galvins, Listowel; Ui Loinsighs, Cork; Jus de Vine, Portmarnock

Price	€9–€12
Region	McLaren Vale
Grape	Grenache/Shiraz/ Mourvèdre
Alc/vol	14%

Taserra

€12–€15

Bird in the Hand Two in the Bush Merlot Cabernet 2004

Good, full-on, rounded chocolate and ripe cassis with plenty of power and some depth. Flavoursome, big, tasty wine.

Eugene's, Kenmare; Karwigs; Redmonds, Ranelagh; Wine & Co, Dalkey

Price	€12–€15
Region	Adelaide Hills
Grape	Merlot/Cab Sauv
Alc/vol	15.5%

Karwigs

d'Arenberg The Footbolt Shiraz 2003

Delicious, pure damson fruit aromas; a big wine with a fiery touch but also really seductive, smooth damson fruit and some minerals on a dry finish. Very easy-drinking, rich wine.

O'Driscolls, Cahirciveen; McHughs, Artane and Kilbarrack; Harvest Off Licences, Galway; Next Door Off Licences; O'Brien's; Jus de Vine, Portmarnock; The Vintry, Rathgar; Uncorked, Rathfarnham; McCabes, Blackrock

Price	€12–€15
Region	McLaren Vale
Grape	Shiraz
Alc/vol	14.5%

Taserra

Jip Jip Rocks Shiraz 2004

Dangerous wine—soft, succulent, sweet, ripe dark fruits, helped along by some spicy new oak. It all comes together in a smooth, rich, heady glass of wine.

Price	€12–€15
Region	Limestone Coast
Grape	Shiraz
Alc/vol	15%

Karwigs

Mitchelton Shiraz 2003

Very good, honest, forthright Shiraz
with slightly rustic plum fruits; fills
the mouth very nicely and has a lovely
spicy finish. Dangerously drinkable
wine.

Selected branches Dunnes Stores

Price **€12–€15**
Region **Victoria**
Grape **Shiraz**
Alc/vol **14.5%**

Dunnes Stores

Pencil Pine Chambourcin 2002

Very pleasant twangy summer fruits
with a hint of barnyard on the nose;
clean, with good concentration of
fruit.

Price **€12–€15**
Region **Hunter Valley**
Grape **Chambourcin**
Alc/vol **14%**

Bacchus

The Black Chook Shiraz Viognier 2005

Youthful colour; big, supple, swarthy
damson fruit, smooth with a fiery
touch and a rounded finish.

*The Lakes Off Licence, Blessington; Gibneys, Malahide;
Village Off Licence, Castleknock; Cheers, The Laurels,
Perrystown; McLoughlins, Manor Street D7; Fallon & Byrne
D2, Red Island, Skerries; Uncorked, Rathfarnham; Slatterys,
Carrick on Shannon; Fahys, Ballina; 4D's Off Licence,
Ballyhaunis; Murty Rabbits Galway; Diceys, Ballyshannon;
Bannons, Cootehill Cavan*

Price **€12–€15**
Region **South Australia**
Grape **Shiraz/Viognier**
Alc/vol **15%**

Taserra

Wakefield Clare Valley Shiraz 2004

Impeccably balanced ripe cherry and
plum fruit offset perfectly by a slightly
savoury note, a touch of vanilla, and a
long, cool finish. Delicious Shiraz.

*Widely available from independents; Londis; Musgraves;
SPAR; SuperValu*

Price **€12–€15**
Region **Clare Valley**
Grape **Shiraz**
Alc/vol **14.5%**

Koala Wines

Wakefield Merlot 2003

This has very decent chunky dark
fruits, supple on the centre palate,
signing off with a pleasing dry note.
Very quaffable.

*Widely available from independents; O'Briens; SPAR;
Superquinn; SuperValu*

Price **€12–€15**
Region **Clare Valley**
Grape **Merlot**
Alc/vol **14.5%**

Koala Wines

Willunga 100 Cabernet Shiraz 2005

Big, broad, ripe, jammy, chocolaty
fruit, with some drying tannins on the
finish, but overlain by cooler herby
notes—gets better. Very good.

Price	€12–€15
Region	McLaren Vale
Grape	Cab Sauv/Shiraz
Alc/vol	14.5%

Donnybrook Fair; Listons; McHughs; O'Donovans; Uncorked   *Liberty Wines*

★ Zonte's Footsteps Shiraz Viognier 2005

Cool but very concen-
trated rich damson and
red cherry fruit with a
certain elegance, but then
the 14.5% alcohol kicks
in to add warmth. It
finishes very smoothly
with a savoury note.

Price	€12–€15
Region	Langhorne Creek
Grape	Shiraz/Viognier
Alc/vol	14.5%

Taserra

*Mr Macs, Limerick; Mortons, Galway; Gibneys, Malahide;
Jus de Vine, Portmarnock; Mortons, Firhouse; Hollands, Bray;
McHughs, Kilbarrack; Wine Shop, Kilkenny; The Vintry,
Rathgar; McCabe's, Blackrock; Next Door Off Licences;
Noffla Off Licences*

€15–€18

Heartland Dolcetto Lagrein 2004

Dolcetto was never like this; a big,
rich, twangy, savoury wine with
powerful alcohol, cassis and dark
cherries; different and dangerous.

Price	€15–€18
Region	Langhorne Creek
Grape	Dolcetto/Lagrein
Alc/vol	15%

*Caprani's; Macs, Limerick; Patrick Stewart, Sligo; Searsons,
Monkstown*   *Searsons*

Lisa McGuigan Tempus Two Merlot 2004

Powerful, big, ripe plum fruit with a
lovely piquant touch. Nice length—a
good food wine.

Price	€15–€18
Region	Langhorne Creek
Grape	Merlot
Alc/vol	14%

Tesco

Mitchelton Crescent Shiraz Mourvèdre Grenache 2001

Showing plenty of development with
leathery touches to the plum fruit and
some minerals and drying tannins on
the finish. Would go down nicely with
rare beef.

Price	€15–€18
Region	Victoria
Grape	Shiraz/Mourvèdre/ Grenache
Alc/vol	14.5%

Dunnes Stores

★ Mitolo The Jester Cabernet Sauvignon 2005

Excellent wine that manages to be big and elegant at the same time; there are full cassis and dark berry flavours that ring true, with plenty of hearty alcohol and dark chocolate notes, but these are balanced by a cool streak of herbs and mint.

Price	€15–€18
Region	McLaren Vale
Grape	Cab Sauv
Alc/vol	14.5%

Liberty Wines

Bailys of Howth

Simon Hackett Old Vine Grenache 2002

Soft, ripe, jammy strawberries in a lush, easy-drinking style. There is just enough acidity coming through to keep it all together. Very moreish, with a lovely sleek finish.

Price	€15–€18
Region	McLaren Vale
Grape	Grenache
Alc/vol	13.5%

Wine Select

The Hole in the Wall, D7; WineOnline.ie; Jus de Vine, Portmarnock

---

Simon Hackett Shiraz 2003

Classy mint and blackcurrants in a very nicely balanced wine with real freshness, a lovely tangy element and good length.

Price	€15–€18
Region	McLaren Vale
Grape	Shiraz
Alc/vol	14%

The Hole in the Wall, D7; Jus de Vine, Portmarnock

Wine Select

★★ Tim Adams The Fergus 2004

This is seriously good stuff; wonderfully balanced, perfectly ripe summer fruits sprinkled with savoury black pepper and subtle spice. Wine that opens up and shows real power—you will keep coming back for more.

Price	€15–€18
Region	Clare Valley
Grape	Grenache/Shiraz/ Cab Franc
Alc/vol	15%

Tesco

Torbreck Woodcutter's Shiraz 2004

Big, rich, intense wine filled with soft, overripe berries and figs—big, beautiful, full-on wine with lush, sweet fruit.

Price	€15–€18
Region	Barossa Valley
Grape	Shiraz
Alc/vol	14.5%

O'Briens

O'Briens

RED WINE OF THE YEAR
FOR UNDER €20

Wolf Blass President's Selection Shiraz 2004

Quite refined ripe strawberry fruits and some fairly subtle chocolaty new oak; good linear flavour with a touch of class.

Price €15–€18
Region South Australia
Grape Shiraz
Alc/vol 14.5%

Tesco; O'Briens Fine Wines; Londis, Bettystown; JC's Supermarket, Swords; Molloy; SuperValu, Blackrock/Kilrush

Dillons

★★ Yering Station Shiraz Viognier 2003

Cool plum and floral aromas; quite elegant, almost delicate, smooth plum fruit with a nice purity, well integrated alcohol, and a beautifully tangy finish. Not your classic Aussie, but good stuff.

Price €15–€18
Region Yarra Valley
Grape Shiraz/Vioqnier
Alc/vol 14%

Ampersand Wines

Deveneys, Rathmines; Gibneys, Malahide; Jus de Vine; Kellys, Vernon Ave; The Vintry, Rathgar

€18–€22

Ainsworth & Snelson
Coonawarra Cabernet Sauvignon 2002

Concentrated and elegant with good acidity and balance, some focused blackberries, an austere touch, and a dry finish.

Price €18–€22
Region South Australia
Grape Cab Sauv
Alc/vol 14.5%

Caprani's; Jus de Vine; Waterford World of Wine

J Donohue

Balgownie Estate Cabernet Sauvignon 2000

Smooth and sweet oak, with plenty of body behind it—full-bodied, rounded wine with some real complexity, and a finish that lasts.

Price €18–€22
Region Bendigo
Grape Cab Sauv
Alc/vol 14%

Tindal

★ Balgownie Estate Shiraz 2001

A maturing wine that offers subtle plum and blackcurrants and a nice mineral and leather note on the finish. No shortage of power, but some complexity too.

Price €18–€22
Region Bendigo
Grape Shiraz
Alc/vol 14.5%

Tindal

★★ Bethany Barossa Shiraz 2002

A behemoth of a wine—huge, massively alcoholic, rich and powerful with great intensity of fruit—dried prunes, plums and figs, with a sweetness too. Meaty, heady stuff.

O'Briens

Price	€18–€22
Region	Barossa Valley
Grape	Shiraz
Alc/vol	14.5%

O'Briens

Cape Mentelle Cabernet Merlot 2003

Cool, herby, minty wine with some fairly burly, concentrated dark fruits and a long tannic finish. This would benefit from decanting an hour or so beforehand.

The Vintry, Rathgar; Next Door, Kinsale; McCabes, Blackrock/Foxrock; Greenacres, Wexford; SuperValu, Churchtown; Londis, Malahide; Martha's Vineyard, Rathfarnham; Jus de Vine, Portmarnock

Price	€18–€22
Region	Margaret River
Grape	Cab Sauv/Merlot
Alc/vol	14.5%

Dillons

Classic McLaren Cabernet Merlot 2001

Rich, very concentrated and powerful wine, full of jammy plum fruits; long, still with some firm, integrated tannins and good length.

Blessings, Cavan; Cana, Mullingar; Claudio's, Drury Street; Foodhall, Portlaoise; Gaffneys, Nenagh; Mitchells, Glasthule; O'Neills, Carrickmacross; Red Island, Skerries

Price	€18–€22
Region	McLaren Vale
Grape	Cab Sauv/Merlot
Alc/vol	14%

Inis Wines

★ d'Arenberg The Bonsai Vine 2001

Fascinating, evolved, sweaty aromas; then a delicious, spicy, herby mouthful of intense, rustic strawberry fruit, with some drying tannins and a great follow-through.

Kellys Wine Vault, Clontarf; Blessings Off Licence, Cavan; McCabes, Blackrock; O'Gormans SuperValu, Carrickmacross; Nolan's, Kilcullen; Jus de Vine, Portmarnock

Price	€18–€22
Region	McLaren Vale
Grape	Grenache/Shiraz/ Mourvèdre
Alc/vol	14.5%

Taserra

d'Arenberg The Cadenzia 2003

A lovely rich red with some tarry, rustic notes to the concentrated dark fruits; big, powerful wine, but one with real class.

Price €18–€22
Region McLaren Vale
Grape Grenache/Shiraz/Mourvèdre
Alc/vol 14.5%

Grenhams Off Licence, Ballinasloe; Fahys Off Licence, Ballina; The Vintry, Rathgar; Fallon & Byrne, Dublin 2; Mr Macs, Limerick; Gaffneys, Nenagh; McCabes, Blackrock; Jus de Vine, Portmarnock

Taserra

★ Green Point Shiraz 2003

Pure dark prunes and liquorice; very nicely balanced cool-climate Shiraz with good liquorice and damson fruits, a lovely soft, ripe centre palate and some black pepper, finishing on a softly tannic note. Beautifully crafted wine.

Price €18–€22
Region Victoria
Grape Shiraz
Alc/vol 14%

Dillons

Londis, Malahide; Chawkes New Mace, Castletroy; Lynch's, Glanmire; Londis, Maynooth; Jus de Vine, Portmarnock; Kellys, Chapelizod; Greenacres, Wexford; Eurospar, Leixlip; Eurospar, Dalkey

Hungerford Hill Orange Merlot 2002

Huge, soft, lush wine with slightly barnyardy sweet cassis, plenty of sweet, spicy oak, and very good length.

Price €18–€22
Region Orange
Grape Merlot
Alc/vol 14%

Classic Drinks

Bailys, Howth; Coopers, Limerick; Kavanaghs, Kildare; Naked Grape, Cork; The Wine Centre, Kilkenny

Jim Barry The Lodge Hill Shiraz 2004

An explosion of deep, overripe, tarry damsons, incredibly ripe and powerful, with sweet coconut oak—a wine that blows you away, but impressive in its own way.

Price €18–€22
Region Clare Valley
Grape Shiraz
Alc/vol 14.5%

Cassidys

Cheers Delgany; Chester Beatty OL, Ashford; Corkscrew, D2; Donnybrook Fair; Fallon & Byrne, D2; Grape Escape, Lucan; Jus de Vine, Portmarnock; Kellys, Clontarf; Macs, Limerick; Marthas Vineyard, Rathfarnham; McCabes; O'Donovans, Cork; On The Grapevine Dalkey & Booterstown; Red Island Wine Co., Skerries; Thomas Martins, Fairview; Thomas Woodberrys, Galway; World Wide Wines, Waterford

Pipers Brook
Pinot Noir - Tasmania

Champagne Jacquart
Brut Mosaique 1996

Excellence in everything we do

| Ninth Island | Vergelegen | Tenuta Del Portale | Villa Bizzarri | Monte Schiavo |
| Tasmania | South Africa | Italy | Italy | Italy |

Gleeson Wines, Unit 16 Cherry Orchard Ind. Est., Ballyfermot, Dublin 10, Tel: + 353 1 62 69787, Fax: + 353 1 62 60652

Leopard's Leap

YOU KNOW YOU WANT TO

★★ Mount Langi Ghiran Cliff Edge Shiraz 2001

Christmas cake spice aromas, medium intensity with a definite liquorice tang becoming stronger by the minute with some tobacco. Very nicely balanced, not overly alcoholic, and quite cool in its own way.

Price	€18–€22
Region	Grampians
Grape	Shiraz
Alc/vol	15%

Ampersand Wines

Callans, Dundalk; Goose Off-Licence, Drumcondra; Martins, Fairview; Sweeneys, Glasnevin

Penfolds Bin 28 Kalimna Shiraz 2003

Firm, concentrated, cool damson fruit with a real savoury edge and some very finely judged tannins on a long finish. Stylish wine.

Price	€18–€22
Region	SE Australia
Grape	Shiraz
Alc/vol	14.5%

Findlater Grants

Bourkes Fine Wine; Gables, Foxrock; Higgins, Clonskeagh; Harvest Off Licence, Galway; McCabe's; O'Briens; O'Donovan's, Douglas; Quinns, Drumcondra; Redmonds of Ranelagh; Sweeneys Wines, Glasnevin

Peter Lehmann The Futures Shiraz 2002

Sweet, big, ripe cassis with a soft, spicy element and a smooth finish; fully mature now, and drinking very nicely.

Price	€18–€22
Region	Barossa Valley
Grape	Shiraz
Alc/vol	14.5%

Comans

Corks of Terenure; Dalys of Boyle; Londis, Castledermot; McHughs of Kilbarrack & Malahide Rd; Mitchell & Son; Mortons, Ranelagh; Unwined Swords

★ Pikes Clare Valley Shiraz 2002

Elegant, ripe damson fruit offset by some black peppery notes. Very stylish wine.

Price	€18–€22
Region	Clare Valley
Grape	Shiraz
Alc/vol	14.5%

Nicholson

Old Stand, Mullingar

★ Rosemount Estate GSM 2002

Masses of smooth, intense, pure, ripe jammy fruits allied to some sweet, spicy notes make for a very seductive, heady wine. Treat yourself to this with grilled red meat.

Price	€18–€22
Region	McLaren Vale
Grape	Grenache/Syrah/Mourvèdre
Alc/vol	14.5%

Findlater Grants

Gables, Foxrock; Joyce, Knocknacarra; McCabe's; O'Briens; O'Donovan's, Douglas; Redmonds of Ranelagh; Terrys, Limerick; Worldwide Wines

Setanta Cabernet Sauvignon 2003

Cool, light and elegant with minty, soft, mature cassis. Now at its best, a smooth attractive wine.

Bunch of Grapes, Clonee; Coach House, Ballinteer; Connoisseur, Dundalk; Jus de Vine; McHughs, Kilbarrack; McHughs, Malahide Road; Mill, Maynooth; Red Island, Skerries; Silver Granite; Thomas's, Foxrock

Price	€18–€22
Region	Adelaide Hills
Grape	Cab Sauv
Alc/vol	13.5%

Inis Wines

Stella Bella Shiraz 2003

Attractive, full-on ripe raspberry and strawberry fruits; rounded, with plenty of body, and an easy, smooth finish.

Price	€18–€22
Region	Margaret River
Grape	Shiraz
Alc/vol	14%

Tindal

★ Tyrrell's Rufus Stone Heathcote Shiraz 2002

A very polished young wine with poised fruits and new oak; a classy, cooler-climate wine with a mass of well-defined savoury damson fruit.

Price	€18–€22
Region	Heathcote
Grape	Shiraz
Alc/vol	15%

Barry Fitzwilliam Maxxium

Londis, Malahide

€22–€30

★ Clairault Cabernet Merlot 2001

A swish, soft, sophisti-cated Cabernet with plenty of concentration and alcohol, showing some maturity and a sweet, minty finish.

Price	€22–€30
Region	Margaret River
Grape	Cab Sauv/Merlot
Alc/vol	14%

Febvre

> **Where to buy the wine**
> If your local retailer does not stock a particular wine, contact the distributor named in italic after the tasting note who will be pleased to give you details of the nearest stockist.

★ Clonakilla Hilltops Shiraz 2004

A very impressive wine with intense, ripe dark fruits, kept well in check by some clean acidity. It all makes for a very elegant, cooler style of Shiraz, but one with plenty of stuffing and real class.

Price	€22–€30
Region	New South Wales
Grape	Shiraz
Alc/vol	13.5%

Liberty Wines

Bailys of Howth; Cellars; Fallon & Byrne; Redmonds

Domain Day One Serious Pinot Noir 2003

Pale colour with some maturing aromas; opens out nicely to show ripe strawberry fruits, good intensity of flavour and a light meatiness. Attractive medium-bodied Pinot.

Price	€22–€30
Region	Barossa Valley
Grape	Pinot Noir
Alc/vol	13.5%

Bacchus

Elderton Barossa Shiraz 2003

A giant swathe of intense chocolate and raisined plums, soft and mature with a barnyardy touch—classic rich Barossa.

Berry Bros & Rudd

Price	€22–€30
Region	Barossa Valley
Grape	Shiraz
Alc/vol	14.5%

Berry Bros & Rudd

★ John Duval Plexus 2004

A wine packed with everything: masses of sumptuous, youthful dark fruits, high levels of toasty, spicy oak, with a sweet/sour kick on the finish. Big and youthful in every way.

Price	€22–€30
Region	Barossa Valley
Grape	Grenache/Shiraz/ Mourvèdre
Alc/vol	14.5%

Liberty Wines

Fallon & Byrne

★ John's Blend No. 6 Margarette's Shiraz 2000

Stinky, maturing mineral nose; very different on the palate—soft and easy, but with a lovely, firm, concentrated finish.

Price   **€22–€30**
Region   **South Australia**
Grape   **Shiraz**
Alc/vol   **14%**

Comans, Rathgar; Donnybrook Fair; Jus de Vine, Portmarnock; O'Donovans, Cork; Shiels, Dorset St

Comans

★★ Kalleske Clarry's Barossa Red 2005

A massive mouthful of ultra-ripe jammy strawberries, plums and dark fruits—full, spicy, heady wine tailor-made for the hedonist.

Price   **€22–€30**
Region   **Barossa Valley**
Grape   **Grenache/Shiraz**
Alc/vol   **14.5%**

Claudio's; Grape Escape, Lucan; McHughs, Kilbarrack; McHughs, Malahide; Morton's, Ranelagh; Morton's, Galway; Nectar Wines; Red Island, Skerries

Nectar Wines

★ Majella Cabernet Sauvignon 2002

A big wine with intense, very ripe black fruits that open out very slowly. There are plenty of well-integrated fine tannins, a leathery touch, and great length. A big but very well-structured Cabernet of high quality.

Price   **€22–€30**
Region   **Coonawarra**
Grape   **Cab Sauv**
Alc/vol   **14%**

Tindal

Millbrook Cabernet Sauvignon Merlot 2002

Refined, elegant, smooth plums and blackcurrants with a light herby edge and some vanilla oak. Showing a pleasing maturity and good length.

Price   **€22–€30**
Region   **Western Australia**
Grape   **Cab Sauv/Merlot**
Alc/vol   **14%**

Claudio's; Grape Escape, Lucan; McHughs, Kilbarrack; McHughs, Malahide; Morton's, Ranelagh; Morton's, Galway; Nectar Wines; Red Island, Skerries

Nectar Wines

Millbrook Shiraz 2002

Smooth, medium-bodied wine with supple fresh plums and subtle spice, with a rounded finish.

Price   **€22–€30**
Region   **Western Australia**
Grape   **Shiraz**
Alc/vol   **14.5%**

Claudio's; Grape Escape, Lucan; McHughs, Kilbarrack; McHughs, Malahide; Morton's, Ranelagh; Morton's, Galway; Nectar Wines; Red Island, Skerries

Nectar Wines

★ Penfolds Bin 407 Cabernet Sauvignon 2001

Concentrated blackcurrant fruit showing some development. A solid tannic shell surrounds the smooth palate and the wine has excellent length. Very good-quality Cabernet.

Price €22–€30
Region South Australia
Grape Cab Sauv
Alc/vol 14%

Findlater Grants

Cheers Off Licence; Eno Wine, Monkstown; Gables, Foxrock; Harvest Off Licence, Galway; Joyce, Knocknacarra; McCabe's; Martha's Vineyard; O'Donovan's, Douglas; Tesco; The Vaults IFSC; Vineyard Galway; Whelans, Wexford Street; Wicklow Wine Co.

Peter Lehmann Mentor Cabernet Sauvignon 2000

Maturing aromas and palate of very nicely developing ripe cassis and plums with a lovely touch of tar and lightly sweet oak. Good wine, and drinking very nicely now.

Price €22–€30
Region Barossa Valley
Grape Cab Sauv/Malbec/ Merlot
Alc/vol 13%

Comans

Comans of Rathgar; Eurospar, Dalkey; SPAR, Saggart; Vineyard Galway; The Lord Mayors, Swords

★ Pipers Brook Vineyard Pinot Noir 2003

Elegant, cool raspberry aromas. Clean, pure summer fruits with just enough spicy oak and a lovely ripe mid-palate; very attractive light Pinot Noir.

Price €22–€30
Region Tasmania
Grape Pinot Noir
Alc/vol 13.5%

Gleesons

Donnybrook Fair; McCabes; McHughs; Red Island Wine Co.; Sweeneys; Selected independent retailers

★★ Red Nectar Shiraz 2005

A young wine with massive power, but also surprising balance; ripe but tight, poised dark fruits, blackcurrants, plums and forest fruits, showing good length and no little style.

Price €22–€30
Region Barossa Valley
Grape Shiraz
Alc/vol 14.5%

Nectar Wines

Claudio's; Grape Escape, Lucan; McHughs, Kilbarrack; McHughs, Malahide; Morton's, Ranelagh; Morton's, Galway; Nectar Wines; Red Island, Skerries

★ The Colonial Estate Envoy 2004

Boom—a huge, ripe, meaty nose leads on to a loaded palate of mega-ripe figs, plums and tar with a burnt character; classic of its style and very nicely balanced.

Price €22–€30
Region Barossa Valley
Grape Grenache/Syrah/
Mourvèdre

Gilbeys

★★ The Colonial Estate L'Explorateur 2003

Big, smooth and rounded in an intensely ripe style—boy, does it have power—but it also has good peppery length. A colossus, with intensity, huge concentration, power and length.

Price €22–€30
Region Barossa Valley
Grape Shiraz
Alc/vol 14.5%

Gilbeys

★ Yalumba Barossa Valley Tricentenary Vines Grenache 2001

Big, jammy, rich strawberries with real intensity and a lovely freshness; rounded, rich and hugely concentrated. Perfect with game and red meats.

Price €22–€30
Region Barossa Valley
Grape Grenache
Alc/vol 14.5%

Cassidys

Cheers Delgany; Chester Beatty OL, Ashford; Corkscrew, D2; Donnybrook Fair; Fallon & Byrne, D2; Grape Escape, Lucan; Jus de Vine, Portmarnock; Kellys, Clontarf; Macs, Limerick; Marthas Vineyard, Rathfarnham; McCabes; O'Donovans, Cork; On The Grapevine Dalkey & Booterstown; Red Island Wine Co., Skerries; Thomas Martins, Fairview; Thomas Woodberrys, Galway; World Wide Wines, Waterford

★★ Yalumba Hand-picked Mourvèdre Grenache Shiraz 2004

Intense, slightly sweaty, very firm, cool, tight dark fruits, with a solid coat of tannins and real length. A wine of amazing proportions, but keeps it all together—just about.

Price €22–€30
Region Barossa Valley
Grape Mourvèdre/
Grenache/Shiraz

Cassidys

Cheers Delgany; Chester Beatty OL, Ashford; Corkscrew, D2; Donnybrook Fair; Fallon & Byrne, D2; Grape Escape, Lucan; Jus de Vine, Portmarnock; Kellys, Clontarf; Macs, Limerick; Marthas Vineyard, Rathfarnham; McCabes; O'Donovans, Cork; On The Grapevine Dalkey & Booterstown; Red Island Wine Co., Skerries; Thomas Martins, Fairview; Thomas Woodberrys, Galway; World Wide Wines, Waterford

€30–€40

Classic McLaren Blend La Testa 2000

Spicy herbs, liquorice and chocolate aromas, leading on to soft ripe plums and milk chocolate, finishing on a spicy note. Amazingly lush, sweet wine with real concentration.

Price	€30–€40
Region	McLaren Vale
Grape	Grenache/Shiraz/Cabernet
Alc/vol	14.4%

Baily Wines, Howth; Jus de Vine, Portmarnock; O'Neills, Carrickmacross

Inis Wines

★ Mitchelton Print Shiraz 2002

Looking for a wine with character? This has intense, leathery, stewed dark fruits with a mineral streak and a lovely tannic bite on the finish. Savoury and austere but packed with fruit. Try it with barbecued red meat.

Price	€30–€40
Region	Victoria
Grape	Shiraz
Alc/vol	15.5%

Dunnes Stores

★ Peter Lehmann Eight Songs Shiraz 2000

Big, hearty Shiraz with those lovely ultra-ripe plums and spice; now fully mature, this would go nicely with game dishes.

Price	€30–€40
Region	Barossa Valley
Grape	Shiraz
Alc/vol	14%

Donnybrook Fair; Gibneys, Malahide; O'Neills, SCR;The Leopardstown Inn

Comans

★ Stella Bella Suckfizzle Augusta Cabernet Sauvignon 2002

Very forward lush aromas of sweet new oak with a herbal touch; very appealing, soft, ripe and lush, with a distinct minty edge, good length and plenty of concentration. Drinking beautifully now.

Price	€30–€40
Region	Margaret River
Grape	Cab Sauv
Alc/vol	14%

Tindal

★ Tahbilk Reserve Shiraz 1994

This is a serious, dark, brooding Shiraz with masses of smoky liquorice and damson fruit, but it finishes cleanly with a surprising fresh note. An opportunity to taste a bit of history.

Price €30–€40
Region Victoria
Grape Shiraz
Alc/vol 12.5%

Comans

Dalys of Boyle; Deveneys, Dundrum; The Bottle Shop (No.1 Vintage), Stillorgan; The Wicklow Arms, Uncorked, Rathfarnham

---

★ Tyrrell's Vat 9 Hunter Shiraz 2001

Light, lean-muscled dark damsons with a definite savoury edge; good acidity and length with lovely gunflint notes. A world away from most other Aussie Shiraz, but great in its own way.

Price €30–€40
Region Hunter Valley
Grape Shiraz
Alc/vol 12%

Barry Fitzwilliam Maxxium

Londis

Wakefield St Andrews Cabernet Sauvignon 1999

Mature bouquet of cedar and roses. Soft, yielding flavours, still with some upfront blackcurrant fruit, but with lovely cedar and oak overtones. One to give your Francophile friends.

Price €30–€40
Region Clare Valley
Grape Cab Sauv
Alc/vol 14.5%

Koala Wines

Cheers, Blackrock; Connoisseur, Dundalk; Next Door, Kinsale; O'Briens; Shannon Knights; Superquinn; SuperValu, Westport; Sweeneys

---

★★ Wirra Wirra RSW Shiraz 2003

Pure elegant cherry fruits with stylish vanilla oak; light, easy drinking with a touch of class.

Price €30–€40
Region McLaren Vale
Grape Shiraz
Alc/vol 14.5%

Straffan

The Connoisseur; The Corkscrew; Donnybrook Fair; Lilac Wines; Red Island, Skerries

---

Rosé

Under €9

Jacob's Creek Shiraz Rosé 2005

Light, refreshing strawberry and raspberry fruits with a ripe kick on the finish. Summer in a glass.

Many branches of: Dunnes Stores; Londis; Mace; SPAR; SuperValu/Centra; Tesco

Special Value!

Price   Under €9
Region   SE Australia
Grape   Shiraz
Alc/vol   12.5%

Irish Distillers

Austria

Are Austrian wines finally starting to make an impact in this country? Let us hope so. Certainly, we have one of the largest representations in years; a number of larger importers and retailers, including O'Briens and Dunnes Stores, have taken the plunge and are listing a few Austrian wines. They and others join a small but faithful band of companies who have always been determined to give us the opportunity to taste the marvels that this country produces. I am not a huge fan of Austrian reds in general, although they have a few very enjoyable Pinot Noirs, but their white wines and dessert wines are superb, wines that are the equal of any other country, and far better than most. Look out for some lip-smacking, rich Rieslings with their wonderful definition and purity of fruit; seek out too the local speciality, Grüner Veltliner with its amazing ginger spice and ripe melon fruits.

White

Under €9

Winzer Krems Sandgrube Grüner Veltliner 2005

Special Value!

What a bargain! Grüner Veltliner's characteristic grapefruit aromas shine through. Satisfying palate of grapefruit with a streak of minerality. Well-made wine with much more complexity than you would expect at this price.

Price	Under €9
Region	Kremstal
Grape	Grüner Veltliner
Alc/vol	13%

Dunnes Stores

Selected branches Dunnes Stores

€9–€12

Salomon Groovey Grüner Veltliner 2005

Special Value!

Light and very fresh with plenty of crisp green fruits and melon; a very pleasant, all-purpose dry white wine at a keen price.

Price	€9–€12
Region	Niederösterreich
Grape	Grüner Veltliner
Alc/vol	12%

Oddbins

Oddbins

€12–€15

Fritsch Riesling 2005

Lively, clean Riesling with some pear and apple fruit, but it is the zippy lemon that gives it a lovely fresh zestiness.

O'Briens

Price	€12–€15
Region	Wagram
Grape	Riesling
Alc/vol	12.5%

O'Briens

Huber Riesling Von den Terrassen 2005

A charming Riesling with plump melon fruit, a touch of honey and nicely balanced acidity. Light and dry, it's perfect as an aperitif or with plain seafood.

Oddbins

Price	€12–€15
Region	Traisental
Grape	Riesling
Alc/vol	12%

Oddbins

€15–€18

Hirsch Zöbing Riesling 2003

Lively, fresh green-apple and lightly floral aromas; a light spritz, elegant, refreshing green fruits with good ripeness, and a lovely lemon zest kick, finishing long and dry—classy wine with real exuberance.

The Hole in the Wall, D7; WineOnline.ie; The Corkscrew, D2

Price	€15–€18
Region	Kamptal
Grape	Riesling
Alc/vol	12%

Wine Select

Wohlmuth Sauvignon Blanc 2005

Very aromatic gooseberry fruit on both nose and palate, with a solid core of refreshing citrus. Good length too—this is a match for most New Zealand Sauvignons.

Eugene's, Kenmare; Karwigs; Redmonds, Ranelagh

Price	€15–€18
Region	Styria
Grape	Sauv Blanc
Alc/vol	13%

Karwigs

€22–€30

Hiedler Thal Novemberlese 2003

Spicy ginger and marzipan with apples in a rich, tropical white wine, finishing on a honeyed note—great by itself or with Asian seafood dishes.

Berry Bros & Rudd

Price	€22–€30
Region	Kamptal
Grape	Grüner Veltliner
Alc/vol	13.5%

Berry Bros & Rudd

Irish Importers of Austrian Wine

Searsons Wine Merchants
Monkstown Crescent, Blackrock,
    County Dublin
Tel 01 280 0405; Fax 01 280 4771
e-mail: info@searsons.com
Website: www.searsons.com
Contact: Mr. Charles Searson,
    Managing Director
Freie Weingärtner Wachau,
    Wachau
Alois Kracher,
    Burgenland

Barry & Fitzwilliam Ltd
Glanmire, Cork
Tel 021 4320900; Fax 021 4320910
also at:
50 Dartmouth Square, Dublin 6
Tel 01 667 1755; Fax 01-660 0479
e-mail: info@bfmws.ie
Website: www.bfmws.ie
Contact: Mr. Michael Barry
Weinkellerei Lenz Moser,
    Kremstal

Terroirs
103 Morehampton Road, Dublin 4
Tel 01 667 1311; Fax 01 667 1312
e-mail: info@terroirs.ie
Website: www.terroirs.ie
Contact: Mr. Seán Gilley;
    Ms. Françoise Gilley-Traineau
Johanneshof Reinisch,
    Thermenregion

Mitchell & Son Wine Merchants
Ltd
54 Glasthule Road,
    Sandycove, Co. Dublin
Tel 01 230 2301; Fax 01 230 2305
also at:
21 Kildare Street, Dublin 2
Tel 01-676 0766; Fax 01-661 1509
e-mail: glasthule@mitchellandson.com
Website: www.mitchellandson.com
Contact: Mr. Peter B. Dunne,
    Director
Domäne Müller Gutsverwaltung,
    Styria

Berry Brothers & Rudd
4 Harry Street, Dublin 2
Tel 01 677 3444; Fax 01 677 3440
e-mail: sales@bbr.com
Website: www.bbr.com
Contact: Ms. Clare Burke or
    Mr. Anthony Jackson
Weingut Franz Hirtzberger,
    Wachau
Weingut Hiedler,
    Kamptal
Weingut Prager,
    Wachau
Weingut Unger,
    Burgenland

Karwig Wines Ltd
Kilnagleary, Carrigaline, Co. Cork
Tel 021 437 2864 / 437 4159
Fax 021 437 2864
e-mail: info@karwigwines.ie
Website: www.karwigwines.ie
Contact: Josef Karwig
Wohlmuth Wine Estate Est. 1803,
    Styria
Weinbau Johann Strauss,
    Kremstal
Weinkellerei Rebenfeld,
    Kosher Wines, Styria

Henry J. Archer & Sons Ltd
White Walls, Ballymoney,
    Gorey, Co Wexford
Tel 053 942 5176; Fax 055 25046
e-mail: info@pauldubsky.com
    paul.dubsky@oceanfree.net
Website: www.pauldubsky.com
Contact: Mr. Paul Dubsky
Fritz Salomon,
    Donauland/Wagram
Jost Hoepler,
    Burgenland
Erzherzog Johann Weine,
    Styria
Weingut Rudolf Bachkönig,
    Burgenland
Johann Kattus,
    Vienna

Irish Importers of Austrian Wine

Oddbins
6b Westend Retail Park
Blanchardstown, Dublin 15
Tel 01 824 3504; Fax 01 824 3506
e-mail:
oddbinsdirectireland@oddbins.com
Website: www.oddbins.com
Weingut Salomon Undhof, Kremstal
Weingut Tegernseerhof, Wachau
Weingut Huber, Traisental

Wineknows Ireland
C/o Ecock Wines and Spirits
Valentia House,
Custom House Square IFSC,
Dublin 1
e-mail: info@wineknows.com
Weingut W. Bründlmayer,
Kremstal

Cabot & Co. Fine Wines
4 Cloghan, Westport, Co. Mayo
Tel 076 602 1302; Fax 01 443 0735
Contact: Mr Liam Cabot
Weingut W. Bründlmayer,
Kremstal

Febvre & Co
Highfield House, Burton Hall Road,
Sandyford Industrial Estate
Dublin 18
Tel 01 2161400; Fax 01 295 9036
e-mail: info@febvre.ie
Website: www.febvre.ie
Contact: Ms Monica Murphy,
Mr David Whelahan
Weingut Sepp Moser,
Burgenland

Burren Fine Wine and Food
Corkscrew Hill Road,
Ballyvaughan, Co. Clare
Tel 065 707 7046 or 087 763 3241
e-mail: wine@burrenwine.ie
Website: www.burrenhampers.com
Contact: Ms Cathleen Connole
Weingut Stift Klosterneuburg,
Donauland
Domäne Wachau, Wachau

Superquinn
Support Office
PO Box 99, Sutton Cross, Dublin 13
Tel 01 816 7239 or 087 9109424
Fax 01 8167150
e-mail: kieran.cody@superquinn.ie
Website: www.superquinn.ie
Contact: Mr Kieran Cody
Weingut Dolle, Kamptal

WineSelect Handels GmbH
& Co KEG
Müllnergasse 9-11/3, Austria
Tel +43 1 406 0445
Fax +43 1 406 0455
e-mail: m.harrison@wineselect.at
Website: www.wineonline.ie
Contact: Mr Michael Harrison
Weingut Pfaffl, Weinviertel
Weingut Gerhard Markowitsch,
Carnuntum
Weingut Krems, Kremstal
Weingut Hirsch, Kamptal

O'Briens Wine Off Licence Group
33 Spruce Avenue, Stillorgan Industrial
Park, Stillorgan, Co Dublin
Tel 01 269 3139; Fax 01 269 7480
E-Mail: sales@obriensgroup.ie
Website: www.obrienswine.ie
Contact: Mr David Whelahan
Weingut Fritsch,
Donauland/Wagram

Dunnes Stores Ltd
Beaux Lane House,
Lower Mercer Street, Dublin 2
Tel 01 475 1111; Fax 01 475 4405
Website: www.dunnesstores.com
Winzer Krems Sandgrube,
Kremstal

Liberty Wines
Tel 087 7966222
e-mail:
peter.roycroft@libertywines.co.uk
Contact: Mr Peter Roycroft
Weingut Fred Loimer, Kamptal
Weingut Heinrich, Burgenland

★★ Hirsch Heiligenstein September 2002

Complex aromas of lightly honeyed pear; rich on the palate but with beautifully defined honeyed apples and pears, nicely textured, with excellent length. As with the best Austrian wines, superb pure fruits and lovely balancing acidity.

The Hole in the Wall, D7; WineOnline.ie

Price	€22–€30
Region	Kamptal
Grape	Riesling
Alc/vol	13%

Wine Select

★ Hirsch Lamm September 2002

Classy maturing honey and lemon aromas; lean, but rich honey, lemon and light ginger in an elegant wine that sings a bit. Long, dry, quite powerful, but impeccably balanced.

The Hole in the Wall, D7; WineOnline.ie

Price	€22–€30
Region	Kamptal
Grape	Grüner Veltliner
Alc/vol	13.5%

Wine Select

★ Sepp Moser Grüner Veltliner Breiter Rain Trocken 2004

Very individual wine with real complexity. Crisp and dry with zesty lemons, but also some rich ginger and grapefruit that last beautifully in the mouth.

Price	€22–€30
Region	Kremstal
Grape	Grüner Veltliner
Alc/vol	13.5%

Febvre

Red

€12–€15

Markowitsch Carnuntum Cuvée 2003

Crunchy, just-ripe fruits—true summer pudding; a nice sappy finish too. Light, easy-drinking wine.

The Hole in the Wall, D7; WineOnline.ie; Jus de Vine, Portmarnock

Price	€12–€15
Region	Carnuntum
Grape	Zweigelt/Pinot Noir
Alc/vol	13%

Wine Select

Chile

As with previous years, Chile has not performed as well as its position in the marketplace would suggest, although this year we list a very creditable 49 wines. The argument remains the same. Chile offers consistency and real value in its wines. But once we move up the quality scale, it does not punch with its full weight. However, things are changing rapidly. There are new cooler regions emerging, such as Bío-Bío in the south, Casablanca, Leyda in the centre and Limarí and Elqui to the north. These diverse areas share one thing—a cooler climate, and therefore very different wines, with well-defined fruits. We list a number of these wines, and look forward to seeing many more in future editions. Even producers from the more established regions are beginning to define regional flavours, and we can expect an even greater range of styles in the future.

White

Under €9

Aresti Estate Selection Chardonnay 2006

Special Value!

Very attractive fresh tropical fruit cut through with lively citrus acidity and the merest hint of oak. Very nicely crafted Chardonnay.

Price	Under €9
Region	Curicó Valley
Grape	Chardonnay
Alc/vol	13.5%

Musgrave

Canepa Sauvignon Blanc 2006

Special Value!

This is good, medium-bodied, broad, ripe Sauvignon, with some pleasant grassy notes and a bit of zip on the finish.

Kelly's Wine Vault, Clontarf

Price	Under €9
Region	Maipo Valley
Grape	Sauv Blanc
Alc/vol	13.5%

Kelly & Co.

> All of the wines in this book are ready to drink now (October 2006), and for the next 12 months. Some will improve further over time and this is mentioned in the tasting note.

Cono Sur Limited Release Gewurztraminer 2005

Classic rose-petal and honeysuckle nose, but not overpowering. Very nicely balanced, smooth, lightly textured, honeyed fruit backed up by some zippy lemons and a dry finish. Very attractive wine.

Price	Under €9
Region	Bío-Bío Valley
Grape	Gewurztraminer
Alc/vol	14%

Findlater Grants

Bennett's, Howth; Eurospar, Dalkey; Higgins, Clonskeagh; Jaynes, Ennis; Martha's Vineyard; Redmonds, Ranelagh; Village, Ballyvaughan

€9–€12

Calbuco Semillon Chardonnay 2005

Forthright, uncomplicated wine with smooth melon and pear fruit; harmonious, and very attractive drinking.

Price	€9–€12
Region	Central Valley
Grape	Chardonnay
Alc/vol	14%

Bailys of Howth; Donnybrook Fair; Fallon & Byrne; Listons; Red Island, Skerries; Uncorked

Liberty Wines

Chileno Gold Sauvignon Blanc 2004

Vibrant, fresh, hugely aromatic nose with gooseberries; the palate has lots of lemon sherbet and nettle flavours; it will certainly wake you up.

Price	€9–€12
Region	Casablanca Valley
Grape	Sauv Blanc
Alc/vol	13%

Galvin

Miguel Torres Don Miguel Gewurztraminer Riesling 2004

Rich rose-petal and grapefruit aromas; clean, light apple fruit with plenty of acidity and a curious honeyed note. Quirky but enjoyable, finishing on a strong mineral note. Very good wine with character.

Price	€9–€12
Region	Curicó Valley
Grape	Gewurztraminer/ Riesling
Alc/vol	13.5%

Woodford Bourne

Donnybrook Fair; McCabes, Blackrock; On the Grapevine, Dalkey

Trio Sauvignon Blanc 2005

Clean pears and lemon zest with a rounded, soft finish; well-made wine with good varietal character and instant appeal. By itself or with fish or seafood.

Bin No 9 Goatstown; Bourkes Fine Wine; Cheers, Wicklow Arms; Donnybrook Fair; Gables, Foxrock; Grapevine, Booterstown; Jus de Vine, Portmarnock; McCabe's; Martha's Vineyard; O'Donovan's, Douglas & Cork; Worldwide Wines

Price €9–€12
Region Casablanca Valley
Grape Sauv Blanc
Alc/vol 13%

Findlater Grants

€12–€15

Millaman Estate Reserva Chardonnay 2004

Wet stones on the nose. Restrained palate with mineral overtones and some citrus notes, growing in complexity through the persistent, focused finish.

Cana; Crouchans, Athlone; Greenacres, Wexford; Jus de Vine

Price €12–€15
Region Curicó Valley
Grape Chardonnay
Alc/vol 13.5%

Vineyard Galway

€15–€18

Concha y Toro Terrunyo Sauvignon Blanc 2003

Plump, rounded pears and tropical fruit set off by some nice grapefruit notes, good concentration, some lovely mid-palate complexity, and a long, stylish finish.

Gables, Foxrock; Gibneys, Malahide; Ivan's, Caherdavin; Jus de Vine, Portmarnock; McCabe's; Martha's Vineyard; Morton's, Galway; O'Donovans, Douglas; The Vaults, IFSC

Price €15–€18
Region Casablanca Valley
Grape Sauv Blanc
Alc/vol 13.5%

Findlater Grants

€18–€22

Montes Alpha Chardonnay 2005

Refreshing, crisp apple fruit contrasting with some subtle charred oak notes, but there is persistence of fruit, a touch of class and an appealing liveliness.

Bourkes Fine Wines; Donnybrook Fair; Egan's Off Licence, Drogheda; Gables, Foxrock; Greenacres, Wexford; Joyce, Knocknacarra; McCabe's; O'Briens; O'Donovan's, Douglas; Redmonds of Ranelagh; Terry's Wines, Limerick

Price €18–€22
Region Casablanca Valley
Grape Chardonnay
Alc/vol 13.5%

Findlater Grants

Santa Rita Floresta Sauvignon Blanc 2004

A very lively dry Sauvignon with pear drops and lean citrus fruit, finishing on a strong mineral note.

Price	€18–€22
Region	Leyda Valley
Grape	Sauv Blanc
Alc/vol	13.5%

Gilbeys

€22–€30

Casa Marin Laurel Vineyard Sauvignon Blanc 2004

A very unusual wine, well worth trying for novelty value alone. Big, rich, aromatic nose with floral, honeysuckle aromas; very powerful, rich and alcoholic, with lychees and almost a beeriness—you wouldn't necessarily guess it was a Sauvignon.

Wines Direct

Price	€22–€30
Region	San Antonio Valley
Grape	Sauv Blanc
Alc/vol	14%

Wines Direct

Red

Under €9

Cono Sur Pinot Noir 2004

Special Value!

Last year's award winner gains a deserved entry once more. Fairly concentrated, slightly earthy wine with plenty of power and some very attractive cherry fruit.

Drink Store, Dublin; Jayne's, Ennis; Joyce's, Headford and Knocknacarra; Jus de Vine, Portmarnock; Londis, Clane; Martha's Vineyard; Martin's, Fairview; Nolan's, Clontarf; O'Donovan's, Douglas; Petrogas, Finglas; Redmond's, Ranelagh; SuperValu

Price	Under €9
Region	Rapel Valley
Grape	Pinot Noir
Alc/vol	13.5%

Findlater Grants

Rio Alto Classic Merlot 2005

Special Value!

Smooth, plump, plummy fruit with a spicy touch and a lovely soft finish. Great easy-drinking wine.

Price	Under €9
Region	Aconcagua Valley
Grape	Merlot
Alc/vol	13.5%

Musgrave

€9–€12

Calbuco Cabernet Merlot 2004

Special Value!

Jammy, rounded, plump damson fruit, with a smooth, peppery finish and a nice lightness.

Bailys of Howth; Donnybrook Fair; Fallon & Byrne; Listons; Uncorked

Price **€9–€12**
Region **Central Valley**
Grape **Cab Sauv/Merlot**
Alc/vol **13%**

Liberty Wines

Casillero del Diablo Cabernet Sauvignon 2005

Special Value!

Soft, mellow dark fruits with a creamy vanilla background. Approachable wine that is almost too easy to drink.

Bennett's, Howth; Bourkes Fine Wine; Dunnes Stores; Higgins, Clonskeagh; McCabe's; McHugh's, Raheny; Martha's Vineyard; O'Briens; O'Donovans, Douglas; Redmonds, Ranelagh; Superquinn

Price **€9–€12**
Region **Central Valley**
Grape **Cab Sauv**
Alc/vol **13%**

Findlater Grants

Pirque Estate Cabernet Sauvignon 2004

A bit of a monster with big, concentrated meaty red fruits, but in a very enjoyable, well-made style.

Price **€9–€12**
Region **Maipo Valley**
Grape **Cab Sauv**
Alc/vol **14.5%**

Marks & Spencer

Porta Carmenère Reserve 2005

A very good and very reasonably priced Carmenère, with plenty of stuffing to complement the light herbaceous notes; fruity, rounded and very gluggable.

Currids Off Licence, Sligo; Kellys Wine Vault, Clontarf; Eldons Off Licence, Cahir; Cheers The Laurels, Perrystown; McLoughlins, Manor Street D7; Martins, Fairview

Price **€9–€12**
Region **Maipo Valley**
Grape **Carmenère**
Alc/vol **13.5%**

Taserra

Porta Pinot Noir Reserve 2004

Very pleasant, smooth, soft, red cherry and slightly jammy fruit; attractive, supple wine.

Harvest Off Licence, Galway; Old Stand Off Licence, Mullingar; The Lakes Off Licence, Blessington; Gibneys, Malahide; Connoisseur Wine Shop, Dundalk; Galvins, Listowel; Knights Off Licence, Shannon; McCabes, Blackrock; Eldons Off Licence, Cahir; Lonergans, Clonmel; Jus de Vine, Portmarnock

Price €9–€12
Region Bío-Bío Valley
Grape Pinot Noir
Alc/vol 13.5%

Taserra

Rio Alto Reserve Cabernet Sauvignon 2003

Refined, restrained pure blackcurrant and plum fruit with subtle vanilla, well-integrated tannins, and just enough structure—very enjoyable wine.

Price €9 €12
Region Aconcagua Valley
Grape Cab Sauv
Alc/vol 13.5%

Musgrave

Secano Pinot Noir 2005 **Special Value!**

Big, rich, concentrated, smooth dark fruits, full-bodied and quite meaty but without losing the purity of fruit. Very good value.

Price €9–€12
Region Leyda Valley
Grape Pinot Noir
Alc/vol 14%

Marks & Spencer

Viña Maipo Carmenère Reserva 2005 **Special Value!**

Very classy, rich dark chocolate and plums with some welcome notes of coconut and spice; smooth and very good at the price.

Most branches Dunnes Stores

Price €9–€12
Region Central Valley
Grape Carmenère
Alc/vol 13.5%

Dunnes Stores

Yali Merlot 2004 **Special Value!**

Juicy, ripe nose; sweet, jammy, ripe cassis and plums with an attractive spiciness and a rounded finish. Slightly astringent on the finish, but more than makes up for it with its bouncy, lively fruit.

Price €9–€12
Region Colchagua Valley
Grape Merlot
Alc/vol 13.5%

Galvin

> **Where to buy the wine**
> *If your local retailer does not stock a particular wine, contact the distributor named in italic after the tasting note who will be pleased to give you details of the nearest stockist.*

Yali Reserve Pinot Noir 2002

Wonderful pure dark cherries and plums; rich, spicy but very sexy ripe raspberries, strawberries and milk chocolate in an open-knit style with plenty of oomph. Very attractive wine, and nicely concentrated too.

Price €9–€12
Region Casablanca Valley
Grape Pinot Noir
Alc/vol 14.5%

Galvin

€12–€15

Carmen Cabernet Sauvignon Reserve 2003

A very attractive full-bodied wine filled with sweet cassis and soft, jammy fruits. A sure-fire crowd-pleaser; needs food to show at its best.

McCabes, Blackrock/Foxrock; Jus de Vine, Portmarnock; McHugh's, Raheny/Artane; Martha's Vineyard, Rathfarnham; McHugh's, Artane; SuperValu, Mullingar; SuperValu, Dunmanway; SuperValu, Churchtown D14

Price €12–€15
Region Maipo Valley
Grape Cab Sauv
Alc/vol 14%

Dillons

Carta Vieja Pinot Noir 2004

Jammy, ripe aromas; some big, vegetal, rounded, sweet cherry fruit—not the most elegant, but a seductive big style.

Price €12–€15
Region Aconcagua Valley
Grape Pinot Noir
Alc/vol 12.5%

Bacchus

Clos Centenaire 2003

Subtle, bordeaux-like, tangy blackcurrants and blackberries, emphasised by a herby note, finishing with black pepper tannins. Very enjoyable wine.

Caprani's; Donnybrook Fair; Waterford World of Wine

Price €12–€15
Region Maule Valley
Grape Cab Sauv/
Carmenère/
Merlot/Cab Franc
Alc/vol 13.5%

J Donohue

Echeverria Reserva Merlot 2003

This is very enjoyable, with cool black pepper, capsicums and lasting dark fruits in a big but stylish wine that finishes on a good dry note.

Price €12–€15
Region Molina
Grape Merlot
Alc/vol 14%

Bacchus

Marqués de Casa Concha Merlot 2004

Dusky damson and plum nose. Very flavoursome palate of inky dark fruits, with fairly strong tannins and a long blackcurrant finish.

Price €12–€15
Region Rapel Valley
Grape Merlot
Alc/vol 14.5%

Cheers, Wicklow Arms; Donnybrook Fair; Fahys Off Licence; Gables, Foxrock; Higgins, Clonskeagh; Jus de Vine, Portmarnock; McCabes Fine Wines; Martha's Vineyard; O'Donovan's, Douglas; Sweeneys Wines, Glasnevin; The Wine Centre; The Vaults IFSC; The Vintry, Rathgar; Vineyard Galway

Findlater Grants

Miguel Torres Tormenta Cabernet Sauvignon Reserva 2004　　　Organic

Big, intense flavours of mint, dark fruits and coffee, in a full-bodied, firmly integrated wine that would improve with decanting.

Price €12–€15
Region Central Valley
Grape Cab Sauv
Alc/vol 14%

Daly's Off-licence, Boyle

Woodford Bourne

Milliman Estate Cabernet Sauvignon Reserva 2004

Swarthy, tangy, herby, dark forest fruits—needs a very bloody steak to keep it under control.

Price €12–€15
Region Curicó Valley
Grape Cab Sauv
Alc/vol 13.5%

Cana Off-licence, Mullingar; Greenacres, Wexford; Jus de Vine, Portmarnock

Vineyard Galway

MontGras Quatro Reserva 2004

Rounded, smooth, soft, lightly spicy fruits, with an easy, chocolate-laden finish.

Price €12–€15
Region Colchagua Valley
Grape Cab Sauv/ Carmenère/ Merlot/Malbec
Alc/vol 14%

Superquinn; SuperValu/Centra

Barry Fitzwilliam Maxxium

MontGras Reserva Merlot 2004

A slightly firmer style of Merlot with nicely balanced ripe plums, a spicy vanilla element and some fine tannins coming through on the finish.

Price €12–€15
Region Colchagua Valley
Grape Merlot
Alc/vol 14%

Superquinn; SuperValu/Centra

Barry Fitzwilliam Maxxium

Tabalí Reserva Shiraz 2002

A very big, concentrated, sweet, alcoholic, oaky wine that fills every corner of the mouth. On second tasting, there is a certain balance to the fruit, but still a huge wine.

Price	€12–€15
Region	Limarí
Grape	Shiraz
Alc/vol	14%

Cassidys

Cheers Delgany; Chester Beatty OL, Ashford; Corkscrew, D2; Donnybrook Fair; Fallon & Byrne, D2; Grape Escape, Lucan; Jus de Vine, Portmarnock; Kellys, Clontarf; Macs, Limerick; Marthas Vineyard, Rathfarnham; McCabes; O'Donovans, Cork; On The Grapevine Dalkey & Booterstown; Red Island Wine Co., Skerries; Thomas Martins, Fairview; Thomas Woodberrys, Galway; World Wide Wines, Waterford

---

€15–€18

Errázuriz Max Reserva Shiraz 2002

A full-bodied, maturing wine with liquorice and damson fruits alongside some smoky notes.

Dunnes; O'Brien's; Superquinn

Price	€15–€18
Region	Aconcagua Valley
Grape	Shiraz
Alc/vol	14%

Allied Drinks

Leon de Oro Merlot Cabernet Sauvignon 2004

Cool, minty, plummy aromas; there are some nicely defined spicy tobacco flavours to go alongside the rich plums. Plenty of alcohol, too, in a full-bodied style.

Price	€15–€18
Region	Rapel Valley
Grape	Merlot/Cab Sauv
Alc/vol	14.5%

Marks & Spencer

Leyda Las Brisas Pinot Noir 2005

A big, broad Pinot with very ripe raspberry fruit—smooth but quite hearty and not without some elegance; attractive, flavoursome wine.

The Drink Store, Manor Street; Redmonds, Ranelagh

Price	€15–€18
Region	Leyda Valley
Grape	Pinot Noir
Alc/vol	14%

Nicholson

Los Vascos Grande Reserve Cabernet Sauvignon 2003

Elegant, cool blackcurrant fruit with some smoky new oak and fine-grained tannins on a dry finish. Try it with roast beef or lamb.

O'Briens

Price	€15–€18
Region	Colchagua Valley
Grape	Cab Sauv
Alc/vol	13.5%

O'Briens

Palo Alto Reserva 2005

Super nose of toast and black fruit. Lovely melange of dark fruits on the palate, with plenty of oak and vanilla support, and smooth tannins.

All branches Dunnes Stores

Price €15–€18
Region Maule Valley
Grape Cab Sauv/
Carmenère/Syrah
Alc/vol 13.5%

Dunnes Stores

Rio Alto Private Collection 2004

Classy, minty blackcurrant fruit with plenty of supporting alcohol; knits together very nicely—quality wine.

Price €15–€18
Region Aconcagua Valley
Grape Cab Sauv/
Carmenère/Syrah
Alc/vol 14%

Musgrave

Tabalí Reserva Especial 2003

A big wine, stuffed with ripe cassis, smoky, toasty new oak and a lovely soft centre palate.

Cheers Delgany; Chester Beatty OL, Ashford; Corkscrew, D2; Donnybrook Fair; Fallon & Byrne, D2; Grape Escape, Lucan; Jus de Vine, Portmarnock; Kellys, Clontarf; Macs, Limerick; Marthas Vineyard, Rathfarnham; McCabes; O'Donovans, Cork; On The Grapevine Dalkey & Booterstown; Red Island Wine Co., Skerries; Thomas Martins, Fairview; Thomas Woodberrys, Galway; World Wide Wines, Waterford

Price €15–€18
Region Limarí
Grape Cab Sauv/Merlot/
Shiraz
Alc/vol 14%

Cassidys

Viña Pérez Cruz Limited Edition Reserva Syrah 2003

Rich dark chocolate and ripe plums in a fairly big, powerful, meaty wine with good purity of fruit, a herbal touch and a soft, easy finish.

Price €15–€18
Region Maipo Valley
Grape Syrah
Alc/vol 14.5%

Celtic Whiskey Shop

Yali Grand Reserve Cabernet Sauvignon 2003

Pleasing cassis and herbal nose; lovely cool blackcurrant fruits balanced by a lightly tannic structure and a spiciness that never dominates.

Price €15–€18
Region Colchagua Valley
Grape Cab Sauv
Alc/vol 14%

Galvin

All of the wines in this book are ready to drink now (October 2006), and for the next 12 months. Some will improve further over time and this is mentioned in the tasting note.

ARGENTINE BEAUTY.
TRAPICHE WINES.

**Trapiche wines reveal the
extraordinary potential held in the wide
variety of Argentina's terroirs.**

www.sterman-viggiano.com

Best Buy - Wine Enthusiast - Trapiche Malbec Oak Cask 2004.

TRAPICHE
ARGENTINA
www.trapiche.com.ar

Mendoza • Argentina

The Best of Wine in Ireland

`€18–€22`

★ Altum Terra Mater Reserve Merlot 1999

Rich, smoky oak aromas; nicely balanced smoky plum fruits with a savoury tang—it has a bit of personality, real refinement and some maturity.

McCambridges, Galway

Price **€18–€22**
Region **Maipo Valley**
Grape **Merlot**
Alc/vol **13%**

McCambridges

`€22–€30`

Casa Lapostolle Merlot Cuvée Alexandre Apalta Vineyard 2002

Beginning to show some maturity, with a vegetal edge to the full-bodied ripe plums and cassis with a smoky nuance.

Gaffneys of Castlebar & Ballina; Jus de Vine, Portmarnock; O'Briens; SPAR, Rathcoole

Price **€22–€30**
Region **Rapel Valley**
Grape **Merlot**
Alc/vol **14.5%**

Comans

Casa Lapostolle Syrah Cuvée Alexandre Requinoa Vineyard 2003

A massive wine, packed with savoury fruit, plenty of heady alcohol and some drying tannins on a lengthy finish. Decant and drink with something equally big, or lay down for a year or two.

Jus de Vine, Portmarnock; O'Neills, SCR; Redmonds, Ranelagh

Price	**€22–€30**
Region	**Rapel Valley**
Grape	**Syrah**
Alc/vol	**14.5%**

Comans

Cousiño Macul Finis Terrae 1997

Fully mature now, but a very pleasant, elegant glass of wine with a good core of solid damson and blackcurrant fruit and a leafy, light finish. Drink up.

Vaughan Johnson

Price	**€22 €30**
Region	**Maipo Valley**
Grape	**Cab Sauv/Merlot**
Alc/vol	**12.5%**

Papillon

★ MontGras Ninquén 2002

Big, rich and concentrated with dark chocolate, mint and dark cassis fruits; plenty of well-integrated tannins too in a softly fruited, powerful wine. Impressive stuff.

B & J Wine; McCambridge's, Galway

Price	**€22–€30**
Region	**Colchagua Valley**
Grape	**Cab Sauv/Malbec**
Alc/vol	**14.5%**

Barry Fitzwilliam Maxxium

★ Santa Rita Floresta Syrah 1999

Good, clean, slightly leathery wine with marked concentration of peppery, somewhat austere fruit; tannic on the finish. It opens out very nicely to reveal a classy wine with excellent contrast between ripe and savoury.

Price	**€22–€30**
Region	**Maipo Valley**
Grape	**Petite Syrah/ Merlot/Cab Sauv**
Alc/vol	**14.5%**

Gilbeys

France

I hate overhearing someone say that they dislike French wine; France produces every style of wine going from the most delicate dry wines on up to the big and powerful. Throw in the great sparkling and dessert wines, and there is something for every wine-lover. France produces more of the world's greatest wines, more of the world's individual wines, in greater quantity than anyone else. It is disappointing to see their market share fall each year, but at least the market is growing.

There are welcome signs that at last the authorities are willing to change some of the more restrictive aspects of French wine law. This would allow French wines to compete on a level footing with New World wines. Let us hope that they improve the overall quality of certain Appellation Contrôlée wines too; at the moment some are inspiring, and others ordinary. The term must come to signify a certain level of quality as well as authenticity.

France has always done well in *The Best of Wine in Ireland*, and this year is certainly no exception: we list a total of 227 wines, including some 88 star wines.

France–Alsace

The Alsace section this year is much smaller than usual, largely because fewer wines were entered, rather than because of any prejudice on the part of the tasters or myself. A mere 12 wines were entered, and 10 gained an entry, not a bad percentage.

Alsace, for so long the source of great un-oaked crisp dry white wines, appears to be making several styles of wine today. Many are richer, more alcoholic and often sweeter than their predecessors. The growers argue this is because they harvest later, with lower yields, giving a must that has more flavour and sugar. Others stick to the more traditional style.

There is no doubt that Alsace produces some great Riesling, and quite a few other very good wines too. In this region you will find Pinot Gris (known as Pinot Grigio in Italy) with real flavour, and some marvellous Gewürztraminer. The Pinot Blancs listed below make a compelling case for a variety often dismissed as second class.

White

€9–€12

Marks & Spencer Pinot Grigio Alsace 2005

Special Value!

Quite plump, ripe peach fruit in a soft, enticingly fruity wine—by itself or with creamy fish.

Price **€9–€12**
Region **Alsace**
Grape **Pinot Gris**
Alc/vol **13%**

Marks & Spencer

€12–€15

Dom. Paul Zinck Pinot Blanc Prestige Alsace 2004

Rich, almost decadent, bruised red-apple fruit with good supporting acidity and a rounded finish. Far removed from your normal Pinot Blanc, and well worth a try.

Price **€12–€15**
Region **Alsace**
Grape **Pinot Blanc**
Alc/vol **12.5%**

Probus Wines

Firhouse Inn; Great Escape, Banna; Next Door, Enfield; The Wicklow Wine Co.; Wine Cluster, Moycullen

Meyer-Fonné Pinot Blanc Vieilles Vignes Alsace 2004

Lively fresh pear aromas; soft, rich pear and orange fruit, with just enough acidity. Very good textured wine with a touch of style, and offering value too.

Celtic Whiskey; The Corkscrew; Fallon & Byrne; Le Caveau

Price €12–€15
Region Alsace
Grape Pinot Blanc
Alc/vol 12.5%

Le Caveau

€15–€18

Dom. Bott-Geyl Pinot d'Alsace Alsace 2002

Sumptuous, textured, honeyed pineapple and pear fruit with some barley sugar and a rich, off-dry finish.

Mill Wine Cellar, Maynooth

Price €15–€18
Region Alsace
Grape Pinot Blanc/Pinot Noir/Pinot Gris/ Pinot Auxerrois
Alc/vol 12.5%

Nicholson

Dom. Zusslin Pinot Auxerrois Alsace 2004

Biodynamic

Rich, plump marzipan, canned peaches and orange peel in a soft, spicy wine with real texture. Developing nicely, this would make a good partner for rich chicken dishes or foie gras.

Centra; George's Delicatessen, Slane; The Kitchen & Food Hall, Portlaoise; Nolan's, Clontarf; O'Tooles, Sandycove

Price €15–€18
Region Alsace
Grape Pinot Auxerrois
Alc/vol 13%

Vendemia

Meyer-Fonné Tokay Pinot Gris Réserve Particulière Alsace 2004

Rich aromas of orange peel and exotic fruits; big, rich, quite powerful mix of luscious fresh pears and orange peel, finishing on a rounded, off-dry note.

Le Caveau

Price €15–€18
Region Alsace
Grape Pinot Gris
Alc/vol 13.5%

Le Caveau

€18–€22

★ Dom. Zusslin Riesling Bollenberg Alsace 2004   **Biodynamic**

Rich, gorgeous, ripe red apples with real power and structure, a mouth-filling mid-palate and a long, slightly spicy finish.

Absolutely Organic; Be Organic; Centra; Ecoshop, Kilmacanogue; George's Delicatessen, Slane; Nolan's, Clontarf; O'Tooles, Sandycove

Price	**€18–€22**
Region	Alsace
Grape	Riesling
Alc/vol	14%

Vendemia

Dopff & Irion Dom. du Ch. de Riquewihr Les Murailles Alsace 2002

Magnificent old Riesling developing light kerosene but lovely nutty honeyed notes too, with rich apples cut through with really vibrant acidity. Drinking beautifully now.

Cheers Delgany; Chester Beatty OL, Ashford; Corkscrew, D2; Donnybrook Fair; Fallon & Byrne, D2; Grape Escape, Lucan; Jus de Vine, Portmarnock; Kellys, Clontarf; Macs, Limerick; Marthas Vineyard, Rathfarnham; McCabes; O'Donovans, Cork; On The Grapevine Dalkey & Booterstown; Red Island Wine Co., Skerries; Thomas Martins, Fairview; Thomas Woodberrys, Galway; World Wide Wines, Waterford

Price	**€18–€22**
Region	Alsace
Grape	Riesling
Alc/vol	12.5%

Cassidys

€22–€30

Dom. Zind-Humbrecht Riesling Gueberschwihr Alsace 2002

An impeccably balanced Riesling with crisp honeyed fruit and excellent length. You could drink it on its own, but fish or roast chicken would be even better.

Price	**€22–€30**
Region	Alsace
Grape	Riesling
Alc/vol	13.5%

Comans

€30–€40

★ Dom. Zind-Humbrecht Pinot Gris Heimbourg Alsace 2002

Intense, rich young wine that is beginning to come out of its shell, revealing a huge concentration of melons and barley sugar with some spice kicking in on a very lengthy finish.

Price	**€30–€40**
Region	Alsace
Grape	Riesling
Alc/vol	14%

Comans

France–Beaujolais

I must admit I was surprised to see that we had seven entries for Beaujolais this year, including two stars. They are not wines that always do well in blind tastings; they are wines for drinking rather than judging. However, we list a few fascinating wines, some with real concentration and complexity. They go some way to convincing cynics such as myself that Beaujolais can rise above simple (but delicious) refreshing jug wines.

Red

€12–€15

Dom. de la Bêche Cuvée Vieilles Vignes Morgon 2004

Light, sweet summer fruits finishing with a concentrated meatiness— elegant but with some real power.

Price **€12–€15**
Region **Beaujolais**
Grape **Gamay**
Alc/vol **13%**

The Bottle Shop; Drink Store; Louis Albrouze Wine; Morton's, Galway; Morton's, Ranelagh; Vanilla Grape, Kenmare

Louis Albrouze

€15–€18

Dom. Jean-Claude Lapalu Cuvée Vieilles Vignes Brouilly 2004

Lightly aromatic nose leading on to very classy, beautifully defined summer fruits, with good length and a pleasing herbaceous touch. Light, elegant but concentrated wine.

Price **€15–€18**
Region **Beaujolais**
Grape **Gamay**
Alc/vol **13%**

Wicklow Wine

Wicklow Wine Co., Jus de Vine, Listons, Michael's Food & Wine

Dom. Jean-Marc Burgaud Les Charmes Morgon 2004

Meaty, perfumed, minerally wine with character; deceptively light at first, but it has good intensity. The overall impression is of real freshness.

Price **€15–€18**
Region **Beaujolais**
Grape **Gamay**
Alc/vol **13%**

Firhouse Inn; Great Escape, Banna; Next Door, Enfield; The Wicklow Wine Co.; Wine Cluster, Moycullen

Probus Wines

Dom. Lucien Lardy Le Vivier Vieilles Vignes Fleurie 2005

Quite young still, but with very attractive, delicate cherry fruits, a peak of acidity to bring real life, and no tannins worth speaking about. Pleasant young Beaujolais.

Price **€15–€18**
Region **Beaujolais**
Grape **Gamay**
Alc/vol **13%**

Inis Wines

Bailys, Howth; Bin No. 9; Breakaway Wines, Kerry; Brechin Watchorn; Caprani's; Dalys, Boyle; Fallon & Byrne; Jus de Vine; Martins, Fairview; Mill, Maynooth; Mortons, Galway; On the Grapevine, Dalkey; On the Grapevine, Booterstown; Red Island, Skerries; SPAR, Bath Avenue; Thomas's, Foxrock; The Wicklow Wine Co.

€18–€22

★ Dom. Jean-Claude Lapalu Cuvée Vieilles Vignes Brouilly 2005

Beautifully poised, well-defined, elegant plums with a mineral edge and a supple but amazingly long, pure finish. Delicious.

Price **€18–€22**
Region **Beaujolais**
Grape **Gamay**
Alc/vol **12.8%**

Wicklow Wine

Wicklow Wine Co., Jus de Vine, Listons, Michael's Food & Wine, Harvest Off-licences, Galway, Hand Made Wines

---

€22–€30

Dom. Jean-Claude Lapalu Cuvée des Fous Brouilly 2004

Ever wondered what oaked Beaujolais would taste like? Here is your chance—elegant, ripe strawberry and blackberry fruit overlain with smoky new oak coming through on the finish.

Price **€22–€30**
Region **Beaujolais**
Grape **Gamay**
Alc/vol **13%**

Wicklow Wine

Wicklow Wine Co., Jus de Vine, Listons, Michael's Food & Wine, Harvest Off-licences, Galway

---

> ### How to use this book
> The wines are listed in order of country/region, colour (red or white), price band, then by name. There are separate chapters for sparkling (including Champagne) and dessert wines. If you can't find the wine you are looking for try the index. The price bands are guidelines only. All of the wines in this book are ready to drink now (October 2006), and for the next 12 months. Some will improve further over time and this is mentioned in the tasting note.

★ Jean-Paul Brun Moulin-à-Vent 2004

Very interesting,
concentrated plum
fruit set off by some
good acidity and
decent length. A very
different wine that
really grows on you.
Made without sulphur.

Wines Direct

Price	€22–€30
Region	Beaujolais
Grape	Gamay
Alc/vol	12%

Wines Direct

France–Bordeaux

Bordeaux has hardly been off the front pages of the wine press and mainstream media all year, for good reasons and bad. The good first: 2005 was an exceptional vintage, hailed by many as the greatest in 50 years. I have tasted only a small selection of the wines and so cannot comment. However, in my relatively short time in the wine trade, I have witnessed no fewer than 11 'vintages of the century'! I would advise a certain amount of caution. The wine trade, and sometimes even the press, have an interest in talking up the wines. I have no doubt that the wines are very good; time will tell just how good. One thing is not in doubt; they are very expensive. As I write, the 2005 vintage of the legendary Pétrus is changing hands at €20,000 a case, about €70 a sip! At the lower end, Bordeaux continues to go through a serious crisis; the bottom has fallen out of the market, and many smaller growers in the peripheral, less fashionable parts of the region are facing bankruptcy.

The advent of a new *vin de pays* that includes Bordeaux may help. But I can't help feeling that drastic changes are necessary to turn things around. And that does not include subsidising over-production, something the growers are demanding.

Value can certainly be found in Bordeaux. There are a host of very affordable *petits châteaux* and *crus bourgeois* on the market, particularly if you are prepared to seek out the less fashionable vintages. The 2001 vintage has always been a favourite of mine, a year that offers the classic restrained dark fruits, structured sometimes dry tannins, but above all balance. These are the kind of wines that are very difficult to find anywhere else in the world of wine, and great wines to drink alongside dinner.

We list a few white wines from Bordeaux, wines that are often overlooked, but can offer the wine-drinker great value. We also have several really delicious *clairets* and other rosé wines—this is something that Bordeaux does extremely well. It is worth going to a little trouble to find these wines.

White

€9–€12

Mitchell's Sauvignon Blanc
Bordeaux Sec 2005

Special Value!

Delicious, light, crisp, dry Sauvignon with subtle gooseberry and green fruits and a lip-smacking, lemony finish.

Price	€9–€12
Region	Bordeaux
Grape	Sauv Blanc
Alc/vol	12%

Andersons, Glasnevin; Douglas Food, Donnybrook; Mitchells, Kildare Street; Mitchells, Glasthule; Myles Doyle, Gorey

Mitchell & Son

€12–€15

Ch. Bel-Air Perponcher Bordeaux Sec 2005

Impeccably balanced, subtle wine with very attractive lemon and green apple flavours, a hint of spice, and some light floral notes. Beautifully made wine at a great price.

Price	€12–€15
Region	Bordeaux
Grape	Sémillon/Sauv Blanc/ Muscadelle
Alc/vol	12%

Febvre

Ch. Thieuley Bordeaux Sec 2005

This opens with some style to reveal excellent Sauvignon—pears and rich apples with a lovely texture, good balance and a lingering finish. Great food wine.

Wines Direct

Price	€12–€15
Region	Bordeaux
Grape	Sauv Blanc/Sémillon
Alc/vol	12.5%

Wines Direct

€22–€30

★ L'Abeille de Fieuzal Pessac-Léognan 2000

A deep colour with a golden tinge; waxy, toasty aromas and flavours with a lovely core of smoky grilled nuts. Excellent concentration and length. A mature wine with real character and no little class.

Donnybrook Fair; Jus de Vine, Portmarnock; O'Brien's; Redmond's, Ranelagh; Terry's Wines, Limerick

Price	€22–€30
Region	Bordeaux
Grape	Sémillon/Sauv Blanc
Alc/vol	12.5%

Findlater Grants

Red

€9–€12

La Coccinelle de la Grolet Côtes de Bourg 2003   **Organic**

Lovely pure plum and blackcurrant fruit in a beautifully balanced wine; finishes on a very attractive peppery note. Classically styled, very enjoyable bordeaux.

The Grainey, Scariff, Co. Clare; Hudsons, Ballydehob, Co. Cork

Price	€9–€12
Region	Bordeaux
Grape	Merlot
Alc/vol	12.5%

Mary Pawle

€12–€15

Ch. d'Argadens Bordeaux Supérieur 2003

This is the real thing—firm, ripe blackberry fruit shot through with a savoury black pepper element and some nice grippy tannins; don't try it without a roast of lamb or beef.

Mitchells, Kildare Street; Mitchells, Glasthule

Price	€12–€15
Region	Bordeaux
Grape	Merlot/Cab Sauv/ Cab Franc
Alc/vol	13.5%

Mitchell & Son

Ch. La Bertrande Premières Côtes de Bordeaux 2002

Green peppers and light, well-defined cool fruits; a very attractive wine—the finish is smooth; drinking perfectly now.

Firhouse Inn; Great Escape, Banna; Next Door, Enfield; The Wicklow Wine Co.; Wine Cluster, Moycullen

Price	€12–€15
Region	Bordeaux
Grape	Merlot/Cab Sauv/ Cab Franc
Alc/vol	12.5%

Probus Wines

Ch. Larrivaux Haut-Médoc Cru Bourgeois 2001

Light, soft strawberries underpinned by new oak flavours—a very seductive wine that is at its peak now.

Most branches Dunnes Stores

Price	€12–€15
Region	Bordeaux
Grape	Cab Sauv/Merlot
Alc/vol	12.5%

Dunnes Stores

Ch. Le Logis de Sipian Médoc 2002

This is good ordinary decent claret. A spicy nose leads on to some smooth pencil shavings and blackcurrant fruit with a nice piquancy and decent length. Ready to go now.

Next Door @ Bridgebrook Arms, Kilkenny; Kingdom Food & Wine Store; Harvest Off Licences, Galway; Cheers @ The Laurels; Raheny Wine Cellar; Super Valu Killester

Price	€12–€15
Region	Bordeaux
Grape	Cab Sauv/Merlot
Alc/vol	12.5%

Taserra

Ch. Turcaud Bordeaux 2003

Light, pure, elegant wine with an enticing sappiness and some black pepper to go along with the brambly blackcurrant fruits. There is a lovely 'cut' to the wine, making it an ideal partner for food.

Celtic Whiskey; Fallon & Byrne; Le Caveau

Price	€12–€15
Region	Bordeaux
Grape	Merlot/Cab Sauv
Alc/vol	12.5%

Le Caveau

L'Orangerie de Carignan Premières Côtes de Bordeaux 2003

Lovely nose of ripe fruits. Very modern style of bordeaux, with rich, ripe—but not jammy—fruit flavours and fleshy tannins. Very well put together and satisfying.

McCabes, Mount Merrion

Price	€12–€15
Region	Bordeaux
Grape	Merlot/Cab Sauv/ Cab Franc
Alc/vol	13%

Nicholson

M de Plain-Point Fronsac 2003

Ripe, slightly inky nose; chunky, pure blackberries and blackcurrants held together with a lovely freshness and a soothing, light but sappy finish. Very enjoyable wine, but one that needs some grilled food.

Oddbins

Price	€12–€15
Region	Bordeaux
Grape	Merlot/Cab Franc/ Cab Sauv
Alc/vol	12.5%

Oddbins

€15–€18

Ch. Calon Montagne St-Emilion 2000

Damsons and blackberries on the nose. Elegant, structured palate with dusky blackberry fruit and still-firm tannins. Some oaky notes come through. Classic style and versatile with red meats and bean dishes.

McCambridges, Galway

Price	€15 €18
Region	Bordeaux
Grape	Merlot/Cab Sauv
Alc/vol	13%

McCambridge

Ch. Durand-Laplagne Puisseguin-St Emilion 2003

This is very lean but quite classy, with concentrated blackberry fruit, well-integrated but noticeable tannins and good length. Opens out nicely with a fragrant nose and soft plum fruits with a spicy touch.

Wines Direct

Price	€15–€18
Region	Bordeaux
Grape	Merlot/Cab Franc
Alc/vol	13%

Wines Direct

Ch. Haut-Guiraud Côtes de Bourg 2003

Cherry aromas, followed by ripe black cherries on the palate. Lovely balance of fruit, alcohol and tannin with enough acidity to keep it interesting. Sound wine with a fresh, persistent finish.

Claudio's; Louis Albrouze Wine

Price	€15–€18
Region	Bordeaux
Grape	Merlot/Cab Sauv
Alc/vol	13%

Louis Albrouze

Ch. Pey de la Tour Bordeaux Supérieur 2003

Warm, ripe blackcurrant and cassis aromas; good concentration of quite classy plum fruit—rich and ripe, over-lain by some fairly obvious new oak, but a very good, modern, voluptuous style of bordeaux.

O'Briens

Price	€15–€18
Region	Bordeaux
Grape	Cab Sauv/Merlot
Alc/vol	14%

O'Briens

Ch. Pichon Lussac St Émilion 2002

Very nicely balanced, light, brambly redcurrants and blackberries in a toothsome, very enjoyable claret, with a lovely subtle peak of acidity to keep it fresh. Fully ready now.

Price	€15–€18
Region	Bordeaux
Grape	Merlot/Cab Sauv/ Cab Franc
Alc/vol	13%

Taserra

Ch. Tour de Guiet Côtes de Bourg 2002

Not very forthcoming on the nose, but good clean plums and forest fruits on the palate, with a light oakiness and a stylish finish. Very good solid bordeaux.

Price	€15–€18
Region	Bordeaux
Grape	Merlot/Cab Sauv
Alc/vol	13%

Wicklow Wine

Wicklow Wine Co., Listons, Hand Made Wines, Harvest Off-licences, Galway

---

€18–€22

★ Ch. de Malleret Haut-Médoc Cru Bourgeois 2001

Earthy nose of dark fruits. Luxurious flavours of damsons, spice, chocolate and leather. Excellent structure with integrated tannins and a lingering, complex finish. Classic.

Price	€18–€22
Region	Bordeaux
Grape	Bordeaux varieties
Alc/vol	13%

Barry Fitzwilliam Maxxium

Terry's, Limerick

Ch. Troquart St Georges-St Emilion 2001

Fleshy, dusky aromas of black cherries and plums. Rich, velvety palate of blackberries and damsons, rounded tannins and subtle oak. Long, succulent finish.

Price	€18–€22
Region	Bordeaux
Grape	Merlot/Cab Sauv/ Cab Franc
Alc/vol	13%

Louis Albrouze

The Bottle Shop; Louis Albrouze Wine; Morton's, Galway; On the Grapevine, Dalkey; On the Grapevine, Booterstown; Red Island, Skerries

---

Ch. Villa Bel-Air Graves 2003

Dark fruits on the nose. Rounded palate with rich black fruits, fleshy tannins and subtle oak, coming together to make a lovely, harmonious wine that doesn't sock you in the eye with alcohol. Versatile food wine.

Price	€18–€22
Region	Bordeaux
Grape	Bordeaux varieties
Alc/vol	13%

Barry Fitzwilliam Maxxium

The Corkscrew; Portlaoise Wine Vaults

★ **Clos des Templiers Lalande de Pomerol 2004**

Classic, clean, stand-up Médoc; vibrant blackberry and blackcurrant fruit, excellent depth, a gently firm tannic backbone and good length.

Price	€18–€22
Region	Bordeaux
Grape	Merlot/Cab Franc
Alc/vol	12.5%

Mitchells, Kildare Street; Mitchells, Glasthule   *Mitchell & Son*

★ **Le Haut-Médoc de Giscours Haut-Médoc 2001**

Not a classic style, with its soft, sweet, ripe, supple strawberry flavours—but good-quality fruit and lingering, supple length.

Price	€18–€22
Region	Bordeaux
Grape	Cab Sauv/Merlot/ Cab Franc
Alc/vol	13%

Emilia's, Enniskerry; Liston's, Camden Street; On the Grapevine, Booterstown and Dalkey; Vanilla Grape, Kenmare   *WineKnows*

Les Allés de Cantemerle Haut-Médoc 2003

This is evolving nicely, revealing a herby, leafy element to go alongside the cool blackcurrant fruit and fine, elegant dry finish.

Price	€18–€22
Region	Bordeaux
Grape	Bordeaux varieties
Alc/vol	12.5%

Jus de Vine, Portmarnock; Higgins Clonskeagh; The Vintry, Rathgar; The Wicklow Arms   *Comans*

€22–€30

Ch. Caronne Ste Gemme Haut-Médoc Cru Bourgeois 2000

Ripe, soft blackcurrants and spice in a fully mature, rounded and complete red wine—this is what bordeaux is all about.

Price	€22–€30
Region	Bordeaux
Grape	Cab Sauv/Merlot/ Petit Verdot
Alc/vol	13%

Brechin Watchorn; Kellys, Clontarf; Harvest Off Licence, Oranmore; Leopardstown Inn; O'Dwyers, Navan   *Findlater Grants*

Ch. Côtes Trois Moulins St Émilion Grand Cru 2000

Lively, very attractive hedgerow aromas. Smooth, pure dark fruits with a lightly sappy tannic finish; perfect with beef or fatty pork.

Price	€22–€30
Region	Bordeaux
Grape	Merlot/Cab Franc
Alc/vol	12.5%

Corkscrew; Horans, Boyle; Sweeneys, Glasnevin; Searsons, Monkstown   *Searsons*

> **Where to buy the wine**
> If your local retailer does not stock a particular wine, contact the distributor named in italic after the tasting note who will be pleased to give you details of the nearest stockist.

★★ Ch. de la Commanderie St Émilion Grand Cru 2001

Piercing, intense, pure, quite plump plums and blackcurrants on nose and palate with lovely balance and a very long, lightly tannic finish. A class act.

Wines Direct

Price €22–€30
Region Bordeaux
Grape Merlot/Cab Sauv
Alc/vol 13.5%

Wines Direct

★ Ch. Grand Destieu St Émilion Grand Cru 2002

Maturing, slightly vegetal nose. Nice plump plums backed by good tannins, but ripe with very good concentration; some lovely liquorice coming through too.

Price €22–€30
Region Bordeaux
Grape Merlot/Cab Franc
Alc/vol 13%

Gilbeys

Ch. Pique-Caillou Pessac-Léognan 2001

Enticing, dusky aromas of fruits of the forest and blackberries. Mature, soft palate of forest fruits and damsons, exceptionally smooth tannins, not too much alcohol and a long, multi-layered finish.

Berry Bros & Rudd

Price €22–€30
Region Bordeaux
Grape Bordeaux varieties
Alc/vol 12.5%

Berry Bros & Rudd

Ch. Potensac Médoc 2001

Firm, concentrated wine with a very nice balance of peppery dark fruits and a drying, long finish. Don't try drinking it without food, but this is both classy and classic.

The Corkscrew; Fallon & Byrne; Le Caveau

Price €22–€30
Region Bordeaux
Grape Bordeaux varieties
Alc/vol 13%

Le Caveau

Ch. Rolland de By Cru Bourgeois Médoc 2000

Ripe cassis and blackcurrants; supple wine with good-quality fruit and some stylish tannins.

Wines Direct

Price €22–€30
Region Bordeaux
Grape Merlot/Cab Sauv/
Petit Verdot
Alc/vol 12.5%

Wines Direct

★ Ch. Teyssier St Emilion Grand Cru 2002

Classy, maturing nose of figs and
spice; soft, ripe, mature plum fruit
overlain with some new oak. The
finish is easy. Voluptuous, silky claret.

Price €22–€30
Region Bordeaux
Grape Merlot/Cab Franc
Alc/vol 13%

*Cheers, Coach-house; Harvest Off Licence, Oranmore;
Higgins, Clonskeagh; McCabe's; Redmonds, Ranelagh*

Findlater Grants

★★ Connétable Talbot St Julien 2000

Wonderful mature claret; beguiling
spicy aromas, a palate of quite firm,
ripe blackcurrants with good vanilla
hints, and a lovely, long, peppery
finish.

Price €22–€30
Region Bordeaux
Grape Bordeaux varieties
Alc/vol 12.5%

Comans

*Bin No.9, Goatstown; Comans, Rathgar; Jus de Vine,
Portmarnock; Redmonds, Ranelagh; The Vintry, Rathgar*

Frank Phélan St Estèphe 2001

Approachable style, with creamy
blackcurrant flavours, firmish tannins
and succulent length. Very harmonious and elegant.

Price €22–€30
Region Bordeaux
Grape Cab Sauv/Merlot
Alc/vol 13%

Gilbeys

★ Le Phare de Ch. Beau Rivage Bordeaux Supérieur 2002

Vanilla spice aromas with some clean
blackcurrants; the same crisp blackcurrants on the palate, refreshing with
subtle oaking and a good finish; this
needs food but it's an attractive wine.

Price €22–€30
Region Bordeaux
Grape Merlot/Petit Verdot/
      Malbec
Alc/vol 13.5%

O'Briens

O'Briens

★ Les Pagodes de Cos St Estèphe 1998

This has some of the classic firmness of
St Estèphe, along with developing
tight blackcurrant and vanilla spice;
finishes with some dry, peppery
tannins and good length. Ready to
drink now with roast beef or lamb.

Price €22–€30
Region Bordeaux
Grape Bordeaux varieties
Alc/vol 13%

Comans

*McCabes; Redmonds, Ranelagh; SuperValu, Churchtown;
The Vintry, Rathgar*

€30–€40

Ch. Bel-Air Marquis d'Aligre Margaux 1996

Classic aromas of cedarwood and pencil shavings. On the palate, the wine is remarkably smooth, with layers of spice and a little bit of prune. Delicious, fruity, spicy length. Mature and drinking beautifully over the next year—but no longer.

Wicklow Wine Co., Listons, Hand Made Wines, The Corkscrew

Price	**€30–€40**
Region	Bordeaux
Grape	Bordeaux varieties
Alc/vol	12.5%

Wicklow Wines

Ch. Petit Bocq St Estèphe 2002

Good, well-made claret, with medium-bodied redcurrants and blackberries and some very correct drying tannins. Try it with lighter red meats.

Fallon & Byrne; The Hole in the Wall; Paploe's; PubVia

Price	**€30–€40**
Region	Bordeaux
Grape	Merlot/Cab Sauv
Alc/vol	13%

PubVia

★ Le Jardin de Petit Village Pomerol 2001

Warm, ripe, quite pure plum fruit leading to a fairly concentrated palate with a supple, mature finish. This has a touch of real class. I like this.

O'Briens

Price	**€30–€40**
Region	Bordeaux
Grape	Merlot
Alc/vol	13%

O'Briens

★★ Sarget de Gruaud Larose St Julien 2000

Very classy ripe style with cassis and sweet vanilla always held in check by some firm tannins; very nicely made wine that will improve further for a year or two.

Donnybrook Fair; Jus de Vine, Portmarnock; Redmonds, Ranelagh; The Vintry, Rathgar

Price	**€30–€40**
Region	Bordeaux
Grape	Bordeaux varieties
Alc/vol	12.5%

Comans

All of the wines in this book are ready to drink now (October 2006), and for the next 12 months. Some will improve further over time and this is mentioned in the tasting note.

Rosé

€9–€12

Ch. de la Bretonnière
Bordeaux Clairet 2004

Special Value!

An unusual but delicious wine—big, quite broad raspberry and strawberry fruit with a distinct touch of caramel; fairly full-bodied, powerful wine, with good length. This would go nicely with full-flavoured fish or lighter meats.

Price €9–€12
Region Bordeaux
Grape Merlot
Alc/vol 13%

Wicklow Wine

Wicklow Wine Co., Listons, Harvest Off-licences, Galway, Hand Made Wines, The Corkscrew, Red Island Wine Co.

€15–€18

Le Rosé de Clarke Bordeaux Rosé 2005

A posh rosé, with clean, defined light strawberry fruit, a rich centre palate and a long, dry finish with a subtle caramel edge.

Price €15–€18
Region Bordeaux
Grape Merlot/Cab Sauv
Alc/vol 13.5%

Mitchell & Son

Mitchells, Kildare Street; Mitchells, Glasthule; Thyme Out, Dalkey

France–Burgundy

Burgundy is going through some exciting times. The 2004 vintage is excellent, and reports of the 2005 are very promising. Add in the delicious 2002s and you can understand why fans of the region have smiles on their faces. Even the very hot and dry 2003 vintage produced some very decent wines.

However, it is a region that continues to tease and tantalise—that such a small area can produce such variation in style is fascinating. That you can still shell out €40 for a very ordinary wine is disappointing; but the overall quality of burgundy, red and white, has never been so high.

Burgundy at its best, whether red or white, is one of the truly great wines of the world, able to thrill the senses like few others. Chardonnay does not get much better outside Burgundy, where you will find wines with body and structure, perfect with food. The reds are more delicate, soft and sensuous; wines to delight those who seek more subtle wines. In this edition, we list nearly 50 wines, including 26 star wines.

White

Under €9

La Larme d'Or Chablis 2004   **Special Value!**

Light, fresh, crisp green-apple fruits with a snappy, dry, lemon zest finish.

Price	Under €9
Region	Burgundy
Grape	Chardonnay
Alc/vol	12.5%

Aldi

€9–€12

Les Manants Côtes d'Auxerre Chardonnay Bourgogne 2004   **Special Value!**

Pure, ripe red-apple fruit cut through with an enlivening, really refreshing lemon note. Modern burgundy at a bargain price.

Most branches Dunnes Stores

Price	€9–€12
Region	Burgundy
Grape	Chardonnay
Alc/vol	12.5%

Dunnes Stores

€12–€15

Dom. Chêne Mâcon-La Roche Vineuse 2004

Delicious, ripe, mouth-filling wine, full of quite powerful apples and pears with a honeyed touch; lovely purity, lightly textured and a hint of orange peel. Great value.

Price	**€12–€15**
Region	**Burgundy**
Grape	**Chardonnay**
Alc/vol	**13.5%**

Nectar Wines

Claudio's; Grape Escape, Lucan; McHughs, Kilbarrack; McHughs, Malahide; Morton's, Ranelagh; Morton's, Galway; Nectar Wines; Red Island, Skerries

Dom. Talmard Mâcon-Uchizy 2005

Zesty with really fresh melons and crisp, clean acidity, with lots of minerals on the finish. Very stylish, nicely balanced white wine.

Price	**€12–€15**
Region	**Burgundy**
Grape	**Chardonnay**
Alc/vol	**13%**

Tyrrell

Bin No. 9; Cana; Cheers; The Corkscrew; Deveneys; Donnybrook Fair; Drinks Store; Fallon & Byrne; McCabes; On the Grapevine; Uncorked; Vanilla Grape; World Wines, Wexford

€15–€18

Dom. André Bonhomme Viré-Clessé 2003

A very good wine in what was a difficult vintage in the Mâconnais; full, rich, pure pear and melon fruit, just enough acidity to keep it fresh, and very good length. Not a wine for keeping, but very enjoyable now.

Price	**€15–€18**
Region	**Burgundy**
Grape	**Chardonnay**
Alc/vol	**14%**

Le Caveau

Le Caveau; Liston's

Dom. des Genèves Vieille Vigne Chablis 2004

Forward, youthful, floral aromas; the palate has fresh, ripe fruits—green apples with very good concentration and length—and a long, bone-dry finish. This is very good.

Price	**€15–€18**
Region	**Burgundy**
Grape	**Chardonnay**
Alc/vol	**12.5%**

Inis Wines

Baily Wines, Howth; Bin No. 9; Coach House, Ballinteer; Conoisseur; Foodhall, Portlaoise; Jus de Vine; McHughs, Kilbarrack; McHughs, Malahide Road; Mill, Maynooth; Morton's, Galway; Silver Granite; Thomas's, Foxrock

★ Dom. St Denis Mâcon-Lugny 2004

Opens out wonderfully after a few minutes to reveal some mouth-watering orange and lemon fruits, with a real minerality too; there is a touch of honey, but the overall impression is of a very stylish, perfectly balanced, fresh dry wine.

Price **€15–€18**
Region **Burgundy**
Grape **Chardonnay**
Alc/vol **12.7%**

Wicklow Wine

Wicklow Wine Co., Wicklow Wine Co., Listons, Michael's Food & Wine, On the Grapevine, Dalkey

---

Dom. Thierry Hamelin Chablis 2004

Fresh, forward, youthful wine with ripe green apples and greengages, finishing dry. It will develop further but it's lovely now—try it with seafood.

Price **€15–€18**
Region **Burgundy**
Grape **Chardonnay**
Alc/vol **12.5%**

On the Grapevine, Booterstown and Dalkey

WineKnows

Jean Manciat Mâcon 2005

Lean, light, crisp green apples but with very good length and a lovely zestiness. Loads of minerals coming through on the finish. Great food wine—try it with chicken or all sorts of fish.

Price **€15–€18**
Region **Burgundy**
Grape **Chardonnay**
Alc/vol **12.5%**

Louis Albrouze

Dunnes Stores; Louis Albrouze Wine; Vanilla Grape, Kenmare; World Wide Wines, Waterford

---

★ Jean-Paul & Benoît Droin Chablis 2005

Really lively, fresh, pure apple and melon fruit with a touch of orange peel; nice concentration and lovely purity. Stylish stuff.

Price **€15–€18**
Region **Burgundy**
Grape **Chardonnay**
Alc/vol **12.5%**

Louis Albrouze

The Bottle Shop; Claudio's; Louis Albrouze Wine; Vanilla Grape

---

Laroche Chablis 2004

Forward, quite rich honeyed nose; clean, lean, minerally, with nice ripe green apples on the centre palate; good length too.

Price **€15–€18**
Region **Burgundy**
Grape **Chardonnay**
Alc/vol **12.5%**

Galvin

★ Merlin Vieilles Vignes Mâcon-La Roche Vineuse 2004

Impeccably made burgundy—nicely textured green fruits with very subtle toasty influences and a lovely citric minerality throughout. Delicious wine—perfect with roast chicken or fuller fish dishes.

Price	**€15–€18**
Region	**Burgundy**
Grape	**Chardonnay**
Alc/vol	**13%**

Tyrrell

Jus de Vine, Portmarnock; Redmonds, Ranelagh; Vanilla Grape, Kenmare.

Nicolas Potel Cuvée Gérard Potel Burgundy 2004

Good, very youthful, vibrant, fresh Chardonnay with clean mineral and wet stone flavours, assisted by some subtle vanilla oak; balanced, stylish and very attractive.

Price	**€15–€18**
Region	**Burgundy**
Grape	**Chardonnay**
Alc/vol	**13%**

Celtic Whiskey Shop

Sylvain Dussort Cuvée des Ormes Bourgogne 2004

Delicious, mouth-watering yellow fruits with quite complex length and some rich-ness. The very subtle oak flavours add to the enjoyment. Lovely wine.

Price	**€15–€18**
Region	**Burgundy**
Grape	**Chardonnay**
Alc/vol	**13%**

Inis Wines

Arc, Liffey Valley; Bailys, Howth; Foxhunter; Gaffneys, Nenagh; Mill, Maynooth; Mortons, Galway; Silver Granite

€18–€22

★ Bret Brothers La Martine Mâcon-Uchizy 2004

Big, flavour-laden wine, a complex mix of minerals and orange peel filled out by greengages and melons. Excellent length, a wine to savour. Decanting would probably improve it further.

Price	**€18–€22**
Region	**Burgundy**
Grape	**Chardonnay**
Alc/vol	**12.5%**

Wines Direct

Wines Direct

> All of the wines in this book are ready to drink now (October 2006), and for the next 12 months. Some will improve further over time and this is mentioned in the tasting note.

Bret Brothers La Martine Mâcon-Uchizy 2003

Big, powerful, honeyed wine with rich, fat fruits—the acidity just keeps it all together, making for a full-bodied, full-flavoured wine.

Berry Bros & Rudd

Price	€18–€22
Region	Burgundy
Grape	Chardonnay
Alc/vol	14%

Berry Bros & Rudd

★ Dom. Alain Roy Montagny 1er Cru 2005

Unusual but very attractive smooth lanolin flavours with a touch of pineapple and yellow apple; very nicely integrated, stylish wine.

Mitchells, Kildare Street; Mitchells, Glasthule

Price	€18–€22
Region	Burgundy
Grape	Chardonnay
Alc/vol	13%

Mitchell & Son

★ Dom. Daniel Defaix Vieilles Vignes Chablis 2003

Broad, lightly floral nose; lovely, rich, pure Chardonnay flavours with green fruits, lime flowers and a crisp mineral finish; stylish, impeccably balanced wine.

Price	€18–€22
Region	Burgundy
Grape	Chardonnay
Alc/vol	12.5%

Celtic Whiskey Shop

★ Dom. Long-Depaquit Chablis 1er Cru Les Vaillons 2001

Clean, developing nose, then on to a beautifully balanced crisp palate of waxy yellow fruits, lively citrus and a delicious honey/orange juice touch. Drinking beautifully now.

Selected independent retailers

Price	€18–€22
Region	Burgundy
Grape	Chardonnay
Alc/vol	13%

Irish Distillers

★ Dom. Meix-Foulot Mercurey 2004

Very nicely made wine with subtle pineapple and pear fruit, a hint of vanilla spice and a very stylish, lightly creamy texture.

Mitchells, Kildare Street; Mitchells, Glasthule

Price	€18–€22
Region	Burgundy
Grape	Chardonnay
Alc/vol	13%

Mitchell & Son

Dom. Stéphane Aladame Montagny 1er Cru 2004

Light and crisp, with aromas of wet stones and hazelnuts in a young, exuberant style. Very fresh style of wine with plenty of acidity—a great match for plain fish or seafood.

Wines Direct

Price	€18–€22
Region	Burgundy
Grape	Chardonnay
Alc/vol	13%

Wines Direct

★ Roux Père & Fils Clos de la Brannière St Romain 2004

Lovely restrained Chardonnay with a crisp green-apple bite to provide a foil to the easy, lightly creamy texture. Stylish, clean, subtle wine.

Price €18–€22
Region Burgundy
Grape Chardonnay
Alc/vol 13%

Febvre

€22–€30

★★ Bernard Moreau & Fils St Aubin 1er Cru Sur Gamay 2004

Broad grilled nuts, smoky new oak and some butter, offset by good acidity and a dry finish. This is a big, full-bodied wine, full of fruit, that ideally needs a year or two to show its true class.

Price €22–€30
Region Burgundy
Grape Chardonnay
Alc/vol 13.5%

Wicklow Wine

Wicklow Wine Co., Listons

Ch. des Rontets Clos Varambon Pouilly-Fuissé 2003

WHITE WINE OF THE YEAR

Honeyed, rich nose; complex, taut, youthful green fruits. It has plenty of new oak, but excellent length, and some very well-defined lime and toasted nut flavours.

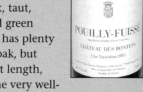

Price €22–€30
Region Burgundy
Grape Chardonnay
Alc/vol 13.5%

Searsons

O'Driscolls, Cahirciveen; Red Island, Skerries; Searsons, Monkstown

---

★ Ch. Fuissé Les Brûlés Pouilly-Fuissé 2002

Deepening colour; lovely rich, honeyed, toasty aromas and flavours too, cut through with incisive lime and minerals, finishing long and dry. Complex, very satisfying wine of real quality.

Price €22–€30
Region Burgundy
Grape Chardonnay
Alc/vol 13%

O'Briens

O'Briens

★ Chanson Père & Fils St Aubin 1er Cru Les Pitengerets 2004

This has a lovely broad centre palate of yellow fruits, opening out slowly to reveal a light oakiness and some honeyed touches—a classy wine still in its youth. Better in a year, but hard to resist now.

Price	€22–€30
Region	Burgundy
Grape	Chardonnay
Alc/vol	13.5%

O'Briens

O'Briens

★ Dom. de la Croix Senaillet Pouilly-Fuissé 2004

Delicious, rich, honeyed green fruits in great concentration and a long, dry finish. Liquid lemons and honey.

Louis Albrouze Wine; Vanilla Grape, Kenmare

Price	€22–€30
Region	Burgundy
Grape	Chardonnay
Alc/vol	13%

Louis Albrouze

Dom. Jaeger-Defaix Rully 1er Cru Mont Palais 2003

Interesting developing flavours, with light lanolin and subtle light new oak, some white flowers, apples and a bone-dry finish.

Firhouse Inn; Great Escape, Banna; Next Door, Enfield; The Wicklow Wine Co.; Wine Cluster, Moycullen

Price	€22–€30
Region	Burgundy
Grape	Chardonnay
Alc/vol	13.5%

Probus Wines

★ Tesco Meursault 2004

Very nicely balanced wine with light vanilla notes and a pleasing richness that never overwhelm the clean, fresh, pure young green fruits; good length in a classy wine. This will improve still further over the next year or so.

Price	€22–€30
Region	Burgundy
Grape	Chardonnay
Alc/vol	13%

Tesco

€30–€40

★ Clos des Quarts Merlin Pouilly-Fuissé 2004

Big, full-bodied flavours of lemon zest and baked apples with cloves and vanilla. The oak is very well integrated and there is plenty of structure. There are minerals too, and a rich flourish at the tail.

Tyrrell (045) 870 882

Price	€30–€40
Region	Burgundy
Grape	Chardonnay
Alc/vol	13.5%

Tyrrell

THE WICKLOW WINE Co.

IMPORTER OF THE YEAR

The Best of Wine in Ireland 2007

SWEET WINE OF THE YEAR

Château Courts-les-Mûts, Saussignac 2001

The Best of Wine in Ireland 2007

BEST VALUE WHITE WINE OF THE YEAR

Cuvée Orélie, Les Vignerons Ardéchois

The Best of Wine in Ireland 2005

IMPORTERS, WHOLESALERS & RETAILERS

Committed to the very best and most interesting in wine

Find us at our shop

THE WICKLOW WINE Co.

Main Street, Wicklow

Or contact us at

Tel +353 404 66767

Fax +353 404 66769

Email wicklowwineco@eircom.net

REPRESENTING THE FOLLOWING OUTSTANDING PRODUCERS

THE WICKLOW WINE Co.

FRANCE
Les Vignerons Ardéchois, **Ardèche**
Domaine Martin, **Rhône**
Moulin de la Gardette, **Gigondas**
Domaine du Tunnel, **Cornas & Saint Peray**
Domaine d'Aupilhac, **Languedoc**
Mas de Chimères, **Languedoc**
Château Dalmeran, **Provence**
Château Court-les-Mûts, **Bergerac**
Clos le Joncal, **Bergerac**
Les Chemins d'Orient, **Pécharment**
Château Beauportail, **Pécharment**
Château Tirecul La Gravière, **Monbazillac**
Domaine d'Homs, **Cahors**
Clos de Gamot & Château du Cayrou, **Cahors**
Château Tour de Guiet, **Côtes de Bourg**
Château La Bretonniere, **Côtes de Blaye**
Château Bel Air Marquis d'Aligre, **Margaux**
Domaine Barat, **Chablis**
Domaine Saint-Denis, **Mâcon**
Domaine Arlaud, **Côte de Nuits**
Domaine Francois Charles, **Côte de Beaune**
Domaine Bernard Moreau, **Côte de Beaune**
Jean Claude Lapalu, **Beaujolais**
J. Mourat Père & Fils, **Fiefs Vendéens**
Domaine Doudeau-Leger, **Sancerre**
Pierre Paillard, **Champagne**

ITALY
La Corte, **Puglia**

GERMANY
Max Ferd. Richter, **Mosel**
Dr. von Bassermann-Jordan, **Pfalz**
Georg Breuer, **Rheingau**

PORTUGAL
Quinta Sá de Baixo, **Douro**
Niepoort, **Douro**
Quinta das Tecedeiras, **Douro**
Quinta de Cabriz, **Dão**
Cortello, **Estremadura**
Casa do Lago, **Ribatejano**
Monte da Cal, **Alentejano**

PORT
Niepoort

LIQUEURS DE BOURGOGNE
Trenel Fils, Crème Cassis, Pêche et Framboise

Deux Montille La Canée Auxey-Duresses 2004

This is an attractive but unusual wine—a nice nose with light spice and some clean fruit, soft and lightly elegant on the palate; opens out very nicely. A wine to seduce over a bottle, rather than at the outset.

Tyrrell (045) 870 882

Price **€30–€40**
Region **Burgundy**
Grape **Chardonnay**
Alc/vol **12.5%**

Tyrrell

Deux Montille St Aubin 1er Cru Sur Gamay 2004

Clean, incisive lemon and pineapple flavours nicely integrated into some vanilla oak; light but attractive wine.

Tyrrell (045) 870 882

Price **€30–€40**
Region **Burgundy**
Grape **Chardonnay**
Alc/vol **12.5%**

Tyrrell

★ Dom. Bernard Moreau & Fils Chassagne-Montrachet 2004

The pure floral green fruits and well-integrated acidity are a perfect foil to the light toasted oak influences in a medium- to full-bodied wine with plenty of concentration and good length.

Wicklow Wine Co., Listons, Red Island Wine Co., The Corkscrew, French Flair, Hand Made Wines

Price **€30–€40**
Region **Burgundy**
Grape **Chardonnay**
Alc/vol **13.5%**

Wicklow Wine

★ Dom. Chandon de Briailles Savigny-lès-Beaune 1er Cru Aux Vergelesses 2003

An unusual but very enjoyable wine, with light mineral notes alongside some distinctive toffee, grilled nuts and lanolin flavours. Very nicely balanced, and finishes with a flourish.

Wines Direct

Price **€30–€40**
Region **Burgundy**
Grape **Chardonnay**
Alc/vol **12.5%**

Wines Direct

★ Sylvain Dussort Meursault 2004

Not the most typical Meursault, but a delicious wine with plenty of fresh acidity to balance out the youthful green fruits and very light toastiness. Clean, crisp and fresh, but with good intensity. Drink now or hold a year or two.

Price €30–€40
Region Burgundy
Grape Chardonnay
Alc/vol 13%

Inis Wines

Bailys, Howth; Breakaway Wines, Kerry; Caprani's; Connoisseur, Dundalk; Donnybrook Fair; Fallon & Byrne; Gaffneys, Nenagh; Mill, Maynooth; Mortons, Galway; Nectar Wines, Sandyford

---

Red

€12–€15

Louis Jadot Bourgogne Pinot Noir 2004

Cool, very seductive pure dark cherries and blackberries in a very supple, easy-drinking style—lovely pure Pinot.

Price €12–€15
Region Burgundy
Grape Pinot Noir
Alc/vol 12.5%

Bottle Shop, Sallins; Halpin Wines, Wicklow; Joyce, Knocknacarra; McCabe's; Martha's Vineyard; O'Brien's

Findlater Grants

€15–€18

Dom. Moissenet-Bonnard Les Maisons Dieu Bourgogne 2004

Clean, fresh summer fruits in a lively but elegant wine; finishes on a lovely ripe note.

Fallon & Byrne; Le Caveau

Price	€15–€18
Region	Burgundy
Grape	Pinot Noir
Alc/vol	12.5%

Le Caveau

Nicolas Potel Cuvée Gérard Potel Bourgogne 2004

Light, pure, forward strawberry aromas; the palate is light, fresh and delicate with nicely integrated acidity. A true summer wine, with fresh, pure strawberry fruit, finishing on a lightly tannic note: very enjoyable wine.

Price	€15–€18
Region	Burgundy
Grape	Pinot Noir
Alc/vol	13%

Celtic Whiskey Shop

€18–€22

★ Dom. Gachot-Monot Les Chaillots Côte de Nuits-Villages 2003

Wonderfully fragrant dark forest fruits with a smoky edge; quite chunky on the palate, with foursquare dark fruits, some chocolate and new oak, but it comes together very nicely in a stylish, seamless wine.

Firhouse Inn; Great Escape, Banna; Next Door, Enfield; The Wicklow Wine Co.; Wine Cluster, Moycullen

Price	€18–€22
Region	Burgundy
Grape	Pinot Noir
Alc/vol	12.5%

Probus Wines

★ Jean-Marc Millot Côte de Nuits-Villages 2003

Cool black fruits, nicely balanced with some lovely concentration of flavour, some subtle vanilla oak, and lots of cloves on the finish. Nice ripeness and excellent plump Pinot fruit.

On the Grapevine, Booterstown and Dalkey

Price	€18–€22
Region	Burgundy
Grape	Pinot Noir
Alc/vol	13%

WineKnows

Joseph Drouhin Maranges 1er Cru 2003

Good ripe summer fruits—redcurrants, blackberries and cherries in a seductive, easy-drinking style.

Price	€18–€22
Region	Burgundy
Grape	Pinot Noir
Alc/vol	13%

Gilbeys

€22–€30

★ Dom. Charles & Fils Clos de la Cache Volnay 2004

Very classy fragrant Pinot with delicious, lush, ripe fruit crossed with sweet vanilla—seductive and very moreish.

Price	€22–€30
Region	Burgundy
Grape	Pinot Noir
Alc/vol	13%

Wicklow Wine Co., Jus de Vine, Listons,, The Corkscrew, Harvest Off-licences, Galway, French Flair, Hand Made Wines

Wicklow Wine

Dom. de Montille Bourgogne 2001

One for the true Pinot fan—light, delicate, mature vegetal aromas and fruit with plenty of dry minerals, as well as a lovely delicacy—hanging on nicely, but drink over the next year. Delicious wine.

Price	€22–€30
Region	Burgundy
Grape	Pinot Noir
Alc/vol	12%

Berry Bros & Rudd

Berry Bros & Rudd

★ Dom. Vincent Girardin Santenay 1er Cru Les Gravières 2004

A very appealing, seductive young burgundy; relatively rich for a Pinot Noir, with smooth blackberry and blackcurrant fruits, a lovely purity of flavour and excellent length.

Price	€22–€30
Region	Burgundy
Grape	Pinot Noir
Alc/vol	13.5%

Corkscrew; Fallon & Byrne; Le Caveau

Le Caveau

Tesco Nuits St Georges 2001

A solid, meaty mouthful of maturing, firm dark fruits; would certainly improve served alongside a nice beef casserole.

Price	€22–€30
Region	Burgundy
Grape	Pinot Noir
Alc/vol	13%

Tesco

Where to buy the wine
If your local retailer does not stock a particular wine, contact the distributor named in italic after the tasting note who will be pleased to give you details of the nearest stockist.

Market Yard, Kilkenny
Tel: 056 77 52166

Le CAVEAU
THE SPECIALIST WINE MERCHANTS

lecaveau.ie

The shop is packed to the rafters with one of the tastiest selections of French wine in the country. All are hand-chosen wines from the very best small estates, mostly at very affordable prices. **John Wilson**

€30–€40

★★ Dom. Arlaud Gevrey-Chambertin 2002

A bit youthful still, but an excellent wine; full, smoky dark fruits with impeccable balancing acidity and a lingering, lightly tannic, tight finish.

Price	**€30–€40**
Region	**Burgundy**
Grape	**Pinot Noir**
Alc/vol	13%

Wicklow Wine

Wicklow Wine Co., Jus de Vine, Listons, Hand Made Wines, Red Island Wine Co.

★ Dom. Louis Boillot & Fils
Volnay 1er Cru Les Brouillards 2002

Fresh, beautifully defined aromas of raspberries and strawberries; concentrated, ripe, dark fruits—blackcurrants and blueberries in a tight, youthful finish. Great intensity of fruit and good length. Lovely balance too. Best in 1–3 years.

Price	**€30–€40**
Region	**Burgundy**
Grape	**Pinot Noir**
Alc/vol	13%

Le Caveau

Le Caveau

★★ Dom. Vincent Sauvestre Aloxe-Corton
1er Cru Les Maréchaudes 2002

Beautifully fresh redcurrant and raspberry fruit with elegant tannins and excellent length; a very classy wine relying on purity of flavour.

Price	**€30–€40**
Region	**Burgundy**
Grape	**Pinot Noir**
Alc/vol	12.5%

Straffan

The Connoisseur, Dundalk; Fallon & Byrne

France–Loire

The reds from this region are distinctly unfashionable; some of the whites remain as popular as ever. In a world full of rich, powerful red wines, I always enjoy the light, cool refreshing flavours of the red Loires; I am also very partial to Muscadet, which is starting to make a real comeback in terms of quality.

But it is the wines from the far east of the Loire, Pouilly-Fumé and Sancerre, that remain the most popular in this country; fresh, aromatic white wines with their piercing, crisp green fruits and dry finish. They are great all-purpose wines. It is worth remembering that the Loire produces some of the truly great sweet wines of the world; with that refreshing acidity and wonderful balance, they slip so easily across the palate, where other dessert wines cloy.

White

€9–€12

Dom. de la Rochepinal Montlouis-sur-Loire 2003

Delicate, chalky, crisp green fruits with some incisive acidity and a good mineral finish. Attractive, different and a great wine for seafood.

Firhouse Inn; Great Escape, Banna; Next Door, Enfield; The Wicklow Wine Co.; Wine Cluster, Moycullen

Price €9–€12
Region Loire Valley
Grape Chenin Blanc
Alc/vol 12%

Probus Wines

Dom. du Haut Bourg Sauvignon VdP du Jardin de la France 2005

Special Value!

Mineral fruits with lean, green freshness, finishing on a nice chalky note with some pear drops. Very pleasant drinking.

The Bottle Shop; Emilia's Wine Shop, Enniskerry; Hemmingway, Clontarf; Louis Albrouze Wine; World Wide Wine, Waterford

Price €9–€12
Region Loire Valley
Grape Sauv Blanc
Alc/vol 12%

Louis Albrouze

€12–€15

Ch. de Fesles Chenin Sec Anjou 2004

Rich yellow fruits with a honeyed
edge, some grilled nuts and a forthright, solid backbone of mineral acidity, finishing bone dry. I suspect that
this would really shine alongside some
fish in a creamy sauce.

Oddbins

Price €12–€15
Region Loire Valley
Grape Chenin Blanc
Alc/vol 14%

Oddbins

Sébastien Vaillant Valençay 2005

Brisk, cool apple and quince fruit with
a lively kick of flinty acidity; light,
refreshing and a delightful glass of
wine.

Bailys of Howth; Red Island

Price €12–€15
Region Loire Valley
Grape Sauv Blanc/
Chardonnay
Alc/vol 12.5%

Liberty Wines

Terre de Fumée Sauvignon Blanc Terroir de Silex Coteaux du Giennois 2005

This is very good—fresh, grassy wine
with mouth-watering acidity, lean,
green fruits and a really enticing,
moreish mineral, dry finish—excellent stuff.

O'Briens

Price €12–€15
Region Loire Valley
Grape Sauv Blanc
Alc/vol 12.5%

O'Briens

€15–€18

★ Dom. des Ballandores Quincy 2005

Lovely, fresh, bright-
as-a-button nose; deli-
cious, soft green
fruits, but without a
hint of flabbiness.
Very attractive light
wine.

O'Donovans, Cork

Price €15–€18
Region Loire Valley
Grape Sauv Blanc
Alc/vol 12.5%

Liberty Wines

*All of the wines in this book are ready to drink now (October 2006), and
for the next 12 months. Some will improve further over time and this is
mentioned in the tasting note.*

€18–€22

Dom. Célestin Blondeau Cuvée des Rabichottes Pouilly-Fumé 2004

Vibrant, fresh and aromatic with well-defined, zippy green fruits and a clean, dry citrus finish. Loire Sauvignon with some class.

Price	**€18–€22**
Region	Loire Valley
Grape	Sauv Blanc
Alc/vol	12.5%

Costcutters, Tuam; Kelly's Wine Vault, Clontarf; JJ O'Driscoll, Ballinlough Road, Cork

Kelly & Co.

Dom. Célestin Blondeau L'Ancienne Vigne Sancerre 2004

Wonderful, slightly steely, mineral edge to counter the delicious, fresh, crisp, green fruits; lively, dry and very classy wine.

Price	**€18–€22**
Region	Loire Valley
Grape	Sauv Blanc
Alc/vol	12.5%

Kellys Wine Vault, Clontarf

Kelly & Co.

€22–€30

Dom. Célestin Blondeau L'Ancienne Vigne Grande Cuvée Sancerre 2003

Lean, clean, light, aromatic green fruits with nice length. Grassy pea pods with good centre palate richness.

Price	**€22–€30**
Region	Loire Valley
Grape	Sauv Blanc
Alc/vol	12.5%

Kellys Wine Vault, Clontarf

Kelly & Co.

Dom. des Baumard Clos du Papillon Savennières 2000

Maturing pale gold colour with subtle floral honey aromas. Quite full bodied with honeyed notes, but more mineral than anything else with faint yellow apple fruit and a fine dry finish.

Price	**€22–€30**
Region	Loire Valley
Grape	Chenin Blanc
Alc/vol	13%

Tyrrell

Tyrrell (045) 870 882

How to use this book
The wines are listed in order of country/region, colour (red or white), price band, then by name. There are separate chapters for sparkling (including Champagne) and dessert wines. If you can't find the wine you are looking for try the index. The price bands are guidelines only. All of the wines in this book are ready to drink now (October 2006), and for the next 12 months. Some will improve further over time and this is mentioned in the tasting note.

Red

€15–€18

Dom. Bernard Baudry Les Granges Chinon 2004

Classic Cabernet Franc nose of pencil shavings and redcurrant fruits; light, with some tannins but perfectly ripe redcurrants and a lovely elegance.

Price	€15–€18
Region	Loire Valley
Grape	Cab Franc
Alc/vol	12.5%

Bottle Shop, Drummartin Road; On the Grapevine, Booterstown and Dalkey; Vanilla Grape, Kenmare

WineKnows

€18–€22

★ Frédéric Mabileau Les Coutoures St Nicolas de Bourgueil 2004

I love this style of wine: freshly crushed summer berries on the nose; the palate is light, slightly herbaceous, a little tart; there are those same delicious berry fruits on the palate with a sprinkling of black pepper and a dry finish.

Price	€18–€22
Region	Loire Valley
Grape	Cab Franc
Alc/vol	13%

Probus Wines

Firhouse Inn; Great Escape, Banna; Next Door, Enfield; The Wicklow Wine Co.; Wine Cluster, Moycullen

Rosé

€9–€12

La Bretonnière Langlois-Château Cabernet de Saumur 2005

Special Value!

Light strawberry and wet stone aromas; plump, light raspberry fruits with a caramel touch, and good enough length. Very pleasant summer wine.

Price	€9–€12
Region	Loire Valley
Grape	Cab Franc
Alc/vol	13%

O'Briens

O'Briens

€12–€15

Les Ruettes Sancerre Rosé 2005

More a dirty white than a rosé, so pale is the colour; light with the most delicate of cherry fruits balanced by lively acidity—very seductive, different wine.

Price	€12–€15
Region	Loire Valley
Grape	Pinot Noir
Alc/vol	12.5%

Marks & Spencer

France–Rhône

There are a full 38 entries from the north and south of the Rhône this year, an indication of the quality of wines now coming from this region. Of all the areas of France, the Rhône seems to have the greatest proportion of younger growers who are no longer prepared to merely send their grapes to the local co-operative once a year. Instead they are producing their own wine, often with spectacular results. The last two vintages have been kind to the region, with some excellent, balanced wines, not overly alcoholic or jammy.

The wines of the southern Rhône are more immediately appealing, soft and rounded, but packing quite an alcoholic punch. By contrast, the northern Rhône offers more austere, savoury wines, subtle and complex, every bit as, if not more, satisfying than their southern brothers.

White

€12–€15

Terre d'Eglantier Viognier
VdP des Coteaux de l'Ardèche 2005

Classic and very stylish Viognier; fresh, tangy apricot and peach fruit held together nicely by good acidity and a lush, soft finish. Very quaffable stuff indeed.

Wicklow Wine Co, Red Island Wine Co., Listons, Harvest Off-licences, Galway

Price	**€12–€15**
Region	**Rhône**
Grape	**Viognier**
Alc/vol	**13.5%**

Wicklow Wine

€15–€18

Dom. Alary La Font d'Estévenas
Côtes du Rhône Villages Cairanne 2004

Lively, lemon-spiked aromas; broad-textured, rich apricots, nicely concentrated, dry with good length—this is lovely wine with a real citrus zestiness throughout.

Egan's Too; McHugh's; Uncorked

Price	**€15–€18**
Region	**Rhône (South)**
Grape	**Viognier/ Roussanne/ Clairette**
Alc/vol	**14%**

Tyrrell

Dom. Mourgues du Grès Terre d'Argence VdP du Gard 2004

A very deep colour; intense pineapple and peach fruit with a bitter finish, big and powerful with some honey and marzipan coming through at the tail.

Mill Wine Cellar, Maynooth

Price	€15–€18
Region	Rhône (South)
Grape	Marsanne/ Roussanne/ Grenache Blanc
Alc/vol	14%

Nicholson

€18–€22

★ Michel & Stéphane Ogier Viognier de Rosine VdP des Collines Rhodaniennes 2004

A delicate balancing act between juicy apricots, citrus acidity and under-stated vanilla oak. It works very well in a classy, beautifully fruity, elegant wine.

Donnybrook Fair; Fallon & Byrne; Redmond's, Ranelagh; Sweeneys

Price	€18–€22
Region	Rhône (North)
Grape	Viognier
Alc/vol	12.5%

Tyrrell

Over €40

Dom. de la Janasse Châteauneuf-du-Pape 2004

Excellent, youthful wine with elegant, floral, delicate fruits underpinned by vanilla oak, which comes through on the long finish. Soft in texture, and very subtle wine—you have no idea how high the alcohol is.

Bin No. 9; Lilac Wines; Lord Mayor's Off Licence; Vanilla Grape, Kenmare

Price	Over €40
Region	Rhône (South)
Grape	Grenache Blanc/ Roussanne/Clairette
Alc/vol	14.5%

Tyrrell

Red

€9–€12

Dom. Alary La Gerbaude Côtes du Rhône 2005

Special Value!

Lovely fragrant nose; piquant rasp-berries and summer fruits; beautifully defined elegant wine, yet backed up with real power. Value wine *par excellence*.

Cana; Donnybrook Fair; Jus de Vine; McCabes; Next Door, @ Myles Creek; On the Grapevine; Uncorked; World Wide Wines, Waterford

Price	€9–€12
Region	Rhône (South)
Grape	Grenache/Syrah/ Carignan
Alc/vol	14%

Tyrrell

M Chapoutier Belleruche Côtes du Rhône 2004

A big, herby, intense wine with some unresolved tannins and a long, chewy finish. Good centre-palate concentration.

Price	€9–€12
Region	Rhône (South)
Grape	Grenache/Syrah
Alc/vol	13.5%

Hogan's, Rathfarnham; Joyce, Knocknacarra; Nolan's, Clontarf; O'Brien's; Redmond's, Ranelagh; Superquinn; SuperValu, Skibbereen

Findlater Grants

Santa Duc Les Plans VdP de Vaucluse 2004

Special Value!

Very attractive juicy raspberry and blackcurrant fruit with a lively edge, finishing on a lightly sappy note—nicely crafted wine, drinking well now.

Price	€9–€12
Region	Rhône (South)
Grape	Grenache/Syrah/ Merlot/Alicante/ Cinsault
Alc/vol	13.5%

Celtic Whiskey; The Corkscrew; Gourmet Food, Dun Laoghaire; Harvest, Lismore; Le Caveau; Listons

Le Caveau

€12–€15

Cave des Vignerons de Rasteau Prestige Côtes du Rhône Villages Rasteau 2003

Sweet summer fruits on the nose; plump and powerful with liquorice and a tarry intensity. Finishes a little hot, but with good compact tannins and nice jammy length.

Price	€12–€15
Region	Rhône (South)
Grape	Grenache/Syrah/ Mourvèdre
Alc/vol	14%

O'Briens

O'Briens

★ Dom. Alary Côtes du Rhône Villages Cairanne 2004

A wonderful blend of piquant black olives crossed with just enough warm southern ripeness. Well-integrated tannins on a lingering finish. True quality wine that needs a bit of food.

Price	€12–€15
Region	Rhône (South)
Grape	Grenache/Syrah/ Mourvèdre
Alc/vol	14.5%

Bin No. 9; French Flair, Tralee; Lilac Wines; McHugh's; On the Grapevine; Redmond's; Sweeneys

Tyrrell

Dom. Cheze Syrah VdP des Collines Rhodaniennes 2004

Vanilla and plums mix in a relatively delicate, cool wine without any austerity; good concentration of fruit.

Price	€12–€15
Region	Rhône (North)
Grape	Syrah
Alc/vol	12.5%

The Bottle Shop; Louis Albrouze Wine; Red Island, Skerries

Louis Albrouze

Dom. de la Janasse Terre de Bussière
VdP de la Principauté d'Orange 2005

Sweet cherry aromas; smooth, concentrated dark cherry and plum fruit with a hint of liquorice and some tarry notes, finishing sweetly with a lovely heady ripeness.

Price	€12–€15
Region	Rhône (South)
Grape	Syrah/Merlot
Alc/vol	14.5%

Tyrrell

Cheers, Wicklow; Deveneys, Dundrum; French Flair, Tralee; Jus de Vine; Lilac Wines; McCabe's; McHugh's; Next Door, Myles Creek; On the Grapevine; Red Island, Skerries; Redmond's; Vanilla Grape, Kenmare; The Vintry, Rathgar

Dom. des Remizières Crozes-Hermitage 2004

Stylish, restrained wine with some classy, cool plum fruit.

McCambridges, Galway

Price	€12–€15
Region	Rhône (North)
Grape	Syrah
Alc/vol	12.5%

McCambridges

Dom. St Martin Plan de Dieu
Côtes du Rhône Villages 2004

Big, rounded, sweet, ripe strawberries with a whiff of black pepper, plenty of oomph, but excellent length. Delicious wine and great value.

Price	€12–€15
Region	Rhône (South)
Grape	Grenache/Syrah/ Mourvèdre
Alc/vol	13.5%

Wicklow Wine Co., Listons, Michael's Food & Wine, Red Island Wine Co., Harvest Off-licences, Galway, Hand Made Wines

Wicklow Wine

Guigal Côtes du Rhône 2003

Light, easy liquorice and plum fruit; the warming alcohol comes through on the finish, but a nicely crafted, easy-drinking wine.

O'Brien's; SuperValu/Centra

Price	€12–€15
Region	Rhône (South)
Grape	Syrah/Grenache/ Mourvèdre
Alc/vol	13%

Barry Fitzwilliam Maxxium

€15–€18

★ Dom. Alary La Brunote
Côtes du Rhône Villages Cairanne 2004

Beautiful, long, elegant, peppery fruit with some lightly dry tannins—this is well-crafted, subtle wine with substance and a lovely floral touch.

McHugh's; Next Door @ Myles Creek

Price	€15–€18
Region	Rhône (South)
Grape	Grenache/ Mourvèdre
Alc/vol	14.5%

Tyrrell

Dom. de Fondrèche Nadal Côtes du Ventoux 2004

This is very good. Broad, Grenache-based strawberries and excellent warmth and intensity on the palate; rounded and very satisfying wine.

Donnybrook Fair; Jus de Vine; Vanilla Grape, Kenmare

Price	€15–€18
Region	Rhône (South)
Grape	Grenache/Syrah/ Mourvèdre
Alc/vol	14.5%

Tyrrell

Dom. des Anges L'Archange Côtes du Ventoux 2003

A bit of a bully-boy with very firm liquorice and tar, but the fruit comes pouring through on the finish, as does the heady alcohol. Firm, concentrated and long.

O'Briens

Price	€15–€18
Region	Rhône (South)
Grape	Syrah/Grenache
Alc/vol	15%

O'Briens

Dom. Le Clos de Caveau Vacqueyras 2003   Organic

Big, concentrated, firm, youthful dark fruits, with a substantial tannic structure, finishing very dry. All very tight at the moment—decant for an hour or two, or lay down.

The Corkscrew; Fallon & Byrne; Le Caveau

Price	€15–€18
Region	Rhône (South)
Grape	Grenache/Syrah/ Cinsault/Mourvèdre
Alc/vol	14.3%

Le Caveau

Dom. Roger Perrin Châteauneuf-du-Pape 2004

Big, soft, ripe primary red fruits, with a rounded, easy finish.

All branches Dunnes Stores

Price	€15–€18
Region	Rhône (South)
Grape	Grenache/Syrah/ Mourvedre
Alc/vol	14.5%

Dunnes Stores

€18–€22

★ Alain Graillot Crozes-Hermitage 2001

Beautiful drawn-out savoury plums with good acidity and a maturing note; still very fresh, though, with lovely savoury balance, ending with black pepper.

Mitchell & Sons; Molloys

Price	€18–€22
Region	Rhône (North)
Grape	Syrah
Alc/vol	13%

Barry Fitzwilliam Maxxium

★ Dom. Martin VdP de Vaucluse 2004

A big, solid, youthful
wine with savoury
plum fruit in a shell of
structured, firm
tannins; excellent
length. Decant or lay
down for a year or two.

Price €18–€22
Region Rhône (South)
Grape Syrah
Alc/vol 13.5%

Wicklow Wine

*Wicklow Wine Co., The Corkscrew, Listons, Harvest Off-
licences, Galway, Michael's Food & Wine*

★ Michel & Stéphane Ogier La Rosine VdP des Collines Rhodaniennes 2004

This has excellent, cool, linear plum
fruit, a lovely elegance and some sweet
vanilla oak. Light in alcohol but beautifully concentrated. Côte-Rôtie in all
but name.

Price €18–€22
Region Rhône (North)
Grape Syrah
Alc/vol 12.5%

Tyrrell

*Bin No. 9; Donnybrook Fair; Lilac Wines; Redmond's,
Ranelagh; Sweeney's*

★ Yann Chave Crozes-Hermitage 2005

This has delicious, light, savoury but
piquant dark plums—very stylish with
excellent balance. A great food wine.

Price €18–€22
Region Rhône (North)
Grape Syrah
Alc/vol 13%

*Fallon & Byrne; Jus de Vine; McCabes; Next Door @ Myles
Creek; Redmonds, Ranelagh; Sweeneys; The Vintry, Rathgar*   *Tyrrell*

€22–€30

★ Dom. de la Citadelle Gouverneur St Auban Côtes du Lubéron 2001

Not for the faint of heart—this is a bit
of a monster, with dark, brooding,
leathery, earthy flavours to complement the rustic dark fruits; full of character and with lots of tannic length—
a wine with attitude.

Price €22–€30
Region Rhône (South)
Grape Syrah/Grenache
Alc/vol 15%

Tyrrell

Tyrrell (045) 870 882

---

*All of the wines in this book are ready to drink now (October 2006), and
for the next 12 months. Some will improve further over time and this is
mentioned in the tasting note.*

★ Dom. du Monteillet Cuvée du Papy St Joseph 2003

Rich, savoury damsons crossed with some light, smoky oak. Fruit is concentrated with good lively acidity and there are some nice peppery tannins on the finish.

Price	€22–€30
Region	Rhône (North)
Grape	Syrah
Alc/vol	13%

Tyrrell

McCabes, Blackrock; Vanilla Grape, Kenmare

Les Challeys Delas St Joseph 2002

Elegant, savoury liquorice and plum fruit with a lovely cool streak; medium-bodied and nicely balanced. Fully mature now, but would go nicely with game or maybe a steak.

Price	€22–€30
Region	Rhône (North)
Grape	Syrah
Alc/vol	12.5%

Febvre

★ Mas Neuf La Mourvache Costières de Nîmes 2003

A huge, tight, intensely flavoured wine with piercing dark fruits, dark coffee, smoky new oak, and plenty of alcohol to keep them company—a massive, impressive wine that needs an hour in the decanter or a year in the cellar.

Price	€22–€30
Region	Rhône (South)
Grape	Grenache/ Mourvèdre
Alc/vol	14%

Febvre

★★ Yann Chave Le Rouvre Crozes-Hermitage 2004

Black pepper on the nose leads on to a good concentration of savoury, tangy liquorice with lovely balancing acidity; lots of cool plum fruits too. Wonderful wine—*à point* now, and an exercise in balance.

Price	€22–€30
Region	Rhône (North)
Grape	Syrah
Alc/vol	13.5%

Tyrrell

Jus de Vine; Redmond's

Where to buy the wine
If your local retailer does not stock a particular wine, contact the distributor named in italic after the tasting note who will be pleased to give you details of the nearest stockist.

€30–€40

★ Dom. du Tunel Cornas 2004

Sweet new oak on the nose; the palate has very young, elegant, piercing, pointed damsons—very classy, but closed. Great concentration in a beautifully balanced wine with potential.

Price	**€30–€40**
Region	**Rhône (North)**
Grape	**Syrah**
Alc/vol	**13.5%**

Wicklow Wine

Wicklow Wine Co., Listons, Michael's Food & Wine, Red Island Wine Co., Harvest Off-licences, Galway, French Flair

---

★★ Dom. du Vieux Télégraphe La Crau Châteauneuf-du-Pape 2004

A wine of huge structure and immense class; very youthful, with intense, herby, spicy dark fruits and an amazing, concentrated core, with peppery dry tannins on a very long, lingering finish. Brilliant.

Price	**€30–€40**
Region	**Rhône (South)**
Grape	**Grenache/ Mourvèdre/Syrah/ Cinsault**
Alc/vol	**14.5%**

Findlater Grants

Gibneys Dublin; Greenacres, Wexford; Halpin's Wines; Harvest, Galway; Jus de Vine, Portmarnock; Morton's, Ranelagh; McCabe's; Vineyard, Galway

---

Dom. Gourt de Mautens Côtes du Rhône Villages Rasteau 2004

An explosion of intense, tarry, baked, ultra-ripe dark fruits with a coat of sleek new oak; a monster of a wine—huge levels of extract and alcohol.

Fallon & Byrne; Redmonds, Ranelagh; Red Island Wine Co.; Wickow Wine.

Price	**€30–€40**
Region	**Rhône (South)**
Grape	**Grenache/Syrah/ Mourvèdre/ Carignan**
Alc/vol	**14%**

Tyrrell

★★ La Crau de ma Mère Châteauneuf-du-Pape 2001

Wonderful, soft, over-ripe, heady aromas—a hedonistic wine with sweet, ripe strawberries, real power and great length, with some balancing dry tannins coming through on the finish. Controlled power in a big, rich wine.

Price	**€30–€40**
Region	**Rhône (South)**
Grape	**Syrah/Grenache/ Mourvèdre/Cinsault**
Alc/vol	**14.5%**

Wines Direct

Wines Direct

★★ Les Aphillanthes Mourvèdre Côtes du Rhône 2003

Big, ripe, sweet, very sweaty and leathery—it's not oaky. This is a megamonster of huge extract, weight and length. Don't try it without some meat.

Jus de Vine, Portmarnock.

Price	€30–€40
Region	Rhône (South)
Grape	Mourvèdre
Alc/vol	14.5%

Tyrrell

★★ Le Vieux Donjon Châteauneuf-du-Pape 2003

Rich, deeply concentrated dark leathery fruits with a mineral edge, very high levels of well-integrated tannins and excellent length. A great wine that needs a few years.

Cheers; Fallon & Byrne; Redmond's, Ranelagh

Price	€30–€40
Region	Rhône (South)
Grape	Grenache/Syrah/ Mourvèdre
Alc/vol	14%

Tyrrell

★ Michel & Stéphane Ogier L'Ame Soeur Terres de Seyssuel VdP des Collines Rhodaniennes 2004

Smooth, jammy plums with some cloves; easy, supple wine with very good fruit behind it. Delicate and fragrant.

Donnybrook Fair; Fallon & Byrne; Sweeney's; Vanilla Grape

Price	€30–€40
Region	Rhône (North)
Grape	Syrah
Alc/vol	12.5%

Tyrrell

Over €40

★ Dom. de la Vieille Julienne Châteauneuf-du-Pape 2003

This is quite classy, big, alcoholic and very concentrated—a bit uneven on the finish, but it certainly has plenty of oomph.

www.jnwine.com

Price	Over €40
Region	Rhône (South)
Grape	Grenache/Syrah/ Mourvèdre/ Counoise
Alc/vol	15.5%

Nicholson

★ Patrick & Christophe Bonnefond Côte-Rôtie 2004

Fragrant new oak on the nose—big and rich with plenty of alcohol; the sweet oak is matched by some savoury plums and a firm, tannic finish. Graceful, stylish Syrah.

Tyrrell (045) 870 882

Price	Over €40
Region	Rhône (North)
Grape	Syrah
Alc/vol	13%

Tyrrell

France–South

The vinegrowers of Languedoc have been getting plenty of publicity over the last year, but sadly for all the wrong reasons. Faced with falling grape prices, the more radical fringe has been planting bombs and incendiary devices, as well as destroying stocks of wine. Overall, the demand seems to be for greater subsidies, something the French government and the EU are determined to resist.

There is no doubt that the better vinegrowers have a bright future. But, like many farmers in this country, the smaller producers must either aim for higher quality or go out of business. The world is awash with wine, and the bigger producers will always have lower costs. This is an emotive issue in France, where winemaking is the lifeblood of many communities. But violence is hardly the way to solve the problem.

In an area so large, it is hardly surprising that quality is mixed. However, the best wines of the Languedoc are world-class, often at very reasonable prices. The reds in particular are worth seeking out for their rich, robust flavours; perfect winter warmers as the nights close in.

White

€9–€12

Ch. de Gourgazaud Chardonnay VdP d'Oc 2004

Special Value!

Very attractive, evolving wine with some delicious rich peach and subtle grilled nut flavours kept nicely in balance by the well-integrated citrus notes.

Dunnes Stores; SuperValu

Price	€9–€12
Region	Languedoc-Roussillon
Grape	Chardonnay
Alc/vol	13.5%

Kelly & Co.

Dom. de la Cessane Marsanne Viognier VdP d'Oc 2004

Ripe, mouth-filling peaches and apricots, balanced nicely by some well-integrated acidity. Try it with Asian dishes.

Berry Bros & Rudd

Price	€9–€12
Region	Languedoc-Roussillon
Grape	Marsanne/Viognier
Alc/vol	12.5%

Berry Bros & Rudd

Dom. Terre à Verre Carnaval Viognier
VdP d'Oc 2004

Fresh primary tropical fruits—pine-apple and apricots in a full-bodied, fruity, dry wine.

Firhouse Inn; Great Escape, Banna; Next Door, Enfield; The Wicklow Wine Co.; Wine Cluster, Moycullen

Price	€9–€12
Region	Languedoc-Roussillon
Grape	Viognier
Alc/vol	13%

Probus Wines

La Bastide Chardonnay VdP d'Oc 2005

Pleasant, quite rich red apples with a sweetish touch, but good, smooth, easy drinking.

Mitchells, Kildare Street; Mitchells, Glasthule

Price	€9–€12
Region	Languedoc-Roussillon
Grape	Chardonnay
Alc/vol	13.5%

Mitchell & Son

★ Le Moulin des Nonnes
Cuvée Inés Minervois 2004   Organic **Special Value!**

Rounded, creamy, slightly waxy nose. Broad, round flavours on the palate—hazel-nuts and baked apples contribute to the depth of flavour. Long, very flavoursome finish.

Fahys, Ballina; Next Door

Price	€9–€12
Region	Languedoc-Roussillon
Grape	Roussanne/Grenache Blanc/Muscat
Alc/vol	14%

Woodford Bourne

Les Trois Poules VdP d'Oc 2005   **Special Value!**

Fresh, crisp, racy dry white with deli-cious young green fruits—a great aperitif, or with seafood.

Price	€9–€12
Region	Languedoc-Roussillon
Grape	Vermentino
Alc/vol	12%

Bacchus

Simone Joseph Chardonnay
VdP d'Oc 2005   **Special Value!**

Vibrant quince and waxy apples in a very finely balanced, crisp, dry wine; this would make a great food wine, especially with fish or seafood.

Fallon & Byrne; McCabes, Blackrock; Next Door @ Myles Creek; Redmond's, Ranelagh; Uncorked; Vanilla Grape, Kenmare; The Vintry, Rathgar

Price	€9–€12
Region	Languedoc-Roussillon
Grape	Chardonnay
Alc/vol	13.5%

Tyrrell

Viognier de Pennautier
VdP d'Oc 2005

Special Value!

A very nicely crafted Viognier, with rich but not overbearing apricot fruit, a bitter twist and good supporting citrus notes. Delicious, pure wine.

Mitchells, Kildare Street; Mitchells, Glasthule

Price	€9–€12
Region	Languedoc-Roussillon
Grape	Viognier
Alc/vol	13.5%

Mitchell & Son

€12–€15

Delphine de Margon Chardonnay
VdP des Côtes de Thongue 2005

Pure, lightly textured apple and pear fruit and a touch of spice, with a nice acidic kick to give it life.

Mitchells, Kildare Street; Mitchells, Glasthule

Price	€12–€15
Region	Languedoc-Roussillon
Grape	Chardonnay
Alc/vol	13%

Mitchell & Son

Dom. du Tabatau Geneviève
VdP des Montes de la Grage 2004

Luscious apricots and pears, good acidity, and some spicy elements coming through on the finish. A good food wine that offers real character.

Firhouse Inn; Great Escape, Banna; Next Door, Enfield; The Wicklow Wine Co.; Wine Cluster, Moycullen

Price	€12–€15
Region	Languedoc-Roussillon
Grape	Chardonnay/Rolle Blanc
Alc/vol	13%

Probus Wines

€15–€18

★ Laurent Miquel Verité Viognier VdP d'Oc 2005

Rich, very primary fruits—cantaloupe melons and peaches in a full-bodied, lightly spicy wine. Big but refreshing in style. Doesn't have the delicacy of a Viognier from the Rhône, but very well-made wine.

Main Dunnes Stores branches

Price	€15–€18
Region	Languedoc-Roussillon
Grape	Viognier
Alc/vol	13.5%

Dunnes Stores

€18–€22

Ch. Rives-Blanques Cuvée de l'Odyssée Chardonnay Limoux 2003

This is very different; grilled nuts and lanolin in a generous, rich wine that seems to be showing some development; plenty of power, and not short on the finish.

Price	€18–€22
Region	Languedoc-Roussillon
Grape	Chardonnay/Mauzac
Alc/vol	14%

Febvre

Red

Under €9

Plume Bleue Grenache Syrah VdP d'Oc 2004

Special Value!

Very satisfying, rounded, lightly spicy wine with soft plums and strawberries.

Cana; Cellars; Cheers; Drinks Store; French Flair; Kitchen Project; McCabes; The Mill, Maynooth; Next Door @ Myles Creek; On the Grapevine; Red Island, Skerries; Redmonds; Uncorked; Vanilla Grape; The Wicklow Wine Co.

Price	Under €9
Region	Languedoc-Roussillon
Grape	Grenache/Syrah
Alc/vol	13.5%

Tyrrell

€9–€12

Ch. de Gourgazaud Minervois 2004

Special Value!

Soft, rounded, slightly leathery, sweet strawberry fruit with fine-grained tannins, plenty of oomph and good length.

Bin No. 9; Dunnes Stores; Kelly's Wine Vault, Clontarf; SPAR, Milltown; SuperValu

Price	€9–€12
Region	Languedoc-Roussillon
Grape	Mourvèdre/Syrah
Alc/vol	13%

Kelly & Co.

Ch. du Donjon Tradition Minervois 2004

Big, quite meaty dark aromas, juicy, ripe cherries with tobacco notes and a medium-bodied, easy, dry finish.

Firhouse Inn; Great Escape, Banna; Next Door, Enfield; The Wicklow Wine Co.; Wine Cluster, Moycullen

Price	€9–€12
Region	Languedoc-Roussillon
Grape	Grenache/Syrah/Mourvèdre
Alc/vol	14.5%

Probus Wines

> **Where to buy the wine**
> *If your local retailer does not stock a particular wine, contact the distributor named in italic after the tasting note who will be pleased to give you details of the nearest stockist.*

Ch. Quartironi de Sars
St Chinian 2003

Special Value!

Very fine, intense, firm, savoury dark fruits, with plenty of well-integrated fine dry tannins. A structured wine that needs a little time, or certainly a bit of air before drinking. The quality, however, is there to see.

Bin No. 9; Connoisseur, Dundalk; Daly's, Boyle; Gibney's, Malahide; McHughs, Kilbarrack; McHughs, Malahide Road; O'Neills, Carrickmacross; Red Island, Skerries; Silver Granite; Slatterys, Carrick on Shannon; SPAR, Bath Avenue

Price	€9–€12
Region	Languedoc-Roussillon
Grape	Syrah/Grenache/Carignan
Alc/vol	13%

Inis Wines

Ch. Ste Eulalie Plaisir d'Eulalie Minervois 2004

Good, soft, very supple, pure blackcurrant fruit and a lovely smooth finish.

Dowlings; Fallon & Byrne; The Hole in the Wall, Castleknock; Paploe's; PubVia

Price	€9–€12
Region	Languedoc-Roussillon
Grape	Carignan/Syrah/Mourvèdre/Cinsault
Alc/vol	13.5%

PubVia

Delphine de Margon Sarabande
VdP des Côtes de Thongue 2005

Special Value!

This has nice, plump, juicy blackcurrant fruit, a hint of herbs and light, drying tannins on the finish. Very pleasant, inexpensive dinner wine.

Mitchells, Kildare Street; Mitchells, Glasthule

Price	€9–€12
Region	Languedoc-Roussillon
Grape	Merlot/Cab Franc
Alc/vol	13.5%

Mitchell & Son

Dom. Comte de Margon
VdP des Côtes de Thongue 2005

Lifted black fruit aromas; rich, soft, sweet, ripe damson and cassis; supple, soft and easy with a lovely rounded finish.

Mitchells, Kildare Street; Mitchells, Glasthule

Price	€9–€12
Region	Languedoc-Roussillon
Grape	Merlot/Cab Sauv
Alc/vol	13%

Mitchell & Son

> **How to use this book**
> The wines are listed in order of country/region, colour (red or white), price band, then by name. There are separate chapters for sparkling (including Champagne) and dessert wines. If you can't find the wine you are looking for try the index. The price bands are guidelines only. All of the wines in this book are ready to drink now (October 2006), and for the next 12 months. Some will improve further over time and this is mentioned in the tasting note.

Dom. de Chamans Hegarty Chamans No. 3 Minervois 2004

Ripe, rounded, quite supple raspberries and strawberries, with a barnyardy hint and a great finish. More
modern style, but very nicely made.

Price	€9–€12
Region	Languedoc-Roussillon
Grape	Carignan/Grenache/Syrah
Alc/vol	13.5%

Celtic Whiskey Shop

Dom. de l'Arjolle Cuvée Cabernet Merlot VdP des Côtes de Thongue 2004 — **Special Value!**

Beautifully balanced blackberry and
blackcurrant fruit, with very nicely
integrated dry tannins kicking
through on the finish.

Selected branches Dunnes Stores

Price	€9–€12
Region	Languedoc-Roussillon
Grape	Cab Sauv/Merlot
Alc/vol	13%

Dunnes Stores

La Chapelle de Castelmaure Corbières 2004 — **Special Value!**

Maturing, meaty, barnyardy strawberry fruits with a pleasing peppery
finish.

Oddbins

Price	€9–€12
Region	Languedoc-Roussillon
Grape	Carignan/Grenache/Syrah/Cinsault
Alc/vol	13.5%

Oddbins

Laurent Miquel Nord Sud Syrah VdP d'Oc 2004 — **Special Value!**

This has a good concentration of ripe
damsons and dark fruits, balancing
out the smoky oak, and a surprisingly
long finish for a wine at this price.

Most branches Dunnes Stores

Price	€9–€12
Region	Languedoc-Roussillon
Grape	Syrah
Alc/vol	13.5%

Dunnes Stores

Le Moulin des Nonnes Cuvée Inés Minervois 2003 — **Organic Special Value!**

Cool, clean, concentrated dark fruits
with a black peppery edge and some
fine tannins. Long, dry length, which
opens out beautifully to reveal a very
stylish modern French wine with tasty
cassis and real elegance.

Fahys, Ballina; O'Donovans; The Gables, Foxrock

Price	€9–€12
Region	Languedoc-Roussillon
Grape	Syrah/Mourvèdre
Alc/vol	13%

Woodford Bourne

€12–€15

Ch. de Caunettes Cabardès 2001

Rich, intense, savoury dark plums with a bit of svelte new oak and a supple finish; big, modern and very good.

Mitchells, Kildare Street; Mitchells, Glasthule

Price	€12–€15
Region	Languedoc-Roussillon
Grape	Cab Sauv/Merlot/Syrah/Grenache
Alc/vol	13.5%

Mitchell & Son

Ch. de Flaugergues Cuvée La Méjanelle Coteaux du Languedoc 2003

Supple but concentrated, inky, dark, tight plum fruit, with a fair whack of alcohol; a big, burly wine with plenty of character. Try it with a casserole.

Most branches Dunnes Stores

Price	€12–€15
Region	Languedoc-Roussillon
Grape	Syrah/Grenache/Mourvèdre
Alc/vol	13.5%

Dunnes Stores

Ch. Grès St Paul Cuvée Antonin Coteaux du Languedoc 2003

Opens out after a few minutes to reveal rich, concentrated dark fruits with some smoky new oak, savoury liquorice notes, and a lingering finish.

The Corkscrew; Fallon & Byrne; Le Caveau

Price	€12–€15
Region	Languedoc-Roussillon
Grape	Syrah/Grenache/Mourvèdre
Alc/vol	13.5%

Le Caveau

Dom. Borie de Maurel Rêve de Carignan Minervois 2005

This has some nice, very spicy, cool fruity flavours, and plenty of them, with a long, cool, peppery finish. Delicious.

Oddbins

Price	€12–€15
Region	Languedoc-Roussillon
Grape	Carignan

Oddbins

Dom. des Jougla Cuvée Classique St Chinian 2004

Big, foursquare, intense dark fruits on the nose; very nicely balanced wine with real character and body. It opens out to show off some lovely cherry fruit and a certain delicacy.

Baily Wines; Caprani's; Fallon & Byrne; McHughs, Kilbarrack; McHughs, Malahide Road; Morton's, Galway; O'Neills, Carrickmacross; Silver Granite; The Wicklow Wine Co.

Price	€12–€15
Region	Languedoc-Roussillon
Grape	Syrah/Grenache/Mourvèdre/Carignan
Alc/vol	12.5%

Inis Wines

★ Dom. Luc Lapeyre L'Amourier Minervois 2004

This is big and ripe with very concentrated strawberry fruit and a lovely savoury finish. Supple, but with enough structure to make it stand up.

Wines Direct

Price	€12–€15
Region	Languedoc-Roussillon
Grape	Syrah/Grenache/Mourvèdre
Alc/vol	14.5%

Wines Direct

Dom. Mas de Martin Cuvée Roi Patriote VdP du Val de Montferrand 2004

Juicy blackcurrant pastilles on the nose. Robust, well-structured palate with damsons, plums and spice supported by nicely judged tannin and alcohol. Long finish with touches of cinnamon. A real food wine that would go with most roasts.

Price	€12–€15
Region	Languedoc-Roussillon
Grape	Grenache/Syrah/Mourvèdre
Alc/vol	14.5%

WineKnows

★ Dom. St Jean de l'Arbousier Mourvèdre VdP d'Oc 2004

I do like this wine! Elegant but full-bodied, with rich, pure cherry and damson fruits and very smooth tannins. It all hangs together beautifully.

Firhouse Inn; Great Escape, Banna; Next Door, Enfield; The Wicklow Wine Co.; Wine Cluster, Moycullen

Price	€12–€15
Region	Languedoc-Roussillon
Grape	Mourvèdre
Alc/vol	13%

Probus Wines

La Jasse Castel Les Intillières Coteaux du Languedoc 2005

Forward, tarry, liquorice aromas; the palate is rich and smooth, revealing dark fruits and a savoury, liquorice note. Big but very ripe in style.

Fallon & Byrne; Le Caveau

Price	€12–€15
Region	Languedoc-Roussillon
Grape	Grenache/Cinsault/Syrah
Alc/vol	13%

Le Caveau

Prieuré de St Jean de Bébian La Chapelle de Bébian Coteaux du Languedoc 2000

Elegant, nicely balanced maturing dark fruits and liquorice, good concentration on the centre palate, with light drying tannins on the finish.

Price	€12–€15
Region	Languedoc-Roussillon
Grape	Grenache/Syrah/Mourvèdre
Alc/vol	13%

Celtic Whiskey Shop

€15–€18

Alain Chabanon Campredon Coteaux du Languedoc 2004   Organic

Soft but concentrated ripe jammy fruits with a mineral edge, and a rounded warm finish. Well-made modern Languedoc with a nice savoury twist and well-integrated tannins.

Fallon & Byrne; Le Caveau; Listons

Price	€15–€18
Region	Languedoc-Roussillon
Grape	Syrah/Mourvèdre/Grenache/Carignan
Alc/vol	14%

Le Caveau

Ch. La Bastide Les Cèdres VdP d'Oc 2000

Good, supple, meaty, savoury and dry, yet easy to drink, with pleasing, chunky dark fruits.

Mitchells, Kildare Street; Mitchells, Glasthule

Price	€15–€18
Region	Languedoc-Roussillon
Grape	Syrah/Malbec
Alc/vol	13%

Mitchell & Son

Ch. L'Euzière L'Amandin Coteaux du Languedoc Pic St Loup 2004

A deeply inky, savoury wine with well-defined dark fruits, finishing on a very nice supple note. Try it with duck or other game birds.

Bailys of Howth; Uncorked

Price	€15–€18
Region	Languedoc-Roussillon
Grape	Syrah
Alc/vol	14%

Liberty Wines

Clos Marie L'Olivette Coteaux du Languedoc Pic St Loup 2004

Solid liquorice and coolish dark fruits in a broad, reasonably concentrated wine. There is an attractive pepper-iness to it, though, and good length.

Le Caveau

Price	€15–€18
Region	Languedoc-Roussillon
Grape	Grenache/Syrah/Cinsault
Alc/vol	13%

Le Caveau

★ Dom. d'Aupilhac Montpeyroux Coteaux du Languedoc 2003

Sweet, jammy aromas; ripe but rustic, intense, dark but perfectly ripe fruits, balanced by a mineral edge and some fairly substantial tannins on the dry finish. Great, hearty stuff.

Wicklow Wine Co., Listons, Michael's Food & Wine, Red Island Wine Co., Harvest Off-licences, Galway, French Flair, Hand Made Wines

Price	**€15–€18**
Region	**Languedoc-Roussillon**
Grape	**Syrah/Grenache/Carignan/Mourvèdre/Cinsault**
Alc/vol	**13.5%**

Wicklow Wine

Dom. Gardiés Vieilles Vignes Côtes du Roussillon Villages Tautavel 2003

This is a bit of a monster—raw power, huge extract of dark fruits, with prunes, leather and dry tannins kicking in on the finish. Certainly not a wine for wimps.

Wines Direct

Price	**€15–€18**
Region	**Languedoc-Roussillon**
Grape	**Grenache/Syrah/Mourvèdre**
Alc/vol	**14.5%**

Wines Direct

La Cave Berlou Vignes Royales Les Coteaux du Rieu-Berlou 2000

Broad, ripe, forward nose leading on to a well-made foursquare wine with liquorice and dark fruits, and a nice tannic bite on the finish. Good, well-made, firm Languedoc that will improve a bit too.

Epicurean Fine Food & Wine

Price	**€15–€18**
Region	**Languedoc-Roussillon**
Grape	**Grenache/Carignan/Syrah**
Alc/vol	**13.5%**

Epicurean Fine Food & Wine

Laurent Miquel Bardou St Chinian 2001

Big, very alcoholic, powerful wine with good plum flavours edged with a smoky, savoury note; at its peak now—drink up.

Dunnes Stores branches in: Bandon Road, Cork; Blanchardstown; Cornelscourt; Donaghmede; Douglas; Ennis; Kilkenny; Terryland, Galway

Price	**€15–€18**
Region	**Languedoc-Roussillon**
Grape	**Syrah**
Alc/vol	**14%**

Dunnes Stores

Les Hauts de l'Enclos des Bories Minervois La Livinière 2002

Warm, meaty, rich wine with real herby, intense stuffing; big, foursquare and full of southern promise.

Mitchells, Kildare Street; Mitchells, Glasthule

Price	**€15–€18**
Region	**Languedoc-Roussillon**
Grape	**Syrah/Mourvèdre/Grenache**

Mitchell & Son

Les Terres Rouges Carignan VdP des Coteaux de Peyriac 2003

This is very stylish wine, showing an unusual delicacy, with some fragrant light cherry fruit, an appealing, easy manner and no tannins to get in the way. Lovely wine.

French Flair

Price	**€15–€18**
Region	**Languedoc-Roussillon**
Grape	**Carignan**
Alc/vol	**13.5%**

Approach Trade

★ Villa Symposia L'Equilibre Coteaux du Languedoc 2003

A very elegant, smooth, impeccably defined wine with plenty of fine tannins and good length. Intensely herby, smooth and elegant.

wineonline.ie

Price	**€15–€18**
Region	**Languedoc-Roussillon**
Grape	**Syrah/Grenache**
Alc/vol	**14%**

WineOnline

€18–€22

Ch. Haut-Gléon Corbières 2002

Solid, foursquare, meaty wine with some nice strawberries and dark fruits; the dry finish calls out for meat or cheese. Fully mature and drinking nicely.

Jus de Vine; Waterford World of Wine; Wine Centre, Kilkenny

Price	**€18–€22**
Region	**Languedoc-Roussillon**
Grape	**Grenache/Mourvèdre**
Alc/vol	**13.5%**

J Donohue

★ Clos Canos Les Cocobrious Corbières 2003

Big, statuesque nose of figs and ripe plums; very powerful but soft ultra-ripe plums, figs and silky dark fruits, overlain with a smoky toastiness; not a shrinking violet, in fact the opposite, but very good indeed of its style.

Price	€18–€22
Region	Languedoc-Roussillon
Grape	Grenache/Carignan/Syrah
Alc/vol	14.5%

Bacchus

Dom. de la Marfée Les Gamines VdP de l'Hérault 2004

Chewy black pepper and liquorice in a youthful, tight wine with firm tannins showing through on the finish. Decant before drinking or keep a year.

Fallon & Byrne; Le Caveau

Price	€18–€22
Region	Languedoc-Roussillon
Grape	Mourvèdre/Syrah/Grenache/Cab Sauv
Alc/vol	14%

Le Caveau

Dom. Luc Lapeyre Les Clots Minervois 2002

Very modern style of wine with a deep colour, intense cassis and ripe plums, backed up by some seductive oak and plenty of hearty alcohol. Big, mouth-filling wine.

Wines Direct

Price	€18–€22
Region	Languedoc-Roussillon
Grape	Grenache/Syrah/Carignan
Alc/vol	14.5%

Wines Direct

Dom. Seguela Cuvée Jean Julien Côtes du Roussillon Villages 2003

Leathery, slightly rustic wine with plenty of dark jammy fruits, warming alcohol, good length and drying tannins kicking through on the finish.

Cheers Delgany; Chester Beatty OL, Ashford; Corkscrew, D2; Donnybrook Fair; Fallon & Byrne, D2; Grape Escape, Lucan; Jus de Vine, Portmarnock; Kellys, Clontarf; Macs, Limerick; Marthas Vineyard, Rathfarnham; McCabes; O'Donovans, Cork; On The Grapevine Dalkey & Booterstown; Red Island Wine Co., Skerries; Thomas Martins, Fairview; Thomas Woodberrys, Galway; World Wide Wines, Waterford

Price	€18–€22
Region	Languedoc-Roussillon
Grape	Carignan/Grenache/Syrah
Alc/vol	13.5%

Cassidys

€22–€30

★ Dom. d'Aupilhac Les Cocalières
Coteaux du Languedoc 2004

Clean, beautifully defined flavours of damsons, cherries and dark fruits, balanced by some good savoury notes and a light spiciness; it is still a little tight, but I can imagine this with a barbecued steak or pork.

Price	€22–€30
Region	Languedoc-Roussillon
Grape	Syrah/Mourvèdre/Grenache
Alc/vol	13.5%

Wicklow Wine

Wicklow Wine Co., Listons, Michael's Food & Wine, Red Island Wine Co., French Flair, Hand Made Wines

€30–€40

★ Dom. Gardiés La Torre
Côtes du Roussillon Villages Tautavel 2002

Very ripe, sweet cassis aromas; tight, concentrated dark fruits coated in a shell of dry tannins with good peppery length. It has plenty of style, firm and savoury, with warming alcohol to back it up.

Price	€30–€40
Region	Languedoc-Roussillon
Grape	Grenache/Syrah/Mourvèdre
Alc/vol	14%

Wines Direct

Wines Direct

★ Prieuré de St Jean de Bébian
Coteaux du Languedoc 2001

Maturing leafy undergrowth with a lovely sweet ripeness; big, intense liquorice and sweet raspberries in a complex, perfectly balanced wine that is drinking beautifully now. Long, stylish and classy.

Price	€30–€40
Region	Languedoc-Roussillon
Grape	Grenache/Syrah/Mourvèdre
Alc/vol	14.5%

Celtic Whiskey Shop

All of the wines in this book are ready to drink now (October 2006), and for the next 12 months. Some will improve further over time and this is mentioned in the tasting note.

★★ Villa Symposia L'Origine Coteaux du Languedoc 2003

Sweet, oh-so-ripe and oaky, with huge levels of drying tannins, but silky soft on the centre palate. Needs air and/or time, but a great example of modern Languedoc. A second taste 10 minutes later was even better.

wineonline.ie

Price	€30–€40
Region	Languedoc-Roussillon
Grape	Syrah
Alc/vol	14%

WineOnline

Rosé

Under €9

Dom. Begude Pinot Rosé VdP de l'Aude 2004

Special Value!

Very light, vibrant, refreshing strawberry fruit, lovely crisp acidity and a dry finish. A charming summer wine.

Molloys

Price	Under €9
Region	Languedoc-Roussillon
Grape	Pinot Noir
Alc/vol	12.5%

Molloys

Laurent Miquel Cinsault Syrah VdP d'Oc 2005

Special Value!

Big, ripe strawberry nose; attractive ripe strawberries on the palate too, with good length and nice acidity. Very stylish rosé.

All branches Dunnes Stores

Price	Under €9
Region	Languedoc-Roussillon
Grape	Cinsault/Syrah
Alc/vol	13%

Dunnes Stores

France–South West

The South West has done even better this year, after last year's sterling performance. We have 19 entries, including wines of virtually every style. I have always been a huge fan of this region, as I believe it offers different and unusual flavours at very acceptable prices.

The South West has always been in the shadow of Bordeaux, and in the past was punitively taxed by the canny Bordelais. In addition to the Bordeaux grape varieties, there are plenty of local specialities, from the Malbec of Cahors, the Gros and Petit Manseng of Jurançon, the Loin d'Oeuil of Gaillac, Tannat, Fer and Négrette. This year I was delighted to see the dessert wines of the South West do so well—like the sweet wines of the Loire, they offer fantastic fresh refreshing fruit balanced by a cleansing acidity.

White

€9–€12

Alain Brumont Gros Manseng Sauvignon VdP des Côtes de Gascogne 2005   **Special Value!**

Zingy, fresh gooseberry aromas jump out of the glass, followed by a palate of pure primary fresh pineapple fruit cut through with lemon peel and a rounded dry finish. Perfect aperitif, or with lightly spicy/herby fish.

Price	€9–€12
Region	South West
Grape	Gros Manseng/ Sauv Blanc
Alc/vol	13%

Le Caveau

Fallon & Byrne; Le Caveau; Listons

Ch. des Eyssards Bergerac Sec 2005   **Special Value!**

Classy, floral, grassy Sauvignon with an attractive delicacy—a nice centre palate and fruity length. Great all-rounder by itself or with lighter fish and seafood.

Price	€9–€12
Region	South West
Grape	Sauv Blanc/Sémillon
Alc/vol	13%

Wines Direct

Wines Direct

Ch. Moulin-Caresse Premières Vendanges Montravel 2005

Special Value!

This is a delicious, firmly mineral wine with crisp green fruits and lovely integrated acidity. All at a great price too.

Baily Wines, Howth; Bin No. 9; Caprani's, Ashford; Dicey Reillys; Fallon & Byrne; Foodhall, Portlaoise; Mill, Maynooth; Morton's of Galway; Silver Granite; Slatterys, Carrick on Shannon

Price €9–€12
Region South West
Grape Sauv Blanc/Sémillon
Alc/vol 13%

Inis Wines

Dom. de Jöy Sauvignon Gros Manseng VdP des Côtes de Gascogne 2005

Special Value!

Very enjoyable wine with delicious, luscious fruits—oranges and ripe pears, shot through with mouth-watering, tangy lemon.

Oddbins

Price €9–€12
Region South West
Grape Sauv Blanc/
Gros Manseng
Alc/vol 12.5%

Oddbins

Jacques Frelin Caylus VdP des Côtes de Gascogne 2004

Organic Special Value!

Mouth-watering, lively lime, yellow apples and crisp pears; this really awakens the senses and gets the salivary glands going. A good aperitif or with plain seafood.

Harrington's, Ardgroom, Cork; Quay Co-op, Cork

Price €9–€12
Region South West
Grape Colombard/
Ugni Blanc
Alc/vol 12%

Mary Pawle

€12–€15

Dom. de Pialentou Les Gentilles Pierres Gaillac 2004

Clean, fresh and zippy with yellow apples and pears, in a well-made, individual, lively, refreshing dry white. A good aperitif, or with seafood.

Firhouse Inn; Great Escape, Banna; Next Door, Enfield; The Wicklow Wine Co.; Wine Cluster, Moycullen

Price €12–€15
Region South West
Grape Sauv Blanc/Mauzac
Alc/vol 12.5%

Probus Wines

Where to buy the wine
If your local retailer does not stock a particular wine, contact the distributor named in italic after the tasting note who will be pleased to give you details of the nearest stockist.

Red

€9–€12

Ch. Tour des Gendres Le Classique Bergerac 2004

Forward spice and plum fruits; delicious pure plum and blackcurrant fruit with a lightly spicy note, good acidity and a dry finish.

Price	€9–€12
Region	South West
Grape	Merlot
Alc/vol	12.5%

Le Caveau; Listons

Le Caveau

€12–€15

Dom. du Pech Buzet 2001

A delicious, big, ripe, softly fruited wine with cassis and an intriguing herby touch.

Price	€12–€15
Region	South West
Grape	Merlot/Cab Franc/ Cab Sauv
Alc/vol	13%

Brechin Watchorn; Kellys, Clontarf; O'Neills, Carrickmacross; Red Island, Skerries

River Wines

€15–€18

Ch. Baudare Fronton 2003

Forward, very seductive ripe cassis and smoky spice with a well-integrated tannic structure. Drinking nicely now but will improve further over the next year.

Price	€15–€18
Region	South West
Grape	Négrette/Cab Sauv/ Cab Franc
Alc/vol	12.5%

Dowlings; Fallon & Byrne; The Hole in the Wall, Castleknock; Paploe's; PubVia

PubVia

★ Ch. du Cèdre Le Prestige Cahors 2003

Cool dark berry fruit aromas; the palate is broad, with brambly, slightly plummy fruits, finishing with some vanilla. There is a lovely concentration of fruit on the centre palate too. Very well-made wine that would go nicely with roasted red meats.

Price	€15–€18
Region	South West
Grape	Malbec/Tannat
Alc/vol	14%

Le Caveau

Celtic Whiskey; The Corkscrew; Fallon & Byrne; Le Caveau; Listons

Dom. des Costes Cuvee Tradition Pécharmant 2000

Forward spice and plum fruit aromas. Delicious pure plum and blackcurrant flavours with a lightly spicy note, good acidity and a dry finish.

Price	€15–€18
Region	South West
Grape	Cab Sauv/Merlot/ Cab Franc
Alc/vol	12.5%

Blessings, Cavan; Foodhall, Portlaoise; Gibneys, Malahide; O'Neills, Carrickmacross

Inis Wines

€18–€22

Clos Triguedina Cahors 2002

Attractive spicy nose; firm but nicely balanced dark fruits, just ripe, with some spice and tobacco, finishing well with finely grained tannins.

Price	€18–€22
Region	South West
Grape	Malbec
Alc/vol	13.1%

Firhouse Inn; Great Escape, Banna; Next Door, Enfield; The Wicklow Wine Co.; Wine Cluster, Moycullen

Probus Wines

Rosé

€12–€15

Ch. Baudare Fronton 2005

A rosé with lovely smooth, textured strawberries and summer fruits carrying through to a dry finish.

Price	€12–€15
Region	South West
Grape	Négrette/Cab Sauv
Alc/vol	12.5%

Fallon & Byrne; The Hole in the Wall, Castleknock

PubVia

Germany

Once again, a very impressive performance from Germany. As with Austria, it appears that we may be starting to realise the fantastic quality available. This year we have 14 excellent wines, including six star wines. The Breuer Terra Montosa was just pipped at the post for Old World White Wine of the Year, and the Marks & Spencer Mineralstein Riesling is our Best Value White. All of the wines listed below are Riesling, and most are dry.

White

€9–€12

Mineralstein Riesling Deutscher Tafelwein 2005

Delicious, fresh, crisp green-apple fruit set off by some racy acidity— summery, delightful—how could anyone fail to like it?

Price €9–€12
Region Rhein-Mosel
Grape Riesling
Alc/vol 12.5%

Marks & Spencer

BEST VALUE WHITE WINE OF THE YEAR

€12–€15

Carl Ehrhard Rüdesheimer Riesling Trocken 2005

This is a wonderful balance of crisp Granny Smith apples with lemony acidity, finishing on a dry, very mineral note. Classic Riesling with concentration, real style and brio.

Price €12–€15
Region Rheingau
Grape Riesling
Alc/vol 12.5%

Karwigs

Eugene's, Kenmare; Karwigs; Redmonds, Ranelagh

Dr von Bassermann-Jordan Riesling Trocken 2005

A very pale colour, lightly spritzy; light, delicate pineapple and pear flavours in harmony with some vibrant mineral acidity; finishes dry and with good length. Charming, elegant wine.

Price €12–€15
Region Pfalz
Grape Riesling
Alc/vol 12%

Wicklow Wine

Wicklow Wine Co., Listons, Redmonds Wines & Spirits, Baily Wines, Jus de Vine, On the Grapevine, Dalkey, On the Grapevine, Booterstown, Donnybrook Fair, Morton's Supermarkets, Hand Made Wines, Michael's Food & Wine, Fallon & Byrne, Sheridans Cheesemongers, Food Hall, Arnotts

★ Dr von Bassermann-Jordan Rupertsberger Reiterpfad Riesling Kabinett Trocken 2002

A subtle, light wine that opens out to show off some impressive pear and grapefruit flavours, finishing dry, with a lovely minerality. Seductive wine that improves with every sip.

Wicklow Wine Co., On the Grapevine, Dalkey, Listons, On the Grapevine, Booterstown, Red Island Wine Co., The Corkscrew, Michael's Food & Wine, Fallon & Byrne

Price €12–€15
Region Pfalz
Grape Riesling
Alc/vol 12%

Wicklow Wine

Dr Wagner Saarburger Rausch Riesling Halbtrocken 2004

Bracing, but delicate and charming wine with the lightest of body, subtle floral fruits and perfect, lively acidity. Very attractive, classic Mosel Riesling.

Karwigs; O'Brien's; Wine & Co, Dalkey

Price €12–€15
Region Mosel-Saar-Ruwer
Grape Riesling
Alc/vol 11.5%

Karwigs

Georg Breuer Riesling Sauvage 2004

Light, fresh, crisp, racy wine with mouth-tingling acidity and a light, dry finish.

Wicklow Wine Co., On the Grapevine, Dalkey, Listons, On the Grapevine, Booterstown, Red Island Wine Co., The Corkscrew, Michael's Food & Wine, Donnybrook Fair, Redmonds Wines & Spirits, Baily Wines, Probus Wines, Fallon & Byrne, Jus de Vine, Hand Made Wines

Price €12–€15
Region Rheingau
Grape Riesling
Alc/vol 11.5%

Wicklow Wine

Schloss Schönborn Hattenheimer Nussbrunnen Riesling Kabinett Trocken 2005

The freshest of noses, followed by a really zippy floral, lightly honeyed wine brimful of lemon zest and finishing bone dry.

O'Briens

Price €12–€15
Region Rheingau
Grape Riesling
Alc/vol 12.5%

O'Briens

€15–€18

Max Ferdinand Richter Brauneberger Juffer-Sonnenuhr Riesling Kabinett Trocken 2005

Soft pear and apple fruit with honey, flowers and very attractive refreshing acidity. Light, lifted—perfect sipping wine.

Wicklow Wine Co., Listons, Baily Wines, Michael's Food & Wine, Redmonds Wines & Spirits, On the Grapevine, Dalkey, The Corkscrew, Fallon & Byrne, Hand Made Wines, Sheridans Cheesemongers, Food Hall, Arnotts

Price €15–€18
Region Mosel-Saar-Ruwer
Grape Riesling
Alc/vol 12.5%

Wicklow Wine

€18–€22

★★ Georg Breuer Riesling Terra Montosa 2004

A delicious mouthful of clean pineapple fruits laid bare by rapier-like, taut, mineral acidity. There is more than a hint of honey and an exotic touch too, but the lingering finish is bone dry. Excellent wine that will improve.

Price €18–€22
Region Rheingau
Grape Riesling
Alc/vol 12.5%

Wicklow Wine

Wicklow Wine Co., On the Grapevine, Dalkey, Listons, Redmonds Wines & Spirits, Baily Wines, Probus Wines, Red Island Wine Co., On the Grapevine, Booterstown, The Corkscrew, Michael's Food & Wine, Fallon & Byrne

---

Where to buy the wine
If your local retailer does not stock a particular wine, contact the distributor named in italic after the tasting note who will be pleased to give you details of the nearest stockist.

Max Ferdinand Richter Brauneberger Juffer-Sonnenuhr Riesling Spätlese 2004

Delicate honeysuckle aromas. A beautifully gentle wine with subtle pears, lemons and ripe peach fruit, finishing off-dry. This would make a wonderful light aperitif.

Price **€18–€22**
Region **Mosel-Saar-Ruwer**
Grape **Riesling**
Alc/vol **7.5%**

Wicklow Wine

Wicklow Wine Co., Listons, Michael's Food & Wine, Power & Smullen Wine Merchants

---

€22–€30

★★ Georg Breuer Berg Roseneck Riesling 2004

Wonderful pure honeycomb, apple and pineapple fruit in a perfectly defined dry wine, with plenty of cleansing acidity balanced by the weight of fruit. Drink now with great pleasure or lay down for a year or two.

GEORG BREUER

BERG ROSENECK

2004

RHEINGAU

Price **€22–€30**
Region **Rheingau**
Grape **Riesling**
Alc/vol **12.5%**

Wicklow Wine

Wicklow Wine Co., Donnybrook Fair, Jus de Vine, Listons, Michael's Food & Wine

---

★ Reichsrat von Buhl Forster Jesuitengarten Riesling Spätlese 2003

Light, luscious, honeyed peach fruit with a refreshing tang and a medium-dry finish—a bit like eating a ripe piece of fruit, dripping with juices.

Price **€22–€30**
Region **Pfalz**
Grape **Riesling**
Alc/vol **9%**

McCabes; Redmonds of Ranelagh; www.jnwine.com

Nicholson

★ Schloss Schönborn Erbach Marcobrunn Rheingau Riesling Erstes Gewächs 2004

Rich, complex pineapple and yellow fruits with a lovely waxy, honeyed touch. A wine of some power and great concentration, finishing with a real flourish.

Price **€22–€30**
Region **Rheingau**
Grape **Riesling**
Alc/vol **13%**

O'Briens

O'Briens

★ Vam Volxem Wiltinger Kupp Riesling 2003

Bracing pineapple fruit with a lovely freshness and a soft, but very long, off-dry finish. Mouth-watering, delicious, subtle wine.

Berry Bros & Rudd

Price €22–€30
Region Mosel-Saar-Ruwer
Grape Riesling

Berry Bros & Rudd

Italy

Italy has it all. The only question is why we Irish have yet to fully embrace Italian wines. Like France, there are wines available in every style and price; the international varieties are there, but so too are a host of unknown local indigenous grapes. Virtually every part of Italy produces wine of some kind. Barring a few exceptions, most of what arrives on these shores is of pretty good quality. In fact, over the last few years, a crop of new companies has sprung up, bringing with them a range of fascinating, individual wines.

This year, there are over 80 wines from Italy, including 17 star wines, although there are no Wines of the Year. There are wines to suit every wine-lover; crisp dry whites from the north, as well as a few from the far south; cool, elegant wines from Piedmont; stylish, refined reds from Tuscany, and richer, more powerful fare from the deep south. Add in the delightful sparkling wines, and a few delicious sweet wines, and you have an irresistible range to excite the most jaded of palates.

White

€12–€15

Borghi IGT Pinot Grigio della Venezie 2005 Organic

Stuffed with rich red-apple and juicy pear fruits. Long, dry finish with a lovely succulence and a funky touch.

The Bottle Shop; Louis Albrouze Wine; Morton's, Ranelagh; Vanilla Grape, Kenmare

Price **€12–€15**
Region **Veneto**
Grape **Pinot Grigio**
Alc/vol **12%**

Louis Albrouze

Borgo dei Vassalli Pinot Grigio IGT Venezia Giulia 2005

Clean, quite light melons and green-gages with very good intensity and a snappy, crisp finish. Light Pinot Grigio with a touch of class.

The Bottle Shop; Fallon & Byrne; O'Donovans

Price **€12–€15**
Region **Veneto**
Grape **Pinot Grigio**
Alc/vol **12%**

Liberty Wines

All of the wines in this book are ready to drink now (October 2006), and for the next 12 months. Some will improve further over time and this is mentioned in the tasting note.

Cristina Ascheri Arneis Langhe 2005

Very pleasant textured ripe pears and peach fruit with a grapey freshness. Very good, fresh, moreish wine with a pleasant delicacy and some real interest.

O'Briens

Price	€12–€15
Region	Piedmont
Grape	Arneis
Alc/vol	12.5%

O'Briens

Feudo Zirtari Bianco IGT Sicilia 2005

A white with real character—some spicy ginger notes, but mostly ripe pineapples and other soft fruits in a fresh, vibrant wine.

Café di Napoli; Donnybrook Fair; Louis Albrouze; The Wicklow Wine Co.

Price	€12–€15
Region	Sicily
Grape	Grillo/Inzolia/Chardonnay
Alc/vol	13%

Select Wines from Italy

Gorgo Podere San Michelin Bianco di Custoza 2005

Quite luscious yellow fruit aromas; clean, lightly textured pears with a bitter edge. Refreshing and enjoyably different.

Donnybrook Fair

Price	€12–€15
Region	Veneto
Grape	Garganega/Tocai/Cortese/Trebbiano
Alc/vol	13.5%

Vinitalia

Plozner Pinot Grigio Friuli 2005

Very clean, light, elegant wine with fine peach fruit. Dry, with a chalky mineral finish. Delicate, but delicious fresh drinking.

Wines Direct

Price	€12–€15
Region	Friuli-Venezia Giula
Grape	Pinot Grigio
Alc/vol	12.5%

Wines Direct

Tramin Pinot Grigio Südtiroler Ruländer/Pinot Grigio dell'Alto Adige 2005

Spritzy, fresh, ripe pear aromas, broad, rounded, quite concentrated pear fruit with an orange citrus note and good length. Very full-flavoured for a Pinot Grigio.

Price	€12–€15
Region	Trentino-Alto Adige
Grape	Pinot Grigio
Alc/vol	13.5%

Celtic Whiskey Shop

Where to buy the wine
If your local retailer does not stock a particular wine, contact the distributor named in italic after the tasting note who will be pleased to give you details of the nearest stockist.

Vigneti Mancini Verdicchio dei Castelli di Jesi 2004

Good concentration of apples and
nuts, bags of vibrant acidity and some
complexity on the nutty finish.

Next Door

Price	€12–€15
Region	Marches
Grape	Verdicchio
Alc/vol	12%

Woodford Bourne

€15–€18

Contini Tyrsos Vermentino di Sardegna 2005

A very interesting wine with lots to
offer—big, powerful, savoury minerals
and chalky flavours; quite a mouthful,
and with good, very dry length. Needs
food, but a lovely wine.

Café di Napoli; Claudio's; Probus; Vanilla Grape, Kenmare

Price	€15–€18
Region	Sardinia
Grape	Vermentino
Alc/vol	13%

Select Wines from Italy

Franz Haas Pinot Bianco Südtirol-Alto Adige 2005

Lovely pure fruit—peaches and
pears—but never a hint of confection.
Vibrant, cleansing acidity and a good
dry finish.

Fallon & Byrne; Hole in the Wall

Price	€15–€18
Region	Trentino-Alto Adige
Grape	Pinot Bianco
Alc/vol	13%

Liberty Wines

La Ghersa Sivoy Monferrato 2003

Smooth, soft peaches with an acidic
spike, fresh, lightly nutty. Very interesting wine, quite lemony too.

Price	€15–€18
Region	Piedmont
Grape	Cortese/Chard/ Sauv Blanc
Alc/vol	13.5%

Bacchus

Loggia della Serra Terredora Greco di Tufo 2005

This has lovely concentrated fruit—
rich, firm melons and a very dry, very
mineral finish. Big, too.

Oddbins

Price	€15–€18
Region	Campania
Grape	Greco di Tufo
Alc/vol	13%

Oddbins

Mastroberardino Sannio 2005

A seductive, soft, distinctive palate of
canned pineapples, pears and pear
drops. Lengthy, dry mineral finish and
a lively freshness overall.

Bradleys, Cork; Dunne & Crescenzi

Price	€15–€18
Region	Campania
Grape	Falanghina
Alc/vol	12.5%

Select Wines from Italy

Mentio Riva Arsiglia Gambellara 2005

Fresh pear fruit, a touch of almonds with excellent length, and a nice dry finish. This is lovely refreshing wine.

The Bottle Shop, Goatstown

Price **€15–€18**
Region **Veneto**
Grape **Garganega**
Alc/vol **12.5%**

Vinitalia

★★ Pieropan Soave Classico 2005

Fresh, beautifully defined minerals and cool, clean green fruits with a lovely crisp, dry finish. Bracing, fresh and very moreish. A previous wine of the year that is still going strong.

Price **€15–€18**
Region **Veneto**
Grape **Garganega/ Trebbiano**
Alc/vol **12%**

Liberty Wines

Bailys of Howth; Donnybrook Fair; Hole in the Wall; McHughs; Michael's Wine; Mortons; Red Island, Skerries

---

Regaleali IGT Sicilia 2004

This is delicious—fresh but full, with a complex mix of almonds, pears and luscious fruits, all cut through by some lively acidity. Yum.

Dunne & Crescenzi; McCambridges, Galway; Probus; The Wicklow Wine Co.

Price **€15–€18**
Region **Sicily**
Grape **Inzolia/Grecanico Dorato/Catarratto**
Alc/vol **12.5%**

Select Wines from Italy

Santa Margherita Pinot Grigio Valdadige 2005

Really lively, fresh, zesty nose; crisp, well-defined, lightly textured and rather delicious pears. Good length.

Donnybrook Fair; McCabes, Blackrock; Probus; The Wicklow Wine Co.

Price **€15–€18**
Region **Trentino-Alto Adige**
Grape **Pinot Grigio**
Alc/vol **12%**

Select Wines from Italy

St Michael-Eppian Pinot Grigio Südtirol-Alto Adige 2005

Appealing, fresh, medium-bodied yellow fruits with plenty of flavour and a clean, tangy finish; lively with some real class.

Jus de Vine, Portmarnock; On the Grapevine, Booterstown and Dalkey

Price **€15–€18**
Region **Trentino-Alto Adige**
Grape **Pinot Grigio**
Alc/vol **13%**

WineKnows

€18–€22

Bonci San Michele
Verdicchio dei Castelli di Jesi 2004

Very unusual but enjoyable wine with rich, textured, luscious soft fruits and a honeyed touch; big in style but full of personality. Try it with richer fish dishes or chicken.

Price	€18–€22
Region	Marches
Grape	Verdicchio
Alc/vol	14%

Select Wines from Italy

Bradleys, Cork; Donnybrook Fair; Vanilla Grape, Kenmare

★ Nova Serra Greco di Tufo 2005

Pineapples, peaches and luscious fruits balanced by some pronounced mineral acidity, with a lovely bite on the lengthy finish.

Price	€18–€22
Region	Campania
Grape	Greco di Tufo
Alc/vol	12.5%

Select Wines from Italy

Bradleys, Cork; Claudio's

Rovereto Chiarlo Gavi di Gavi 2005

A textbook Gavi with the lightest of zesty lemon fruits overlain with a light nuttiness and a fresh, clean, dry finish.

Price	€18–€22
Region	Piedmont
Grape	Cortese
Alc/vol	12%

Ui Loinsighs, Cork; SuperValu, Killester; Blessings, Cavan; JJ Carvil & Sons, D2; Patrick Stewart, Sligo; Sweeneys, Hartes Corner; Jus de Vine, Portmarnock

Taserra

€30–€40

★ Antinori Castello della Sala
Cervaro della Sala IGT Umbria 2004

Subtle, smoky oak wrapped round a core of classy, concentrated, honeyed pear fruit. Finishes with a real flourish.

Price	€30–€40
Region	Umbria
Grape	Chardonnay/ Grechetto
Alc/vol	13%

Bin No 9, Goatstown; Cana Wines, Mullingar; Gables, Foxrock; Jus de Vine, Portmarnock; Martha's Vineyard; O'Brien's; Superquinn; Vineyard Galway

Findlater Grants

How to use this book
The wines are listed in order of country/region, colour (red or white), price band, then by name. There are separate chapters for sparkling (including Champagne) and dessert wines. If you can't find the wine you are looking for try the index. The price bands are guidelines only. All of the wines in this book are ready to drink now (October 2006), and for the next 12 months. Some will improve further over time and this is mentioned in the tasting note.

Red

€9–€12

Contessa Camilla Montepulciano d'Abruzzo 2000

A swish, complex mix of coffee, chocolate and mint in a soft, smooth wine
with plenty of maturing damson
fruits.

wineonline.ie

Price	**€9–€12**
Region	**Abruzzo**
Grape	**Montepulciano**
Alc/vol	**13%**

WineOnline

Monte Schiavo Sassaiolo
Rosso Piceno Superiore 2003

Broad, concentrated, maturing plums
and figs on an elegant, well-structured
palate with good tannic length.
Jammy, and overlaid with roasted
coffee beans.

*Donnybrook Fair; McCabes; The Tower Mini Market;
Selected independent retailers*

Price	**€9–€12**
Region	**Marche**
Grape	**Montepulciano/ Sangiovese**
Alc/vol	**13%**

Gleesons

Regolo Sartori IGT Veronese 2002   **Special Value!**

Rich dark cherry nose. Melting black cherry and chocolate palate with firmish tannins, balanced alcohol and refreshing acidity. Savoury, lasting finish.

Most branches Dunnes Stores

Price	€9–€12
Region	Veneto
Grape	Corvina/Rondinella
Alc/vol	13.5%

Dunnes Stores

Rocca delle Macie Vernaiolo Chianti 2004

Warm, ripe cherry nose; soft, easy cherry fruit on the palate as well. A bouncy easy drinker finishing with a light tanginess.

Kellys Wine Vault, Clontarf

Price	€9–€12
Region	Tuscany
Grape	Sangiovese
Alc/vol	12.5%

Kelly & Co.

Valpanera IGT Rosso di Valpanera 2004

Very light coffee notes to some cool, slightly austere blackcurrant and redcurrant fruit; there is a touch of refreshing acidity and lingering length. Very nicely made, elegant wine.

Amelia's, Enniskerry; Bunch of Grapes, Clonee; Callans, Dundalk; Connoisseur, Dundalk; Jus de Vine; Londis, Bray; Swan's, Naas; Sweeneys; Wicklow Wine Co.

Price	€9–€12
Region	Veneto
Grape	Refosco/Cab Sauv/ Merlot
Alc/vol	12.5%

Koala Wines

Valpanera Refosco dal Penduculo Rosso 2004

Want to try something different? This has very attractive, piquant, elegant raspberry fruit with a very light palate, finishing dry, with no shortage of acidity. Try it lightly chilled with fatty pork.

Amelia's, Enniskerry; Bunch of Grapes, Clonee; Callans, Dundalk; Connoisseur, Dundalk; Jus de Vine; Londis, Bray; Swan's, Naas; Sweeneys; Wicklow Wine Co.

Price	€9–€12
Region	Veneto
Grape	Refosco
Alc/vol	12.5%

Koala Wines

Villa Bizzarri Girone dei Folli Montepulciano d'Abruzzo 2003   **Special Value!**

Smooth, rich dark cherries and plums with a classy fresh edge—this is good, with some snappy, peppery tannins on the finish. Smooth, possibly a bit heavy on the oak, but still pretty good.

Ballymaloe; Donnybrook Fair; Foxwell Taverns; Kelly's; McCabes; The Tower Mini Market; Selected independent retailers

Price	€9–€12
Region	Abruzzo
Grape	Montepulciano
Alc/vol	13.5%

Gleesons

€12–€15

Agricole Vallore Vigna Flaminio Brindisi 2001

Sweet, ripe raspberries and strawberries in a soft, easy-drinking, jammy wine.

Eugene's, Kenmare; Karwigs; Redmonds, Ranelagh

Price	€12–€15
Region	Puglia
Grape	Negroamaro/ Malvasia Nera/ Montepulciano
Alc/vol	13%

Karwigs

Bellamarsilia Morellino di Scansano 2004

Lovely, supple ripe damsons and cherries with a lively tangy note and a smooth, long finish. Seductive, easy-drinking wine with real character.

Egan's, Liscannor; Grapevine, Booterstown, Halpins, Wicklow; Higgins, Clonskeagh; Lilac Wines; McHugh's; O'Brien's

Price	€12–€15
Region	Tuscany
Grape	Sangiovese
Alc/vol	13.3%

Findlater Grants

Carpineto Chianti 2004   Organic

Light- to medium-bodied classic Chianti with savoury, tangy dark cherries, just enough tannin and a clean finish. Very good, easy-drinking wine.

Ardkeen Quality Foodstore, Waterford; Bin No. 9, Goatstown; Diceys Bottle Shop, Ballyshannon; Fallon & Byrne, Dublin 2; McCambridges, Galway; The Vintry, Rathgar; Wine Centre, Kilkenny

Price	€12–€15
Region	Tuscany
Grape	Sangiovese
Alc/vol	12.5%

Taserra

Castello del Trebbio Chianti 2004

Soft, easy, luscious dark cherry fruit with a smoky touch; fresh and moreish.

Claudio's; Grape Escape, Lucan; McHughs, Kilbarrack; McHughs, Malahide; Morton's, Ranelagh; Morton's, Galway; Nectar Wines; Red Island, Skerries

Price	€12–€15
Region	Tuscany
Grape	Sangiovese
Alc/vol	13%

Nectar Wines

Colli della Murgia Selvato IGT Puglia 2003   Organic

Soft, broad, heady, earthy flavours mingle with some coffee and spice with a lovely, soft, easy finish. Perfect for a barbecue or with grilled meats.

Centra; George's Delicatessen, Slane; The Kitchen & Food Hall, Portlaoise; Nolan's, Clontarf; Wild Harvest, Tullamore

Price	€12–€15
Region	Puglia
Grape	Aglianico/ Sangiovese
Alc/vol	13%

Vendemia

Falesco Vitiano IGT Umbria 2004

Light, smooth, herby, dark cherry fruit with a mouth-watering tangy touch that makes you want another mouthful straight away—great food wine.

O'Briens

Price €12–€15
Region Umbria
Grape Vermentino/ Verdicchio
Alc/vol 13%

O'Briens

Feudo Zirtari IGT Sicilia 2004

Interesting, complex nose of prunes and tobacco. Rich, soft dark fruits on the palate with finely judged acidity and firm tannins. Coffee and spice flavours come through on the long finish. Super wine and a great match for pasta or anything meaty.

Café di Napoli; Donnybrook Fair; Louis Albrouze; The Wicklow Wine Co.

Price €12–€15
Region Sicily
Grape Nero d'Avola/ Merlot/Syrah/ Cab Sauv
Alc/vol 13.5%

Select Wines from Italy

Fortediga Cabernet Syrah IGT Maremma Toscana 2005

This is very classy wine, with enjoyable pure cherries on a lively palate, with some slightly sappy tannins coming through on the finish.

The Bottle Shop; Morton's; Red Island, Skerries

Price €12–€15
Region Tuscany
Grape Syrah/Cab Sauv/ Cab Franc
Alc/vol 13.5%

Liberty Wines

Le Bine Campagnolla Valpolicella Classico Superiore Ripasso 2003

Deliciously smooth, quite rich damson and piquant dark cherry fruit with a smoky edge and good length. Very satisfying, rounded wine.

Next Door @ Olwyn Mahon, Enfield; Peter Matthews Off Licence, Drogheda; Ardkeen Quality Foodstore, Waterford; Lonergans, Clonmel; Bin No 9, Goatstown, Uncorked, Rathfarnham; The Vintry, Rathgar; Jus de Vine, Portmarnock

Price €12–€15
Region Veneto
Grape Corvina/Rondinella
Alc/vol 13%

Taserra

Le Orme Michele Chiarlo Barbera d'Asti 2003

Light, cool, brambly, fresh red fruit, smooth and easy-drinking—perfect with charcuterie or salami.

Next Door @ Valentine, Longford; Burkes Londis, Kinvara; The Vintry, Rathgar; Sweeneys Off Licence, Hartes Corner; Kingdom Food & Wine Store, Tralee; Jus de Vine, Portmarnock; Uncorked, Rathfarnham

Price €12–€15
Region Piedmont
Grape Barbera
Alc/vol 13%

Taserra

Le Tobele Valpolicella Classico 2004

Piquant, dark cherry fruit of some class with a herby touch, light spice and a solid tannic finish. Very nicely crafted wine.

Liston's, Camden Street; On the Grapevine, Booterstown and Dalkey; World Wide Wines, Waterford

Price	€12–€15
Region	Veneto
Grape	Corvina/Rondinella
Alc/vol	12.5%

WineKnows

Masi Campofiorin IGT Rosso del Veronese 2003

Smooth, ripe, soft cherry fruit masking a piquant note; lovely, lightly tannic finish.

Cork's Drink & Food; Joyce, Knocknacarra; Martha's Vineyard; Nolan's, Clontarf; O'Brien's; Redmonds of Ranelagh; Superquinn; Tesco

Price	€12–€15
Region	Veneto
Grape	Corvina/Rondinella/Molinara
Alc/vol	13%

Findlater Grants

Renato Ratto Nebbiolo Langhe 2004

Fairly full-bodied, cool, pure Nebbiolo fruit—tar, liquorice, plums, then coffee and vanilla—possibly a bit over-oaked but a pretty good introduction to the Nebbiolo grape. Good, savoury wine.

Price	€12–€15
Region	Piedmont
Grape	Nebbiolo
Alc/vol	14.5%

Marks & Spencer

Stefan Accordini Valpolicella Classico 2005

Big, bouncy, fresh primary fruit and a touch of refreshing acidity—delicious classic Valpolicella with plenty of lively cherry fruit.

Wines Direct

Price	€12–€15
Region	Veneto
Grape	Corvina Veronese/Rondinella/Molinara
Alc/vol	12.5%

Wines Direct

Terradavino Ansisa Barbera d'Asti 2004

Fresh, ripe raspberry and blackberry fruits in a light, smooth, very appealing wine.

Jaynes, Ennis; Next Door; Searsons, Monkstown

Price	€12–€15
Region	Piedmont
Grape	Barbera
Alc/vol	13%

Searsons

Velenosi Il Brecciarolo Rosso Piceno Superiore 2003

Lovely, quite concentrated dark cherries with some prunes and coffee; balanced and long with some dry tannins kicking in on the finish.

Eugene's, Kenmare; Karwigs; Redmonds, Ranelagh

Price	€12–€15
Region	Marches
Grape	Montepulciano/Sangiovese
Alc/vol	13.5%

Karwigs

€15–€18

Boroli Madonna di Como Dolcetto d'Alba 2004

Sweet cassis aromas turn into medium-bodied brambly fruit with a lovely core of cool fruits and a bitter twist on the finish—good stuff in a savoury style, with a vibrant fruitiness.

Price **€15–€18**
Region **Piedmont**
Grape **Dolcetto**
Alc/vol **14%**

WineKnows

Bottle Shop, Drummartin Road; Celtic Whiskey Shop; On the Grapevine, Booterstown and Dalkey; Red Island, Skerries

Camparo' Cascina la Ghersa Barbera d'Asti 2003

Cool, clean, fresh, dark bramble fruits, good acidity and nice length—no pretensions but a very enjoyable wine with lovely incisive purity of fruit.

Price **€15–€18**
Region **Piedmont**
Grape **Barbera**
Alc/vol **13.5%**

Bacchus

Carpineto Chianti Classico 2003

This has clean, piquant cherry and damson fruit, a spicy edge and some drying tannins on a long, classy finish.

Price **€15–€18**
Region **Tuscany**
Grape **Sangiovese**
Alc/vol **13%**

Fahys Ballina, Salthill Liqour Store, Lord Mayors Off Licence, Bin No. 9, Goatstown; Gerrys Supermarket, Skerries. The Gables Foxrock, McCabes Blackrock, Jus de Vine

Taserra

Elisabetta Geppetti Le Pupille Morellino di Scansano 2005

Grippy, youthful wine with some lovely tight blackcurrant fruit on the centre palate, and lively throughout. Will certainly improve, and calls out for food.

Price **€15–€18**
Region **Tuscany**
Grape **Sangiovese/Alicante Bouschet/ Malvasia Nera**
Alc/vol **13.5%**

Michael's Wines

Liberty Wines

Pèppoli Chianti Classico 2003

A very correct, light-bodied, stylish Chianti with a slightly tart note to the dark cherry fruits.

Price **€15–€18**
Region **Tuscany**
Grape **Sangiovese/ Cab Sauv**
Alc/vol **13.5%**

Findlater Grants

Poliziano Rosso di Montepulciano 2004

Nicely poised, well-defined dark cherry fruit with a spicy edge, a bit of toffee and some drying tannins on the finish. Elegant, classically acidic Sangiovese.

Price €15–€18
Region Tuscany
Grape Sangiovese/Merlot
Alc/vol 13.5%

WineKnows

Bin No. 9; Connoisseur Wines, Dundalk; Liston's, Camden Street; On the Grapevine, Booterstown and Dalkey

Tenuta del Portale Aglianico del Vulture 2001

Slightly faded aromas of black cherries. Ultra-smooth flavours on the palate—rich dark cherries, coffee, liquorice—firmly underpinned by ripe tannins and enough acidity to keep it interesting.

Price €15–€18
Region Basilicata
Grape Aglianico
Alc/vol 13%

Gleesons

Donnybrook Fair; McCabes; Selected independent retailers

★ Volpi Barbera Colli Tortonesi 2003

This is classic, fresh, juicy Barbera, with lively blackberry and dark cherry fruit and a clean, piquant finish. Lovely quality of fruit throughout.

Price €15–€18
Region Piedmont
Grape Barbera
Alc/vol 13.5%

Wine Obsessed

€18–€22

★ Allegrini Palazzo della Torre IGT Veronese 2003

Delicious, light, very pure, ripe cherry and damson fruit with a lovely clean finish.

Price €18–€22
Region Veneto
Grape Corvina/Rondinella/
Sangiovese
Alc/vol 13.5%

Fallon & Byrne; Le Caveau; McHughs; On the Grapevine

Liberty Wines

Bricco 4 Fratelli Barbera d'Alba 2003

Lovely, savoury, freshly crushed blackcurrant aromas; smooth and ripe on the centre palate with light spiciness and cooked plums; finishes on a spicy coffee note.

Price €18–€22
Region Piedmont
Grape Barbera
Alc/vol 13.5%

WineKnows

Bottle Shop, Drummartin Road; Celtic Whiskey Shop; On the Grapevine, Booterstown and Dalkey

Cabanon Prunello Oltrepò Pavese 2001

Light, delicate, elegant cherry fruit with some crisp acidity and good length. Classic Piedmontese-style winemaking.

Corkscrew; Grape Escape; Lilac; Redmonds; Vaughan Johnson

Price €18–€22
Region Lombardy
Grape Barbera
Alc/vol 13.5%

Papillon

Cos Cerasuolo di Vittoria 2003

Super nose of fragrant black cherries. Ultra-ripe, soft palate of black cherries and blackcurrants. Extremely drinkable wine with no harsh tannins

Liston's, Camden Street; Martin's, Fairview; On the Grapevine, Booterstown and Dalkey; World Wide Wines, Waterford

Price €18–€22
Region Sicily
Grape Nero d'Avola/
         Frappato
Alc/vol 13%

WineKnows

Foradori Teroldego Rotaliano 2004

Vibrant redcurrants and plums in a beautifully poised light red wine; refreshing and stylish—with food only.

Nectar Wines, Sandyford; On the Grapevine, Booterstown and Dalkey; Red Island, Skerries

Price €18–€22
Region Trentino-Alto Adige
Grape Teroldego Rotaliano
Alc/vol 13%

WineKnows

Il Falcone Castel del Monte Riserva 2001

Tobacco and coffee to the fore in a pleasantly different foursquare wine with some good chewy dark fruits and a touch of leather.

The Corkscrew; Redmonds; Vaughan Johnson

Price €18–€22
Region Puglia
Grape Uva di Troia/
         Montepulciano
Alc/vol 13.5%

Papillon

Lamùri Nero d'Avola IGT Sicilia 2003

A big mouthful of pure, ultra-ripe cassis and damsons with a lovely kick on the finish; lovely, rich, meaty fruit. Perfect with red meats or hard cheese.

Claudio's; Probus

Price €18–€22
Region Sicily
Grape Nero d'Avola
Alc/vol 13.5%

Select Wines from Italy

Le Tobele Valpolicella Classico Ripasso 2003

Cherry pie aromas; enjoyable, light, pure bramble fruit, some real class and concentration. Not as sweet or rich as some in this style, and all the better for it.

Cana Wines, Mullingar; Le Caveau, Kilkenny; On the Grapevine, Booterstown and Dalkey; Wicklow Wine Co.; World Wide Wines, Waterford

Price €18–€22
Region Veneto
Grape Corvina/Rondinella
Alc/vol 14%

WineKnows

Masottina Ai Palazzi Piave Riserva 2000

Lovely, fully mature, herby dark fruits with some cedarwood and a beautifully smooth, dry finish.

Cellars; Coopers, Limerick; Deveneys, Dundrum; Gibneys; The Wine Centre, Kilkenny

Price	€18–€22
Region	Veneto
Grape	Cab Sauv
Alc/vol	14%

Classic Drinks

★ Ruffino Ducale Chianti Classico Riserva 2001

Lots of juicy black cherries with some maturing gamey flavours, yielding tannins and quite a bite of acidity. Great structure and a super match for rich meat dishes—bring on the roast pork!

Fine Wine Shops

Price	€18–€22
Region	Tuscany
Grape	Sangiovese

Allied Drinks

Sogno Mediterraneo Casadei IGT Toscano 2004

Intense, soft, easy, ripe fruit with some plums, dark fruits, an attractive piquancy and some firm tannins on the finish. Good stuff.

Claudio's; Grape Escape, Lucan; McHughs, Kilbarrack; McHughs, Malahide; Morton's, Ranelagh; Morton's, Galway; Nectar Wines; Red Island, Skerries

Price	€18–€22
Region	Tuscany
Grape	Syrah/Petit Verdot/ Merlot/Cab Sauv/ Alicante/Sangiovese
Alc/vol	13.5%

Nectar Wines

Vivaio dei Barbi Morellino di Scansano 2003

Quite wild, brawny aromas, but creamy cherry fruit with a tangy bite and rich, slightly earthy, length. Overall, good smooth wine.

Mitchell & Son; The Wicklow Wine Co.

Price	€18–€22
Region	Tuscany
Grape	Sangiovese
Alc/vol	13.5%

Select Wines from Italy

€22–€30

★ Allegrini La Grola IGT Veronese 2003

Wonderful, pure, ripe but cool dark cherry fruit in great concentration and some perfectly integrated tannins on a lasting finish.

Donnybrook Fair; Fallon & Byrne; McCabes; O'Donovans; On the Grapevine, Dalkey

La Grola
Veronese
Indicazione Geografica Tipica
Allegrini

Price	€22–€30
Region	Veneto
Grape	Corvina/Rondinella/ Syrah/Sangiovese
Alc/vol	13.5%

Liberty Wines

★ Ca'Rugate Campo Lavei Valpolicella Superiore 2004

Cherries galore on the nose. Fruit on the palate is a slightly darker hue, with black cherries and some quite meaty flavours. Tannins are exceptionally soft, and the finish is persistent and flavoursome.

Price €22–€30
Region Veneto
Grape Corvina/Rondinella

Febvre

La Luna del Rospo Gil Storni Monferrato 2003   Organic

Maturing, attenuated dark cherries with an earthy edge and a mouth-watering finish. A unique wine with real character.

George's Delicatessen, Slane

Price €22–€30
Region Piedmont
Grape Barbera/Nebbiolo
Alc/vol 14%

Vendemia

Lamole di Lamole Vigneto di Campolungo Chianti Classico Riserva 2000

Pleasant, maturing, broad cherry and blackberry fruit with a seam of slightly austere acidity and a firm, dry finish. Good solid length.

McCambridges, Galway; Mitchell & Son

Price €22–€30
Region Tuscany
Grape Sangiovese
Alc/vol 13%

Select Wines from Italy

★ Montalupa di Bra Langhe 2001

Cool, quite fragrant liquorice and violet aromas; broad, smooth, concentrated savoury fruits with some spice and a really velvety, smooth finish.

O'Briens

Price €22–€30
Region Piedmont
Grape Syrah
Alc/vol 14%

O'Briens

★★ Poliziano Vino Nobile di Montepulciano 2003

Huge coffee and dark fruit aromas; big and concentrated, with distinctive clove and spice flavours and very intense dark fruits and plums; nicely balanced, but young with telling length and real style.

Baily Wines, Howth; Bin No. 9, Farmhill Ave; Le Caveau, Kilkenny; Liston's, Camden Street; On the Grapevine, Booterstown and Dalkey

Price €22–€30
Region Tuscany
Grape Sangiovese
Alc/vol 14%

WineKnows

Rovero Rouve Barbera d'Asti Superiore 2000   Organic

Piercing nose of blackcurrant fruit with some smoky aromas; the oak is there, perhaps a little heavy, but this is still an excellent wine with fresh blackcurrants, good acidity and real concentration. It is beginning to show some complexity on the finish.

Mannings Emporium, Cork

Price	**€22–€30**
Region	**Piedmont**
Grape	**Barbera**
Alc/vol	**14.5%**

Mary Pawle

Ruffino Ducale Chianti Classico Riserva 2000

Fresh red fruit aromas. Juicy fruit on the palate, with lively acidity and almost invisible tannins. Soft and easy drinking.

Fine Wine Shops

Price	**€22–€30**
Region	**Tuscany**
Grape	**Sangiovese**

Allied Drinks

Valdipiatta Vino Nobile di Montepulciano 2002

Pleasant, medium-bodied wine with smooth oaky and tangy dark cherry pie flavours. Drying tannins on the finish. Ready to drink now.

Mitchell & Son; Vanilla Grape, Kenmare; The Wicklow Wine Co.

Price	**€22–€30**
Region	**Tuscany**
Grape	**Sangiovese/ Canaiolo**
Alc/vol	**13.5%**

Select Wines from Italy

★ Vigna Casi Castello di Meleto Chianti Classico Riserva 2001

Forward, leafy tobacco aromas; well-defined, perfectly ripe damson and dark cherry fruits with some tobacco; quite linear with well-integrated tannins on a very classy finish. Very stylish wine.

Morton's, Ranelagh

Price	**€22–€30**
Region	**Tuscany**
Grape	**Sangiovese**
Alc/vol	**13.5%**

Vinitalia

How to use this book
The wines are listed in order of country/region, colour (red or white), price band, then by name. There are separate chapters for sparkling (including Champagne) and dessert wines. If you can't find the wine you are looking for try the index. The price bands are guidelines only. All of the wines in this book are ready to drink now (October 2006), and for the next 12 months. Some will improve further over time and this is mentioned in the tasting note.

€30–€40

★★ Ascheri Podere di Rivalta de la Morra-Verduno Barolo 2001

Tar, liquorice and some violet aromas; smooth, concentrated, tangy, tarry, intense wine with some cloves and a great kick on a fairly tannic finish. Overall a very welcoming and very good Barolo—not as elegant as some, but very enjoyable.

O'Briens

Price	**€30–€40**
Region	**Piedmont**
Grape	**Nebbiolo**
Alc/vol	**13.5%**

O'Briens

★★ Campogiovanni San Felice Brunello di Montalcino 2001

Decidedly classy with beautifully defined, developing, burly dark cherry and blackcurrant fruit, some real vanilla spice, a very intense centre palate, huge length and lots of tannin. Needs a year or two, but very good. Mega in all senses.

O'Briens

Price	**€30–€40**
Region	**Tuscany**
Grape	**Brunello**
Alc/vol	**13.5%**

O'Briens

Castello Vicchiomaggio La Prima Chianti Classico 2003

Morello cherry nose. Soft, dark fruits on the palate with firm acidity and substantial tannins. Drink now or keep for two to three years. Excellent with grilled or roast meats.

Price	**€30–€40**
Region	**Tuscany**
Grape	**Sangiovese/ Canaiolo/Colorino**
Alc/vol	**13%**

Febvre

★★ Nearco Rosso VdT di Toscano 2000

This is marvellous wine—developing, tarry, meaty nose; big and beautiful, with very concentrated plums with light cloves and spice, a creamy texture and plenty of hearty alcohol. It all comes together beautifully in a very classy wine.

Price	**€30–€40**
Region	**Tuscany**
Grape	**Sangiovese/ Cab Sauv**
Alc/vol	**13%**

Bacchus

★ Zenato Amarone della Valpolicella Classico 2001

Heady stuff! Intense, dark, raisined fruit overlain with sweet vanilla, dark chocolate and a silky, smooth finish. Rich, powerful and hard to put down.

Celtic Whiskey Shop; Harvest; Next Door; Searsons, Monkstown

Price	€30–€40
Region	Veneto
Grape	Corvina/Rondinella/Sangiovese
Alc/vol	16%

Searsons

Over €40

★ GD Vajra Barolo 2001

Interesting, multidimensional nose—old roses, violets and red fruits. Yielding palate of fragrant red fruits. Tannins are still quite firm, so this could take a bit of ageing, but it will drink very well at the moment with roasts and grills.

Price	Over €40
Region	Piedmont
Grape	Nebbiolo
Alc/vol	14%

Febvre

★ Monte del Frá Amarone della Valpolicella 2001

Touch of figs with the black fruit on the nose. Wonderful structured palate of figs, liquorice, black fruit and chocolate. Tannins are on the firm side, but the wine is drinking beautifully now, with the plus that it will keep for five years or more.

Price	Over €40
Region	Veneto
Grape	Corvina/Rondinella
Alc/vol	15.5%

Febvre

Lebanon

Just the one wine this year, and one wonders how the budding wine industry will fare over the next few years in this war-torn country.

Red

€22–€30

Ch. Kefraya 2001

Big, broad, rich, intensely herbal, powerful wine—it almost has the cedar pine of Lebanon in it; well made, very menthol, heady and long.

Claudio's; Fahy's of Ballina

Price	€22–€30
Region	Bekaa Valley
Grape	Cab Sauv/ Mourvèdre/ Carignan/Grenache
Alc/vol	13.5%

Nicholson

New Zealand

New Zealand is best known for its vibrant, refreshing Sauvignon Blanc. These days there is far more subtlety to most of the wines, with a variety of styles available. But New Zealand can do far more than Sauvignon Blanc; there are some great wines made from Riesling, Gewurztraminer and Pinot Gris, and some pretty good Chardonnay too.

Red wines have never performed quite so well in the cooler climate, but over the last decade we have seen some very fine Pinot Noirs being produced, including our New World Red Wine of the Year, the Felton Road Pinot Noir, a world-class wine that compares very favourably with many burgundies at the same price.

The immediate future looks pretty good for New Zealand too. The 2006 vintage is large, and of excellent quality; the New Zealand dollar is at an all-time low, so prices have softened considerably, and look set to remain relatively low.

White

€9–€12

Babich Semillon Chardonnay 2004

Very pleasant, rounded, cool apple fruits—with a lime touch too. Clean, classy, lean wine.

Price	€9–€12
Region	East Coast
Grape	Semillon/ Chardonnay
Alc/vol	12%

JC's Supermarkets, Swords; C & T Supermarkets, Swords; Molloys; Eurospar Inchichore; Heaslips Off-Licence D11; O'Neills Off Licence D8

Dillons

Montana Sauvignon Blanc 2005

Gooseberries and pea pods in a delicious, zingy, dry, mouth-watering wine. A great aperitif or with lighter seafood.

Price	€9–€12
Region	Marlborough
Grape	Sauv Blanc
Alc/vol	13%

Many branches of: Dunnes Stores; Londis; Mace; McCabes; SPAR; SuperValu/Centra; Tesco

Irish Distillers

€12–€15

Babich Sauvignon Blanc 2005

Peaches and fresh gooseberries in a vibrant, refreshing, crisp Sauvignon—classic Marlborough.

Tesco; McCabes, Blackrock/Foxrock; Superval; O'Briens Fine Wines; The Vinyard, Ballinasloe

Price €12–€15
Region Marlborough
Grape Sauv Blanc
Alc/vol 13.5%

Dillons

Hanmer Junction Sauvignon Blanc 2005

Light, fresh and racy wine with clean fruit—a touch of gooseberries but more pears and green fruits, a light spritz and dry finish.

Donnybrook Fair

Price €12–€15
Region Waipara
Grape Sauv Blanc
Alc/vol 13.5%

New Zealand Boutique Wines

Matua Valley Sauvignon Blanc 2005

A fairly classic example of Marlborough Sauvignon. It has tasty, clean, fresh green fruits—pea pods and gooseberries—on the rich centre palate and a long finish.

Price €12–€15
Region Marlborough
Grape Sauv Blanc
Alc/vol 12.5%

Gilbeys

Mount Cass Sauvignon Blanc 2005

Soft, quite rich melons and pears, but the acidity is there, gooseberries and citrus; good, fresh, crisp young Sauvignon.

The Bottle Shop; Donnybrook Fair; Ferguson Fine Wines, Clifden; Gibney's, Malahide; Karwig Wines, Carrigaline; Lilac Wines; Masters Wine Warehouse, Waterford; McHugh's, Kilbarrack; McHugh's, Malahide Road; 64 Wine, Glasthule; Sweeneys; The Wine Centre, Kilkenny

Price €12–€15
Region Waipara
Grape Sauv Blanc
Alc/vol 12.5%

New Zealand Boutique Wines

Omaka Springs Sauvignon Blanc 2005

Sound, clean, refreshing wine with pure pear and lime fruits, finishing dry, with very nice balance.

Firhouse Inn; Great Escape, Banna; Next Door, Enfield; The Wicklow Wine Co.; Wine Cluster, Moycullen

Price €12–€15
Region Marlborough
Grape Sauv Blanc
Alc/vol 12.5%

Probus Wines

Seifried Nelson Sauvignon Blanc 2005

Vibrant, intense pea and flower aromas; slightly spritzy, crisp Sauvignon with a lovely lime edge; light, refreshing and lemony. Delicious wine.

Price **€12–€15**
Region **Nelson**
Grape **Sauv Blanc**
Alc/vol **12.5%**

Classic Drinks

Bailys, Howth; The Bottle Shop; Coopers, Limerick; Deveneys; Harvest; Londis; Naked Grape

Waipara Springs Premo Riesling 2005

Pale, youthful colour; lemon verbena and lime-zest aromas, leading on to attractive apple or lemon pie with a lively fruitiness and an off-dry finish. Nicely balanced, richer style of Riesling, but still retaining a vivid acid balance.

Price **€12–€15**
Region **Waipara**
Grape **Riesling**
Alc/vol **10.5%**

New Zealand Boutique Wines

On the Grapevine, Dalkey; On the Grapevine, Booterstown; Redmonds, Ranelagh; Sweeneys

Waipara Springs Sauvignon Blanc 2005

Everything you look for in a Sauvignon; fresh, herbaceous aromas, lively fruits with nice weight and good ripeness, finishing crisp and dry.

Price **€12–€15**
Region **Waipara**
Grape **Sauv Blanc**
Alc/vol **12.5%**

New Zealand Boutique Wines

The Bottle Shop; Clada/Thomas Woodberrys, Galway; Ferguson Fine Wines, Clifden; On the Grapevine, Dalkey; On the Grapevine, Booterstown; Sweeneys

€15–€18

Coney Ragtime Riesling 2005

Fresh stewed-apple nose; something similar on the palate, but with a very seductive honeyed touch that grows, and a rounded, long, off-dry finish.

Price **€15–€18**
Region **Martinborough**
Grape **Riesling**
Alc/vol **13%**

New Zealand Boutique Wines

The Corkscrew; Donnybrook Fair; Lilac Wines; Redmonds, Ranelagh; 64 Wine, Glasthule; Sweeneys; The Wine Centre, Kilkenny

Greenhough Hope Vineyard Riesling 2004

Forward, fresh, rounded primary pears and light tropical fruits with a touch of honey; nicely structured, well-made, easy-drinking, off-dry wine. This would be great with Asian prawn dishes.

Price €15–€18
Region Nelson
Grape Riesling
Alc/vol 11.5%

New Zealand Boutique Wines

Ferguson Fine Wines, Clifden; Lilac Wines; Masters Wine Warehouse, Waterford; 64 Wine, Glasthule; Sweeneys

Greenhough Sauvignon Blanc 2005

This has a nice rich centre palate of green apples and passion fruit, with clean citrus notes keeping a lovely brisk freshness.

Price €15–€18
Region Nelson
Grape Sauv Blanc
Alc/vol 13%

New Zealand Boutique Wines

The Bottle Shop; Clada/Thomas Woodberrys, Galway; The Corkscrew; Ferguson Fine Wines, Clifden; Lilac Wines; Masters Wine Warehouse, Waterford; McHugh's, Kilbarrack; McHugh's, Malahide Road; Redmonds, Ranelagh; 64 Wine, Glasthule; Sweeneys; The Wicklow Wine Co.; The Wine Centre, Kilkenny

★★ Huia Sauvignon Blanc 2005

Subtle, ripe but never heavy, with pure, clean lime, lemon and peach fruits that ring perfectly true; bone dry and very classy; the kind of wine that wins you round slowly over a few glasses rather than impresses straight away.

Price €15–€18
Region Marlborough
Grape Sauv Blanc
Alc/vol 13.5%

Searsons

Fahys, Ballina; Next Door; Searsons, Monkstown

★ Muddy Water Dry Riesling 2004

Wake-up wine— clean, fresh, zippy, very young Riesling, with lime and minerals in a bracing style, alongside lovely tart green-apple fruit. Bone dry and enervating—classy stuff that would appeal to Riesling lovers.

Price €15–€18
Region Waipara
Grape Riesling
Alc/vol 12%

New Zealand Boutique Wines

On the Grapevine, Dalkey; On the Grapevine, Booterstown; The Wicklow Wine Co.

Muddy Water Riesling 2005

Attractive fresh white-
flower nose; spritzy,
bouncy, fresh young
apples, clean with a lip-smacking, rich
finish. Nicely crafted, lively, very
nicely balanced young Riesling.

Price €15–€18
Region Waipara
Grape Riesling
Alc/vol 13%

New Zealand Boutique Wines

Ferguson Fine Wines, Clifden; On the Grapevine, Dalkey; On the Grapevine, Booterstown; The Wicklow Wine Co.

Villa Maria Private Bin Pinot Gris 2005

Succulent, rounded cantaloupe
melons in a rich, off-dry wine that
would make great drinking on its own,
or with fusion dishes.

Price €15–€18
Region Marlborough
Grape Pinot Gris
Alc/vol 13.5%

Next Door; O'Brien's

Allied Drinks

Villa Maria Private Bin Riesling 2005

Soft, ripe, pure peaches and grapefruit
with a rounded finish in a really enjoyable, refreshing wine.

Price €15–€18
Region Marlborough
Grape Riesling
Alc/vol 13%

O'Brien's

Allied Drinks

Villa Maria Private Bin Sauvignon Blanc 2005

Rounded with a nice richness on the
centre palate, creamy, quite complex
pears and subtle gooseberries; good
length and well-integrated acidity.
Stylish, well-priced wine.

Price €15–€18
Region Marlborough
Grape Sauv Blanc
Alc/vol 13.5%

Allied Drinks

Dunnes; Superquinn

Waipara Springs Premo Chardonnay 2004

Very classy lime-
flower and vanilla
nose; richly textured,
smooth but focused
lime and orange to
balance the toasty oak flavours;
already a well-integrated, full-bodied
wine that lingers nicely too.

WAIPARA SPRINGS
CHARDONNAY
2004

Price €15–€18
Region Waipara
Grape Chardonnay
Alc/vol 14%

New Zealand Boutique Wines

The Wine Centre, Kilkenny

★ Woollaston Estates Sauvignon Blanc 2005

Very distinctive, really fresh, zippy pears and light peaches with a cleansing mineral element. Long, racy, classy and different.

Price	**€15–€18**
Region	**Nelson**
Grape	**Sauv Blanc**
Alc/vol	**13.5%**

New Zealand Boutique Wines

The Bottle Shop; Donnybrook Fair; Ferguson Fine Wines; Lilac Wines; Masters Wine Warehouse, Waterford; Redmonds, Ranelagh; Sweeneys; The Wine Centre

---

€18–€22

Bilancia Pinot Grigio 2005

Herbal, grassy nose. Firm flavours from a grape that can often be wishy-washy. Here there is refreshing acidity and good structure, with some lemony notes on the palate. Medium finish with a nice bite of acidity. Good on its own or with fish.

Price	**€18–€22**
Region	**Hawke's Bay**
Grape	**Pinot Grigio**
Alc/vol	**14%**

New Zealand Boutique Wines

Cheers, Delgany; Donnybrook Fair; Karwig Wines, Carrigaline; Redmonds, Ranelagh; Sweeney's Wine Merchants, Glasnevin; Wicklow Wine Co.; The Wine Centre, Kilkenny

---

★ Dog Point Vineyard Sauvignon Blanc 2004

Big, rich, concentrated gooseberries with a broad texture and some real complexity and concentration; creamy, stylish Sauvignon.

Price	**€18–€22**
Region	**Marlborough**
Grape	**Sauv Blanc**
Alc/vol	**13.5%**

Berry Bros & Rudd

Berry Bros & Rudd

Hunter's Marlborough Sauvignon Blanc 2005

This is textbook Marlborough Sauvignon out of the top drawer—fresh, clean, green fruits, light, crisp, balanced and dry—delicious.

Price	**€18–€22**
Region	**Marlborough**
Grape	**Sauv Blanc**
Alc/vol	**13%**

Gilbeys

Millton Gisborne Chenin Blanc 2002   Organic

Deep straw colour. Loads of sweet marshmallow and honey aromas, a sweetness that is reflected in the palate, which is medium-sweet—a mixture of honey, barley sugar and apricots. With its great backing acidity and long, fruity finish, this is a super wine to have on its own or to accompany fish in rich sauce or even blue cheese. One for those who don't like their wines too dry.

Price €18–€22
Region Gisborne
Grape Chenin Blanc
Alc/vol 12.5%

Mary Pawle

Morton's, Galway; Mr Beans, Ennistymon; Quay Co-op, Cork; The Granary, Scarriff

Muddy Water Chardonnay 2004

Rich, concentrated red apples with subtle new oak, nicely textured—a classy wine, with a gentle leesy quality, good softness and substance all the way through. Excellent length too.

Price €18–€22
Region Waipara
Grape Chardonnay
Alc/vol 14%

New Zealand Boutique Wines

The Bottle Shop; Clada/Thomas Woodberrys, Galway; Ferguson Fine Wines, Clifden; Lilac Wines; McHugh's, Kilbarrack; McHugh's, Malahide Road; On the Grapevine, Dalkey; On the Grapevine, Booterstown; Redmonds, Ranelagh; 64 Wine, Glasthule; Sweeneys; The Wicklow Wine Co.

Seresin Sauvignon Blanc 2004

Very floral aromatic nose; clean, fresh gooseberry fruit, good concentration and some complexity, not too big— zippy and dry, light but tasty.

Price €18–€22
Region Marlborough
Grape Sauv Blanc
Alc/vol 13%

Bacchus

Bunch of Grapes; Caprani's; Greenacres; Mitchells; Hand Made Wines; Swans on the Green, Naas

€22–€30

★ Cloudy Bay Chardonnay 2002

Complex, lightly vanilla nose with toast and honey; rich, concentrated lime and fresh apple fruit overlain with toasty new oak. Good length.

Price €22–€30
Region Marlborough
Grape Chardonnay
Alc/vol 14%

Dillons

Donnybrook Fair; Greenacres, Wexford; Redmonds of Ranelagh; McCabes Blackrock/Foxrock; The Vintry, Rathgar; Castleyard, Dalkey; Berry Bros & Rudd, SuperValu, Churchtown

★★ **Felton Road Barrel Fermented Chardonnay 2004**

Full, forward nose with fairly subtle vanilla oak; plenty of racy, crisp lime and pear fruit overlain by plenty of smoky oak—a New World Puligny in style.

Price	€22–€30
Region	Central Otago
Grape	Chardonnay
Alc/vol	14%

WineKnows

Fallon & Byrne; Jus de Vine, Portmarnock; On the Grapevine, Booterstown and Dalkey

Red

€9–€12

Saint Clair Vicar's Choice Pinot Noir 2005

This has delightful pure raspberry and cherry fruit—soft, smooth and silky without a tannin in sight. Lovely pure Pinot.

Price	€9–€12
Region	Marlborough
Grape	Pinot Noir
Alc/vol	13.5%

Findlater Grants

Baileys Wines; Bennett's, Howth; Bottle Shop, Sallins; Drink Store Dublin; Harvest Off Licence Galway; Joyce, Knocknacarra; Lilac Wines; Fairview; Martha's Vineyard; Next Door Off Licence; O'Brien's; O'Sullivan's, Blarney; Redmond's of Ranelagh

€15–€18

Old Coach Road Pinot Noir 2003

Roast coffee beans and piquant dark cherries knit nicely together in a very enjoyable, savoury style of Pinot.

Price	€15–€18
Region	Nelson
Grape	Pinot Noir
Alc/vol	13.5%

Cellars; Coopers, Limerick; Deveneys, Dundrum; Gibneys; Harvest; Jus de Vine; Londis

Classic Drinks

€18–€22

Hunter's Marlborough Pinot Noir 2003

Big, upfront damson and dark cherry fruit with nice balancing acidity, well-judged spicy oak and a good finish; attractive, clean Pinot with a bit of class.

Price	€18–€22
Region	Marlborough
Grape	Pinot Noir
Alc/vol	13.5%

Gilbeys

> *All of the wines in this book are ready to drink now (October 2006), and for the next 12 months. Some will improve further over time and this is mentioned in the tasting note.*

Villa Maria Private Bin Pinot Noir 2004

Pure, well-defined cherries and damsons in a lovely, quite crunchy style—this has nice purity of fruit and good acidity to keep it fresh. Very nice wine.

O'Brien's

Price   €18–€22
Region Marlborough
Grape Pinot Noir
Alc/vol 13%

Allied Drinks

Waipara Springs Premo Pinot Noir 2004

One for true lovers of Pinot; elegant redcurrants and light blackberries are balanced by some liquorice,

Price   €18–€22
Region Waipara
Grape Pinot Noir
Alc/vol 14%

New Zealand Boutique Wines

woodsmoke and light tannins. Excellent ripeness and balance. It would be even better with food.

The Bottle Shop; Karwig Wines; Lilac Wines; McHugh's, Kilbarrack; McHugh's, Malahide Road; On the Grapevine, Dalkey; On the Grapevine, Booterstown; 64 Wine, Glasthule; Sweeneys

---

€22–€30

Bilancia Syrah 2004

Cool, slightly inky damson aromas; sleek, plum pie overlain with plenty of spicy new oak, some black pepper and a peak of acidity. Well made and very clean.

Price   €22–€30
Region Hawke's Bay
Grape Syrah
Alc/vol 13.5%

New Zealand Boutique Wines

The Bottle Shop; Clada/Thomas Woodberrys, Galway; The Corkscrew; Donnybrook Fair; Karwig Wines; McHugh's, Kilbarrack; McHugh's, Malahide Road; On the Grapevine, Dalkey; On the Grapevine, Booterstown; Redmonds, Ranelagh; The Wicklow Wine Co.; The Wine Centre, Kilkenny

---

Cornish Point Vineyard Pinot Noir 2004   **Organic**

Concentrated bramble fruit overlain with intense flavours of coffee and spice; this blows off after a while to reveal a wine with very good-quality, pure fruit.

Jus de Vine, Portmarnock; On the Grapevine, Booterstown and Dalkey

Price   €22–€30
Region Central Otago
Grape Pinot Noir
Alc/vol 14%

WineKnows

Greenhough Hope Vineyard Pinot Noir 2004

Cool, quite chunky damsons and morello cherries with a pleasing dryness, lightly smoky, and very good length. Opens out after a few minutes to reveal class and restraint.

Clada/Thomas Woodberrys, Galway; Redmonds, Ranelagh; Sweeneys

Price €22–€30
Region Nelson
Grape Pinot Noir
Alc/vol 14%

New Zealand Boutique Wines

Hatter's Hill Pinot Noir 2004

Crunchy dark fruits—cherries and damsons—with a nice bite and a long, cool finish. Elegant, satisfying wine.

Fallon & Byrne

Price €22–€30
Region Marlborough
Grape Pinot Noir
Alc/vol 13%

Liberty Wines

★ Muddy Water Pinot Noir 2004

Ultra-ripe raspberry aromas leap out of the glass; pure, intense, heady, ripe raspberries with just enough piquant acidity to even things out, and light oak flavours that remain in the background. Seductive, delicious wine.

The Bottle Shop; Donnybrook Fair; Ferguson Fine Wines; Karwig Wines; Lilac Wines; Masters Wine Warehouse, Waterford; McHugh's, Kilbarrack; McHugh's, Malahide Road; On the Grapevine, Dalkey; On the Grapevine, Booterstown; Redmonds, Ranelagh; 64 Wine, Glasthule; Sweeneys; The Wicklow Wine Co.; The Wine Centre, Kilkenny

Price €22–€30
Region Waipara
Grape Pinot Noir
Alc/vol 14.5%

New Zealand Boutique Wines

★ Palliser Estate Pinot Noir 2003

A wine with depth and concentration, cool damson and dark cherry fruit, a slightly piquant note, and subtle oak spice. Very good New World Pinot.

Le Caveau, Kilkenny, O'Donovan's, Uncorked

Price €22–€30
Region Martinborough
Grape Pinot Noir
Alc/vol 13%

Findlater Grants

> **Where to buy the wine**
> If your local retailer does not stock a particular wine, contact the distributor named in italic after the tasting note who will be pleased to give you details of the nearest stockist.

Waipara Springs Reserve Pinot Noir 2003

Cool, clean, delicate dark cherries and redcurrants in a wonderfully fresh, ripe wine that finishes on a savoury note. Essence of Pinot.

Price €22–€30
Region Waipara
Grape Pinot Noir
Alc/vol 13.5%

New Zealand Boutique Wines

The Corkscrew; Masters Wine Warehouse, Waterford; Redmonds, Ranelagh; Sweeneys; The Wine Centre, Kilkenny

Woollaston Estates Pinot Noir 2004

Light, sweet spice and dark, sultry damsons combining in a smooth, svelte wine, with chocolate notes showing through on a long finish.

Price €22–€30
Region Nelson
Grape Pinot Noir
Alc/vol 13.5%

New Zealand Boutique Wines

Redmonds, Ranelagh

€30–€40

★ Craggy Range Te Muna Road Vineyard Pinot Noir 2004

Smooth, beautifully defined, broad Pinot fruit—dark cherries with a gamey touch and some smoky oak combine to give a voluptuous, silky, toothsome wine of real quality.

Price €30–€40
Region Martinborough
Grape Pinot Noir
Alc/vol 13.5%

Febvre

Felton Road Pinot Noir 2004

Very fragrant perfumed aromas, with some elegant red fruits; this is very good—refined, smooth redcurrants, cherries and blackberries in a juicy, quite concentrated wine, with well-judged new oak. A delicious wine that is a joy to drink.

Price €30–€40
Region Central Otago
Grape Pinot Noir
Alc/vol 14%

WineKnows

NEW WORLD RED WINE OF THE YEAR

Connoisseur Wines, Dundalk; Fallon & Byrne; Jus de Vine, Portmarnock; Le Caveau, Kilkenny; On the Grapevine, Booterstown and Dalkey

Over €40

★ Bilancia La Collina Syrah 2002

Big, savoury, herbal
wine with an earthi-
ness, a sprinkle of
black pepper, and a
firm, dry, tannic
finish. Never clumsy, though; would
do very nicely with game or red meats.

Price   Over €40
Region Hawke's Bay
Grape   Syrah
Alc/vol 14%

New Zealand Boutique Wines

Redmond's, Ranelagh; Sweeneys

Portugal

Personally, I find Portuguese wines amongst the most interesting, and occasionally thrilling, you can buy. Sadly, most of you seem to disagree. Portugal's share of the market still amounts to less than 2 per cent. The good news is that it is growing, and the last few years have seen a welcome increase in the number of wines available.

I do not turn my nose up at Cabernet and Merlot, but neither do I want to drink them all the time. There are very few countries that can offer the range and diversity of grape varieties of Portugal. She has stuck steadfastly to her own varieties while many other parts of the wine world rushed to rip up their traditional vines. There is a host of red grapes, Touriga Nacional, Trincadeira, Baga and Tinta Roriz being the most promising, but there are many more that could surprise. There are fewer whites, but I always look out for the Loureiro from the north or Arinto, a grape that remains remarkably fresh and delicate in the baking heat of the Alentejo.

Probably the most exciting areas are the Douro and Alentejo, followed closely by Ribatejo and Dâo, and then a host of smaller regions such as Palmela, Estremadura, and Bairrada. Taken together, they amount to a rich heritage, one that we will surely see more of in the future. This year's entry from Portugal includes two star wines along with 14 other wines. All are well worth trying out.

White

€9–€12

Prova Regia Bucelas 2005

The Muscadet of Portugal? Better, possibly, with its delightful crisp lemon and intriguing light pear fruit, set off by a slight spritz. Perfect as an aperitif or with seafood.

Price **€9–€12**
Region **Estremadura**
Grape **Arinto**
Alc/vol **12.5%**

Grace Campbell

Bin 9; Cellars; The Corkscrew; Donnybrook Fair; Fallon & Byrne; Fresh; McCabes; Nolans of Vernon Avenue; Redmonds of Churchtown

€15–€18

Encruxado Quinta dos Roques Dão 2004

Light, clean, quite delicate almond and floral notes; nice plump pears with lime and subtle new oak—very different and classy in its own right.

Power & Smullen Wine Merchants Lucan; Redmonds, Ranelagh; Searsons, Monkstown

Price	€15–€18
Region	Dão
Grape	Encruxado
Alc/vol	13.5%

Searsons

Red

€9–€12

Quinta de Cabriz Colección Seleccionada Dão 2004

Special Value!

Big, warm, ripe nose, with an initial whiff of barnyards; on the palate rich, soft and concentrated, with very good acidity, dark cherries and lots of smoke on the finish.

Wicklow Wine Co., Redmonds Wines & Spirits, Probus Wines, Power & Smullen Wine Merchants, Listons, Harvest Off-licences, Galway, Morton's Supermarkets, The Corkscrew, Hand Made Wines, On the Grapevine, Dalkey, Fallon & Byrne, Power & Smullen Wine Merchants

Price	€9–€12
Region	Dão
Grape	Alfrocheiro/ Tinta Roriz/ Touriga Nacional
Alc/vol	13%

Wicklow Wine

Sá de Baixo Douro 2003

Special Value!

Nicely balanced, firm, hearty, meaty fruit with a smoky edge and plenty of flavour. Good substantial wine.

Wicklow Wine Co., Red Island Wine Co., Power & Smullen Wine Merchants, Harvest Off-licences, Galway, Hand Made Wines, Listons

Price	€9–€12
Region	Douro
Grape	Touriga Nacional/ Touriga Francesa/ Tinta Roriz/ Tinta Barroca
Alc/vol	13%

Wicklow Wine

€12–€15

Adriano Ramos Pinto Duas Quintas Douro 2003

A solid core of firm, meaty fruit streaked with dark cherries and coffee; it has a tangy bite and good length. Food essential, but this is good—it opens out nicely to reveal intense, ripe damson fruits.

Harvest; Listons; Power & Smullen Wine Merchants, Lucan; Searsons, Monkstown

Price	€12–€15
Region	Douro
Grape	Touriga Francesa/ Tinta Barroca/ Tinta Roriz
Alc/vol	13%

Searsons

Dom Martinho VR Alentejano 2002

This is very nicely made, easy-drinking wine with cool damson fruits, a herbaceous touch and some fine-grained tannins and spice on the finish.

O'Briens

Price	€12–€15
Region	Alentejo
Grape	Aragonês/ Trincadeira/ Alicante Bouschet
Alc/vol	13%

O'Briens

Herdade Grande VR Alentejano 2003

Some nice, pure blackberry fruit crossed with a mineral edge, and a fine long finish. A wine with a bit of Portuguese character, and very welcome too.

Bin 9; Coach House of Ballinteer; The Corkscrew; Donnybrook Fair; Fallon & Byrne; Fresh; McCabes; Redmonds of Churchtown

Price	€12–€15
Region	Alentejo
Grape	Aragonês/ Trincadeira/ Alicante Bouschet
Alc/vol	14%

Grace Campbell

Pegos Claros Palmela 1999

This has matured nicely into an elegant wine with some lovely ripe cassis fruit and a soft, smooth finish.

Bin 9; Cellars; Claudio's; The Corkscrew; Deveney's of Dundrum; Deveney's of Rathmines; Donnybrook Fair; Fallon & Byrne; Fresh; Grape Escape; Higgins; Jus de Vine; Londis; McCabes; Mortons of Ranelagh; Nectar; Nolans of Vernon Avenue; O'Briens; Shiels of Malahide; Thomas Deli; Wine Corner of Rathgar

Price	€12–€15
Region	Setúbal
Grape	Castelão Francês
Alc/vol	13.5%

Grace Campbell

Quinta de Pancas Assemblage VR Estremadura 2003

Herby, smooth, dark berry fruits with some drying tannins on the finish. Maturing very nicely, this would go very well with most white or lighter red meats.

Bin 9; Claudio's; Coach House of Ballinteer; Coolers; The Corkscrew; Deveneys; Donnybrook Fair; Fallon & Byrne; Fresh; Grape Escape; Higgins of Clonskeagh; Jus de Vine; McCabes; Morton's of Ranelagh; Nectar; Nolans of Vernon Avenue; O'Briens; Redmonds of Churchtown; The Wine Corner; The Wine Shop, Ferrystown

Price	€12–€15
Region	Estremadura
Grape	Touriga Nacional/ Cab Sauv/Merlot
Alc/vol	14%

Grace Campbell

> All of the wines in this book are ready to drink now (October 2006), and for the next 12 months. Some will improve further over time and this is mentioned in the tasting note.

€15–€18

Quinta de Cabriz Reserva Dão 2001

This is a beautifully balanced wine with pure dark cherry and damson fruits, a lovely refreshing edge, and very good length.

Wicklow Wine Co., Redmonds Wines & Spirits, Probus Wines, Power & Smullen Wine Merchants, Listons, Hand Made Wines, On the Grapevine, Dalkey, Power & Smullen Wine Merchants

Price	€15–€18
Region	Dão
Grape	Alfrocheiro/ Tinta Roriz/ Touriga Nacional
Alc/vol	13.5%

Wicklow Wine

€18–€22

Niepoort Vertente Douro 2002

Delicious, developing damson fruit backed up by a good structure— tannins and acidity—to give it length and real interest on the palate. Perfect with roast meats.

Wicklow Wine Co., Jus de Vine, Listons, Probus Wines, Red Island Wine Co., Redmonds Wines & Spirits, On the Grapevine, Dalkey, On the Grapevine, Booterstown, The Corkscrew, Morton's Supermarkets, Louis albrouze, Harvest Off-licences, Galway, Mitchell & Son, Kildare Street & Glasthule, Power & Smullen Wine Merchants

Price	€18–€22
Region	Douro
Grape	Tinta Roriz/Touriga Francesa/Tinta Amarela/Touriga Nacional
Alc/vol	13%

Wicklow Wine

€22–€30

Esporão Reserva VR Alentejano 2002

Rich coffee and cassis kept nicely in check by a subtle acidic touch and a pleasing jamminess. Stylish, rounded, full-bodied wine.

Egan's Too

Price	€22–€30
Region	Alentejo
Grape	Aragonês/Cab Sauv/ Trincadeira
Alc/vol	14%

Approach Trade

★ Quinta do Carmo VR Alentejano 2000

It starts off with some big, broad chocolate aromas and leads on with lots of ripe, gutsy fruit—rich, hearty stuff with some spice and chocolate kicking in on an oaky finish. Very good substantial wine.

O'Briens

Price	€22–€30
Region	Alentejo
Grape	Aragonês/ Trincadeira/ Alicante Bouschet
Alc/vol	13%

O'Briens

€30–€40

★★ Niepoort Redoma Douro 2001

A vibrant, complex
nose followed by
gorgeous cool damson
and blackcurrant
fruit, kept in tight rein
by plenty of fine-grained tannins;
long, very dry and beautifully elegant.
There is a perfect ripeness on the
centre palate.

Price	€30–€40
Region	Douro
Grape	Tinta Amarela/ Tinta Roriz/Touriga Francesa/Touriga Nacional
Alc/vol	13.5%

Wicklow Wine

*Wicklow Wine Co., Listons, Probus Wines, Mitchell & Son,
Kildare Street & Glasthule*

Quinta Vale D Maria Douro 2002

Sweet, ripe plum fruit with a herbal
edge; elegant, smooth and full of spicy
character; soft finish.

Egan's Too

Price	€30–€40
Region	Douro
Grape	Tinta Amarela/ Rufete/Tinta Barroca/others
Alc/vol	13.5%

Approach Trade

Rosé

€12–€15

Niepoort Redoma Rosé Douro 2005

Soft caramel and concentrated
crushed summer fruit, good acidity
with a nice bit of power coming
through on a dry finish. Very tasty
wine—I can see this going down
nicely with a plate of prawns.

*Wicklow Wine Co., Listons, Red Island Wine Co.,
The Corkscrew*

Price	€12–€15
Region	Douro
Grape	Tinta Amarela/ Touriga Nacional/ others
Alc/vol	13%

Wicklow Wine

South Africa

After Australia, South Africa produces the widest range of wines in the New World. The 16 years since Nelson Mandela's release and the fall of apartheid have been full of ups and downs for wine producers. The years of isolation left many with inferior clones in their vineyards, and out-of-date equipment. Since then there has been a real sense of excitement as the country begins to discover its true potential.

To date, it is the white wines that have really impressed me. There are some great Sauvignons, with some of the intense aromas of New Zealand, balanced by the crisp minerality of Sancerre. Try the Springfield Sauvignon, and you'll see what I mean. As well as some very good Chardonnays, we are beginning to see some top-class wines made from Chenin Blanc, a variety that South Africa has in spadefuls.

The red wines that have really impressed me over the last few years have been the Shirazes/Syrahs. There are some lovely savoury wines, with real elegance, alongside some ripe blockbusters. Cabernet Sauvignon, and Merlot have a longer history in South Africa, but are not always so impressive. The best are very good, with real structure allied to ripeness; but many still have stubborn hard tannins that are out of balance. Don't forget the South African dessert wines either; last year's winner, the Paul Cluver, is an excellent wine, this year joined by two wonderful Muscats from Rietvallei in Robertson.

White

Under €9

Leopard's Leap The Lookout Chenin Blanc Chardonnay Colombard 2006   **Special Value!**

Pear and pineapple fruit with muted acidity and a toasty background. Very easy to drink, with some pineapple on the finish. Tasty and good value.

Acheson's, Crumlin; Brackens, Glasnevin; Callans, Dundalk; Coolers, Swords; Currids, Sligo; Deveneys, Dundrum; Galvins, Listowel; Londis, Bray; O'Donovans, Cork

Price	Under €9
Region	Western Cape
Grape	Chenin Blanc/ Chardonnay/ Colombard
Alc/vol	12.5%

Koala Wines

Rietvallei Estate John B Sauvignon Blanc Colombard 2006 — Special Value!

Racy, vibrant, crisp dry wine that will wake you up and tingle your taste-buds; light, zesty lemons with a lovely mineral cut.

Price	Under €9
Region	Robertson
Grape	Sauv Blanc/ Colombard
Alc/vol	12.5%

Rushdale Wines

€9–€12

Clos Malverne Sauvignon Blanc 2006 — Special Value!

Pungent aromas of fresh-cut grass. Full in the mouth, with ripe greengage fruit and lively acidity. Long, rounded, fruity finish.

All branches Dunnes Stores

Price	€9–€12
Region	Stellenbosch
Grape	Sauv Blanc
Alc/vol	13%

Dunnes Stores

De Wetshof Estate Bon Vallon Chardonnay 2004

Light, lemony and zesty—a delicious, easy Chardonnay with a lovely texture and some real complexity. The sort of wine that gets better with every sip.

Fahy's; Gables; Grapevine, Glasnevin; Jus de Vine; Lilac Wines, Fairview; Next Door, Enfield; World Wide Wines; Superquinn

Price	€9–€12
Region	Robertson
Grape	Chardonnay
Alc/vol	14%

Findlater Grants

Leopard's Leap Chenin Blanc 2006

Big, rich, ripe tropical fruits with a touch of marzipan and plenty of power. This would go nicely with spicy fish and seafood dishes.

Acheson's, Crumlin; Brackens, Glasnevin; Callans, Dundalk; Coolers, Swords; Currids, Sligo; Deveneys, Dundrum; Galvins, Listowel; Londis, Bray; O'Donovans, Cork

Price	€9–€12
Region	Western Cape
Grape	Chenin Blanc
Alc/vol	13.5%

Koala Wines

> **Where to buy the wine**
> If your local retailer does not stock a particular wine, contact the distributor named in italic after the tasting note who will be pleased to give you details of the nearest stockist.

Villiera Chenin Blanc 2005

Big, ripe, honeyed melon fruit—rich, with plenty of body, some residual sugar and good length. Try it with rich chicken and seafood dishes.

Gables; Holland's Cheers in Bray; Ivan's of Caherdaniel; Next Door in Boggan & Ennis; Orchard, Redmonds, Uncorked, Veldon's of Letterfrack

Price	**€9–€12**
Region	**Stellenbosch**
Grape	**Chenin Blanc**
Alc/vol	**14.5%**

Findlater Grants

€12–€15

Durbanville Hills Sauvignon Blanc 2005

Broad pear and lemon flavours, quite full-bodied but finishing dry.

Martha's Vineyard, Rathfarnham; Lynch's, Glanmire; Fine Wines, Ballysimon; The Dew Drop, Athboy; C & T Supermarket, Swords; Fitzgeralds, D6; Jus de Vine, Portmarnock; Next Door, Kinsale; Eurospar, Inchicore

Price	**€12–€15**
Region	**Durbanville**
Grape	**Sauv Blanc**
Alc/vol	**13%**

Dillons

Graham Beck Viognier 2004

Textbook Viognier with full-bodied apricot fruit and a bitter, dry twist coming through on the finish; plenty of concentration and a lingering finish.

Donnybrook Fair; Red Island, Skerries; The Gables, Foxrock

Price	**€12–€15**
Region	**Western Cape**
Grape	**Viognier**
Alc/vol	**14.5%**

Woodford Bourne

Neil Ellis Sauvignon Blanc 2005

Fine, lifted bouquet of gooseberry and elderflower; light in style with very moreish lime zest and delicate, pure green fruits, finishing bone dry and lingering nicely.

Cellars Big Wine Warehouse, Claudio's of Drury St; Fahy's, Ballina; Gables, Grapevine, Higgins, Jus de Vine, Le Caveau, Liston's, O'Brien's, O'Donovan's, Sweeney's, Thomas's

Price	**€12–€15**
Region	**Groenekloof**
Grape	**Sauv Blanc**
Alc/vol	**13%**

Findlater Grants

€15–€18

Mulderbosch Sauvignon Blanc 2005

Vibrant, floral nose; crisp lime and gooseberry fruits with a fine dry finish. Made for seafood dishes.

Vaughan Johnson

Price	**€15–€18**
Region	**Stellenbosch**
Grape	**Sauv Blanc**
Alc/vol	**12.5%**

Papillon

Waterkloof Peacock Ridge Sauvignon Blanc 2005

A slightly baffling wine that manages to be fairly clean and refreshing at 14.5% alcohol; there are ripe melons, a touch of sherbet and good length.

Price €15–€18
Region Stellenbosch
Grape Sauv Blanc
Alc/vol 14.5%

Tindal

€18–€22

Fairview Viognier 2004

A very attractive Viognier, true to type with plenty of ripe apricot fruit cut through with an appetising mineral streak. It would be even better with food, pork or chicken in particular.

Price €18–€22
Region Coastal Region
Grape Viognier
Alc/vol 14.5%

Gilbeys

Springfield Estate Life from Stone Sauvignon Blanc 2005

Very aromatic nose—peas and honeysuckle; intense fruits on the palate too, with delicate, very ripe pea pods and elderflowers, finishing dry; very light, very well made, and no lack of flavour. One to thrill the Sauvignon aficionado.

Price €18–€22
Region Robertson
Grape Sauv Blanc
Alc/vol 12.5%

Papillon

Bin No. 9; Cellars; Corkscrew; Grape Escape; O'Briens; Redmonds

WHITE WINE OF THE YEAR FOR UNDER €20

€22–€30

★ Hamilton Russell Chardonnay 2003

White flowers and lime aromas; nicely elegant, well-defined, lightly toasty vanilla and lime flavours in a very classy wine that lingers beautifully on the palate.

Price €22–€30
Region Hermanus
Grape Chardonnay
Alc/vol 13%

Gilbeys

All of the wines in this book are ready to drink now (October 2006), and for the next 12 months. Some will improve further over time and this is mentioned in the tasting note.

★ Thelema Chardonnay 2003

Light gold colour.
A substantial but
complex wine, the
rich peaches and
yellow fruits cloaked very nicely with
toasty vanilla and a clean core of citrus
acidity. Classy stuff.

Vaughan Johnson

Price	€22–€30
Region	Stellenbosch
Grape	Chardonnay
Alc/vol	14%

Papillon

Red

Under €9

Delheim Three Springs Red 2004   **Special Value!**

Very enjoyable light
wine, with fresh
blackberry fruit, a
clean finish and very
good length.

O'Briens

Price	Under €9
Region	Stellenbosch
Grape	Cab Sauv/Shiraz
Alc/vol	13%

O'Briens

Golden Kaan Shiraz 2003

Warm, ripe, inviting
strawberries and
smooth damsons,
with lightly spicy
oak in a nicely
rounded, supple
wine. A great all
rounder to please everyone; ideal
with most meat and cheese dishes.

Eurospar; Mace; SPAR; SPAR Express

**BEST VALUE RED
WINE OF THE YEAR**

Price	Under €9
Region	Western Cape
Grape	Shiraz
Alc/vol	14%

Greenhills

Hutton Ridge Merlot 2003   **Special Value!**

Jammy, rich plums with a light
peppery touch; big, smooth and very
nicely rounded wine.

The Grapevine; SuperValu/Centra

Price	Under €9
Region	Coastal Region
Grape	Merlot
Alc/vol	14.5%

Barry Fitzwilliam Maxxium

€9–€12

★ Beyerskloof Pinotage 2005 Special Value!

Big, sweet, ripe dark cherries and plums with a lightly savoury bite; spicy new oak too, but the bouncy fruit wins out. Unputdownable.

Price	€9–€12
Region	Stellenbosch
Grape	Pinotage
Alc/vol	14%

Tesco

Clos Malverne Pinotage Reserve 2002

One for the hedonist—big, rich, ripe fruit overlain with sweet new oak and plenty of body—and all at a very reasonable price.

Most branches Dunnes Stores

Price	€9–€12
Region	Stellenbosch
Grape	Pinotage
Alc/vol	14.5%

Dunnes Stores

Goats do Roam 2004

Very drinkable, rounded wine with savoury but ripe damsons, juicy red fruits and a lovely tannic kick on the finish. This would make a great house wine at home.

Price	€9–€12
Region	Western Cape
Grape	Shiraz/Pinotage/ Cinsault/Grenache/ Gamay Noir
Alc/vol	14%

Gilbeys

Nederburg Manor House Shiraz 2004

Quite elegant, very smoky style; plenty of chocolate and dark roast coffee mocha covering the quite delicate cherry fruit. Very good of its style.

Londis, Kinvara; Londis, Malahide; Mace, Milford; WJ Higgins, Clonskeagh; Eurospar, Naas; Eurospar, Inchicore; JCs Supermarket, Swords; Fitzgeralds Off Licence, D6; Joyces Supermarket, Knocknacara; John Flanagan, Castlebridge

Price	€9–€12
Region	Coastal Region
Grape	Shiraz
Alc/vol	14.5%

Dillons

The Wolftrap 2004 Special Value!

Big, gutsy wine with some drying, leathery tannins to match the ripe fruit; needs meat, preferably red and rare.

Oddbins

Price	€9–€12
Region	Western Cape
Grape	Cab Sauv/Pinotage/ Syrah/Cinsault
Alc/vol	14%

Oddbins

€12–€15

Vergelegen Mill Race 2002

Light, soft, elegant wine with leafy
maturing fruit and a rounded finish.

Donnybrook Fair; Halpins Fine Wine; Jus de Vine; McCabes;
Red Island Wine Co.; Vineyard Galway; Selected
independent retailers

Price	€12–€15
Region	Stellenbosch
Grape	Merlot/Cab Sauv/ Cab Franc
Alc/vol	14.5%

Gleesons

Wildekrans Cabernet Franc Merlot 2004

Ripe but elegant forest fruits with an
intriguing herby edge; plenty of
concentration and a good clean finish.

Mitchells, Kildare Street; Mitchells, Glasthule

Price	€12–€15
Region	Walker Bay
Grape	Cab Franc/Merlot
Alc/vol	13.5%

Mitchell & Son

Wildekrans Caresse Marine Red 2005

A very attractive wine with plenty of
ripe fruit and a small dollop of spicy
new oak. It has an attractive elegance
and a nice freshness. Supple, easy-
drinking wine.

Mitchells, Kildare Street; Mitchells, Glasthule

Price	€12–€15
Region	Western Cape
Grape	Pinotage/Shiraz/ Merlot
Alc/vol	13.5%

Mitchell & Son

€15–€18

Diemersfontein Pinotage 2005

Aromas of coffee, dark chocolate and
spice by the spadeful; a massive
mouthful of coffee, sweet milk chocolate, brown sugar and damsons—you
will either love this or hate it. This is
wine, but not as we know it!

Bin No. 9; Nuts About Wine, Tralee; Searsons, Monkstown

Price	€15–€18
Region	Paarl
Grape	Pinotage
Alc/vol	14%

Searsons

Iona Merlot Cabernet Sauvignon 2003

Cool black pepper and capsicum nose;
this is a very stylish little wine—nice
just-ripe blackcurrants, good acidity
giving it a nice freshness, and a herby
twist.

Morton's, Galway; On the Grapevine, Booterstown;
Searsons, Monkstown

Price	€15–€18
Region	Elgin
Grape	Merlot/Cab Sauv
Alc/vol	13%

Searsons

11 Generations of Fine Glassmaking

Sommelier Burgundy Grand Cru

Designed 1958
Claus Riedel
9th Generation

Vinum Bordeaux

Designed 1986
Georg Riedel
10th Generation

O Riesling/Sauvignon

Designed 2003
Maximilian Riedel
11th Generation

THE **O** WINE TUMBLER

Riedel is imported and distributed in Ireland by
Mitchell & Son Wine Merchants.
Available in all good wine shops and off-licences,
nationwide.

Wholesale enquiries: Gerry Gunnigan, Wholesale Manager.
Tel: 086 821 3955. Email: gerry@mitchellandson.com

www.riedel.com

Rupert & Rothschild Classique 2001

Maturing aromas and palate, with plenty of body and firm, chunky concentration in the South African way, with a light pepperiness on the finish.

Cheers, Bray; Jus de Vine; Lakes, Blessington; Londis, Malahide; No 1 Vintage; O'Donovans, Cork; On the Grapevine; Superquinn; Sweeneys

Price €15–€18
Region Coastal Region
Grape Cab Sauv/Merlot/
Pinotage
Alc/vol 14.5%

Koala Wines

★ Springfield Estate Whole Berry Cabernet Sauvignon 2003

Don't let the cool, light, clean Cabernet streak fool you; there is excellent concentration, a lovely mineral streak and crunchy blackcurrant ripeness, signing off with some nice tannins and real length—this is delicious, beautifully crafted wine.

Bin No. 9; Corkscrew; Grape Escape; Nectar Wines; O'Briens; Vaughan Johnson

Price €15–€18
Region Robertson
Grape Cab Sauv
Alc/vol 13.5%

Papillon

Thelema Pinotage 2003

Very pleasant piquant dark cherries and plums showing the true character of the variety at its best.

Corkscrew; Redmonds; Vaughan Johnson

Price €15–€18
Region Coastal Region
Grape Pinotage
Alc/vol 14%

Papillon

Wildekrans Shiraz 2004

Nicely maturing nose; sweet, concentrated and quite structured wine with real complexity—cloves, soft dark fruits with peppercorns and a nice tannic kick on the finish.

Mitchells, Kildare Street; Mitchells, Glasthule

Price €15–€18
Region Walker Bay
Grape Shiraz
Alc/vol 14%

Mitchell & Son

> #### How to use this book
> The wines are listed in order of country/region, colour (red or white), price band, then by name. There are separate chapters for sparkling (including Champagne) and dessert wines. If you can't find the wine you are looking for try the index. The price bands are guidelines only. All of the wines in this book are ready to drink now (October 2006), and for the next 12 months. Some will improve further over time and this is mentioned in the tasting note.

€18–€22

Backsberg Klein Babylons Toren Cabernet Sauvignon Merlot 2002

Powerful, maturing wine with attractive redcurrants and peppery length; a lively tart note gives it freshness and the fruit matches the hearty alcohol.

Vaughan Johnson

Price	**€18–€22**
Region	Paarl
Grape	Cab Sauv/Merlot
Alc/vol	14%

Papillon

★ Laibach The Ladybird 2004   Organic

Big, firm dark fruits with lovely underlying ripeness, overlain with spicy, dark, woody flavours and plenty of well-integrated tannins on the finish.

Rushdale Wines, 021 477 4857 or info@rushdalewines.ie

Price	**€18–€22**
Region	Stellenbosch
Grape	Merlot/Cab Franc/ Cab Sauv
Alc/vol	14%

Rushdale Wines

€22–€30

Bellingham The Maverick Syrah 2003

Sweet, spicy nose; soft, ripe raspberries and strawberries in a hearty, easy-drinking wine, with no shortage of new oak or alcohol.

Cheers Delgany; Chester Beatty OL, Ashford; Corkscrew, D2; Donnybrook Fair; Fallon & Byrne, D2; Grape Escape, Lucan; Jus de Vine, Portmarnock; Kellys, Clontarf; Macs, Limerick; Marthas Vineyard, Rathfarnham; McCabes; O'Donovans, Cork; On The Grapevine Dalkey & Booterstown; Red Island Wine Co., Skerries; Thomas Martins, Fairview; Thomas Woodberrys, Galway; World Wide Wines, Waterford

Price	**€22–€30**
Region	Coastal Region
Grape	Syrah
Alc/vol	14.5%

Cassidys

Diemersfontein Carpe Diem Pinotage 2003

Sultry dark plums and spice, followed by big, very concentrated, but strangely elegant dark, dark plums; long, plenty of spicy oak, but the fruit wins through.

Claudio's; Next Door; Searsons, Monkstown

Price	**€22–€30**
Region	Paarl
Grape	Pinotage
Alc/vol	14%

Searsons

★ Kanonkop Pinotage 2002

This is maturing into a wonderful wine—lovely dark cherry and black-currant fruit, a nicely balanced palate with some milk chocolate and a long, ripe finish. Elegant, fragrant wine that will be at its peak over the next year or so.

Bradley's, Cork; Brady's; Gibney's, Jus de Vine, O'Brien's, Uncorked, Vaughan Johnson's

Price	€22–€30
Region	Stellenbosch
Grape	Pinotage
Alc/vol	14.5%

Findlater Grants

Veenwouden Classic 2001

If you like them big and chewy, this could be the wine for you. Solid meaty nose with some very ripe cassis along-side some concentrated leathery dried plums, plenty of power, and a firmly dry, tannic finish.

The Hole in the Wall, D7

Price	€22–€30
Region	Paarl
Grape	Cab Sauv/Merlot/ Cab Franc/ Petit Verdot
Alc/vol	14%

Wine Select

Spain

Spain has been riding its own economic tiger over the last decade. Travel through any part of the country, and you will see enough cranes to make an Irish building contractor feel very inferior. The wine industry has shared in the boom times, usually with excellent results. Of all the countries I have visited over the last two decades, Spain is the most changed, and has the most new exciting wines too. There are some excellent white wines, light and elegant; modern fruity rosés with real character; and a plethora of stunning reds with unique flavours, often made from little-known grape varieties.

The only downsides are my usual bugbear of over-oaked wines—very popular locally—and the huge number of very expensive, limited-production wines—most are simply not worth the money. In all the excitement of discovering new areas, do not forget Rioja. It is still the powerhouse of Spanish wine (accounting for a large proportion of all quality Spanish wine) and does produce some quite brilliant wines. Rioja has won Red Wine of the Year this year and last year. In total we list some 68 scintillating wines, including 40 star wines.

White

Under €9

Tramoya Verdejo Rueda 2005   **Special Value!**

Delightful lemons and limes on the nose. Sprightly palate of lemons, limes and more than a touch of grapefruit. Light, full of vibrant acidity, carrying its alcohol well. Fresh, zesty and amazing value.

Price Under €9
Region Castilla-León
Grape Verdejo
Alc/vol 13%

Dunnes Stores

Most branches Dunnes Stores

> **Where to buy the wine**
> *If your local retailer does not stock a particular wine, contact the distributor named in italic after the tasting note who will be pleased to give you details of the nearest stockist.*

€9–€12

Mantel Blanco Rueda 2005

Attractive nose of autumnal fruits—
apples and pears. Notes of citrus
appear on the palate, along with ripe
apples. Nicely structured wine, with
easy acidity.

Price €9–€12
Region Castilla-León
Grape Verdejo/Sauvignon
Alc/vol 13%

Approach Trade

*Brechin Watchorn; Egan's Too; French Flair; The Kingdom
Food & Wine; McCambridges; Michael's Wines; Next Door in
Ennis; Next Door @ Myles Creek; Probus Wines; Vanilla
Grape; The Wicklow Wine Co.*

Marqués de Riscal Sauvignon Blanc Rueda 2005

Fresh gooseberries on both nose and
palate; refreshing, clean, almost in a
New Zealand style, with a lingering
finish and a touch of class.

Price €9–€12
Region Castilla-León
Grape Sauv Blanc
Alc/vol 13.5%

Findlater Grants

*Donnybrook Fair; Gables, Foxrock; McCabe's; Nolan's,
Clontarf; O'Brien's; O'Donovan's, Cork; Superquinn; The
Vaults IFSC*

Val do Sosego Albariño Rías Baixas 2005

Lovely aromas of honey and white
flowers with a touch of vanilla. Firm
palate of peaches and citrus, with
vibrant acidity and a long grapefruit
finish. Would go very well with fish or
roast chicken.

Price €9–€12
Region Galicia
Grape Albariño
Alc/vol 12.5%

Oddbins

Oddbins

Viña Cantosán Rueda 2005

Rich pear aromas; clean grapefruit and
pears in a rounded, nicely textured
fresh wine with a bit of real style.

Ballymaloe Shop

Price €9–€12
Region Castilla-León
Grape Verdejo
Alc/vol 13%

Smith & Whelan

Viña Mocen Rueda 2005   **Special Value!**

Super nose of rich gooseberry fruit.
Well-structured palate of intense
gooseberries, zesty acidity, balancing
alcohol and a long, ripe finish.

Eurospar; Mace; SPAR; SPAR Express

Price €9–€12
Region Castilla-León
Grape Sauv Blanc
Alc/vol 13%

Greenhills

SPAIN
in a bottle

Approach Trade

The Specialist in Spanish Wines
offering
an exciting range of top labels
carefully selected from the best
of Spain's wine producers

Discover the taste of Spain

Approach Trade Wine Merchants
Mill River Business Park, Carrick-on-Suir, Co. Tipperary, Ireland
Tel: ++353 51 640164 Fax: ++353 51 641580
E-mail: info@approachwines.com http://www.approachwines.com

We are **HAPPENING** –
right here and now!

Rushdale Wines
021 477 4857
086 104 9879
info@rushdalewines.ie

€12–€15

Albet y Noya Lignum Penedès 2005   Biodynamic

A cool, clean wine with plump but fresh grapefruit and peach fruit, a lovely centre palate, and a slightly minerally dry finish. Very tasty wine with real character.

O'Brien's; O'Donovans; some branches Superquinn

Price	€12–€15
Region	Catalonia
Grape	Sauv Blanc/ Chardonnay
Alc/vol	12.5%

Mary Pawle

Dona Rosa Rías Baixas 2005

Wonderful, soft pure pears and green-gages with some lively citrus flavours to give it a real vibrancy. Captivating wine.

Drinks Store; Jus de Vine; The Mill, Maynooth; Next Door @ Myles Creek; Uncorked; Vanilla Grape, The Vintry, Rathgar

Price	€12–€15
Region	Galicia
Grape	Albariño
Alc/vol	12.5%

Tyrrell

José Pariente Verdejo Rueda 2005

Rich, ripe pears and canned peaches on nose and palate, with a light fizz and a delicious long finish. Very more-ish, opulently fruity wine.

Wines Direct

Price	€12–€15
Region	Castilla-León
Grape	Verdejo
Alc/vol	13%

Wines Direct

Martín Códax Albariño Rías Baixas 2005

Green fruit aromas with a definite touch of sherbet. Light, fresh, zesty wine with concentrated greengage, gooseberry and green-apple fruit, ending with a note of citrus.

Andersons Food Hall & Café; Brackens; The Corkscrew; Egan's Too; Gaffney's; Gibney's; The Grapevine; Harvest; Karwig; The Kingdom Food & Wine; Next Door in Ennis; O'Brien's; O'Driscoll; On The Grapevine; Probus Wines

Price	€12–€15
Region	Galicia
Grape	Albariño
Alc/vol	12.5%

Approach Trade

NavaReal Verdejo Rueda 2005

Gentle aromas of green leaves and vanilla rise from the glass. Very nicely rounded flavours of grapefruit and pears, with beautifully integrated backing acidity and a long, harmonious finish.

Price	€12–€15
Region	Castilla-León
Grape	Verdejo
Alc/vol	13%

Liberty Wines

Fallon & Byrne

€15–€18

Carbalal Albariño Rías Baixas 2005

Forward, floral nose leading on to fresh, crisp, sweet apple fruit, with lively acidity in a delicate but very attractive white wine.

Price	€15–€18
Region	Galicia
Grape	Albariño
Alc/vol	12%

Ballymaloe Shop

Smith & Whelan

Finca de Arantei Albariño Rías Baixas 2004

Shy, floral nose, almost perfumed; zingy, fresh, light, crisp pear fruit with lively lemon zest on the finish. Delicious. Slightly fizzy, but adds to the interest.

Price	€15–€18
Region	Galicia
Grape	Albariño
Alc/vol	12%

Cassidys

Cheers Delgany; Chester Beatty OL, Ashford; Corkscrew, D2; Donnybrook Fair; Fallon & Byrne, D2; Grape Escape, Lucan; Jus de Vine, Portmarnock; Kellys, Clontarf; Macs, Limerick; Marthas Vineyard, Rathfarnham; McCabes; O'Donovans, Cork; On The Grapevine Dalkey & Booterstown; Red Island Wine Co., Skerries; Thomas Martins, Fairview; Thomas Woodberrys, Galway; World Wide Wines, Waterford

★ Guitian Godello Valdeorras 2005

Magnificent, lightly textured, zingy fresh lemon, lemon zest and pear fruits, finishing on a dry note. Light but concentrated wine with real class.

Price	€15–€18
Region	Galicia
Grape	Godello
Alc/vol	12%

Spanishwines.ie

Approach Trade

€18–€22

Enate Gewurztraminer Somontano 2005

Big, rich, rounded Gewurz, with lots of rose petals and a rounded, ripe finish. Clean, well made and unmistakably a Gewurztraminer.

Price	€18–€22
Region	Aragón
Grape	Gewurztraminer
Alc/vol	13.5%

Febvre

€22–€30

Terra Firme Albariño Rías Baixas 2004

A soft, rounded wine showing some very attractive ripe peach and pear flavours; nicely textured, with good length.

Price	**€22–€30**
Region	Galicia
Grape	Albariño
Alc/vol	12.5%

Febvre

Red

€9–€12

Casteller Tinto Barrica Penedès 2001

Sweet, ripe, soft, maturing aromas; lean, quite light mineral and meaty dark fruits, with refined, mature tannins; good stuff. Some nice soft cherry fruit on the centre palate.

Price	**€9–€12**
Region	Catalonia
Grape	Cab Sauv/Merlot
Alc/vol	13%

Bacchus

Chivite Gran Feudo Navarra Crianza 2002

Special Value!

A maturing vegetal nose; cool, elegant but attractive dark fruit with good acidity and a tangy, dry finish.

Widely available

Price	**€9–€12**
Region	Navarra
Grape	Tempranillo/ Garnacha/Cab Sauv
Alc/vol	12.5%

Ampersand Wines

El Burro Garnacha Campo de Borja 2004

Special Value!

Soft summer fruits in a glass. Juicy palate full of redcurrants, strawberries and cherries backed by fleshy tannins and balanced alcohol. Fresh, fruity finish.

Price	**€9–€12**
Region	Aragón
Grape	Garnacha
Alc/vol	13.5%

Kelly & Co.

Black's, Athy; Bourke Fine Wines, Clonskeagh; Egan's, Drogheda; Goose, Drumcondra; Grapevine, Kilbarrack; Grapevine, Ballymun; Londis

Mad Dogs & Englishmen
Jumilla 2004

Special Value!

Cherries and chocolate, smooth and delicious, packed with flavour. Tannins still have a bit of a bite and the oak is quite pronounced, but it's all coming together beautifully.

Cheers, Dun Laoghaire; Gerry's Supermarket, Skerries; Kellys Wine Vault, Clontarf; Londis; O'Donovan's, Cork; JJ O'Driscoll, Cork

Price	€9–€12
Region	Murcia
Grape	Monastrell/Shiraz/ Cab Sauv
Alc/vol	14%

Kelly & Co.

Ochoa Tempranillo Navarra 2002

Plum and damson aromas. Rounded fruit on the palate, dark and soft. Very approachable tannins and a long finish with a touch of cinnamon.

Dunnes Stores; Kellys Wine Vault, Clontarf; SuperValu

Price	€9–€12
Region	Navarra
Grape	Tempranillo
Alc/vol	13%

Kelly & Co.

Raimat Tempranillo Syrah Costers del Segre 2003

Lovely ripe fruit, strawberries and a little blackcurrant. Soft and appealing, smooth tannins and a good fruity finish. On its own or with pasta.

Ivan's of Caherdavin; McGovern's, Ballyvolane; R. & N. Odlum; Tasters Blanchardstown

Price	€9–€12
Region	Catalonia
Grape	Tempranillo/Syrah
Alc/vol	13.5%

Findlater Grants

Sierra Cantabria Rioja 2004

Special Value!

Good, soft, slightly vegetal Rioja, with very nice concentration of red berry fruits and light tannins on the finish. Perfect with white meats and lighter red meats.

O'Briens

Price	€9–€12
Region	Rioja
Grape	Tempranillo/ Graciano
Alc/vol	13.5%

O'Briens

Telmo Rodriguez Viña 105 Cigales 2004

Beautiful, lightly textured strawberry and blackcurrant fruit with a nice peppery edge on the soft, easy finish. Lovely easy-drinking wine.

Brechin Watchorn; Dicey Reillys; Harvest; McCambridges; O'Briens

Price	€9–€12
Region	Castilla-León
Grape	Tempranillo/ Garnacha
Alc/vol	13%

Approach Trade

Tergeo Yecla 2004

Special Value!

Big, fairly pure plums, with a spicy kick, not overripe and with good meaty length.

Bin No. 9; Cana; Drinks Store; McCabes; The Mill, Maynooth; Red Island, Skerries; Uncorked; Vanilla Grape, Kenmare; The Vintry, Rathgar; World Wines, Wexford

Price   €9–€12
Region Murcia
Grape Monastrell/Syrah
Alc/vol 14%

Tyrrell

Viña Cobranza Rueda 2001

Special Value!

A definite structure to this wine, combining cherries and plums with quite solid tannins that will soften over the next year or two; in the meantime, it's a good food wine.

Eurospar; Mace; SPAR; SPAR Express

Price   €9–€12
Region Castilla-León
Grape Tempranillo/
            Cab Sauv/Merlot
Alc/vol 13.5%

Greenhills

€12–€15

Aquilice Cencibel VdlT Castilla y León 2005

Engaging damson/blackberry aromas. Beautifully smooth flavours of ripe black cherries mixed with plums, all backed by supple oak. Tannins are evident, but would disappear beside a rich casserole.

Fallon & Byrne; Wine Well, Dunboyne

Price   €12–€15
Region Castilla-León
Grape Tempranillo
Alc/vol 13.5%

Straffan

Celeste Torres Ribera del Duero 2003

Ripe black cherries and plums with a hint of vanilla from the oak. Beautifully soft and easy to drink, but with a definite personality and structure. Excellent.

Fahys, Ballina; McCabes, Blackrock

Price   €12–€15
Region Castilla-León
Grape Tempranillo
Alc/vol 13.5%

Woodford Bourne

Chivite Gran Feudo Viñas Viejas Navarra Reserva 2000

Light, slightly vegetal, easy fruitiness with good length and dry tannins; there is a nice core of dark, firm blackcurrants too.

McCabes, Blackrock; McHughs: Kilbarrack, Malahide Road; O'Donovans, Cork

Price   €12–€15
Region Navarra
Grape Cab Sauv/Merlot/
            Tempranillo
Alc/vol 12.5%

Ampersand Wines

Dominio de Ugarte Rioja Reserva 1999

Good traditional Rioja, with a scented nose, lifted, elegant fruit, a mature vegetal touch and some light, dry tannins.

Molloys

Price	€12–€15
Region	Rioja
Grape	Tempranillo
Alc/vol	13%

Molloys

El Quintanal Ribera del Duero 2005

Coffee and plum aromas, with a few figs to keep it interesting. On the palate, flavours are mature and developed, with concentrated dark fruits, firm tannins and a dry finish. This hearty wine is still developing.

Oddbins

Price	€12–€15
Region	Castilla-León
Grape	Tempranillo
Alc/vol	14%

Oddbins

Floresta Costa Brava Crianza 2002

Very pleasing, smooth, forthcoming wine with soft blackcurrants and redcurrants and a good dry finish.

Ballymaloe Shop; O'Donovans, Cork

Price	€12–€15
Region	Catalonia
Grape	Tempranillo/ Cab Sauv/Carignan
Alc/vol	13.5%

Smith & Whelan

Lanzado Rioja Crianza 2002

A big, youthful, full-bodied style of Rioja with plenty of alcohol and ripe dark fruits alongside some sweet vanilla oak.

Price	€12–€15
Region	Rioja
Grape	Tempranillo
Alc/vol	14%

Celtic Whiskey Shop

Luis Cañas Rioja Crianza 2003

A fairly full-bodied style of Rioja, but with delicious, ripe, rounded sweet cherry and plum fruits, subtle vanilla oak and a smooth finish. Very stylish wine.

Jus de Vine; Next Door; Searsons, Monkstown

Price	€12–€15
Region	Rioja
Grape	Tempranillo/ Garnacha
Alc/vol	13.5%

Searsons

All of the wines in this book are ready to drink now (October 2006), and for the next 12 months. Some will improve further over time and this is mentioned in the tasting note.

Marqués de Cáceres Vendemia Seleccionado Rioja Crianza 2002

Perfect lighter style of Rioja with deli-cate strawberry fruit, a touch of new oak and a smooth, easy finish. A great all-rounder with food, or by itself.

Price €12–€15
Region Rioja
Grape Tempranillo/
Graciano/Garnacha
Alc/vol 13%

Ardkeen Superstore; Bennett's; Bin No 9, Big Wine Warehouse; Blarney Off-Licence; Cellars; Drinagh Co-op

Findlater Grants

Osoti Rioja Crianza 2003   Organic

Pure, elegant, but nicely concentrated cherry fruit with stylish vanilla oak; smooth, easy drinking with a real touch of class.

Price €12–€15
Region Rioja
Grape Tempranillo/
Garnacha
Alc/vol 13.5%

Connemara Hamper, Clifden; Lettercollum Kitchen Project, Clonakilty

Mary Pawle

Pirineos Somontano Reserva 2001

An understated elegant nose of pure red fruits is followed by a light, smooth palate of cool summer fruits, with subtle refreshing acidity and some faint notes of spice; very attractive, charming wine with real character.

Price €12–€15
Region Aragón
Grape Tempranillo/
Cab Sauv/Moristel
Alc/vol 13.5%

Searsons

Next Door; Patrick Stewart, Sligo; Searsons, Monkstown

★ Telmo Rodriguez Dehesa Gago Toro 2005

Closed, ultra-ripe, firm damsons and spicy herbal flavours; shocks the palate a bit—very concentrated and ripe—but give it time.

Price €12–€15
Region Castilla-León
Grape Tempranillo
Alc/vol 14%

Approach Trade

Egan's Too; Gaffney's; Harvest; Kinnegar Wines; Listons; McCambridges; Mitchell & Son; O'Brien's; On the Grapevine; Probus Wines

---

Terrasola Jean León Catalunya 2003

Rich, smooth dark fruits integrate beautifully with the acidity and grainy tannins. Excellent structure and deli-cious length. You could drink this on its own, but it would be better with steaks and roasts.

Price €12–€15
Region Catalonia
Grape Syrah/Garnacha/
Tempranillo
Alc/vol 14%

Woodford Bourne

Daly's Off-licence, Boyle; Fahys, Ballina; Fallon & Byrne, D2

€15–€18

★ Bodegas Carchelo Rico Jumilla Crianza 2003

Lovely figgy depths on
the nose. Does the palate
live up to expectations?
Entirely. A palate of cush-
iony softness, melting
dark fruits, velvety
tannins and enormous,
oaky, creamy length. You
couldn't accuse it of
subtlety. Super.

Fallon & Byrne

Price **€15–€18**
Region **Murcia**
Grape **Monastrell/**
         Tempranillo/
         Cab Sauv
Alc/vol **14%**

Straffan

Emilio Moro Finca Resalso Ribera del Duero 2004

Big, slightly tarry flavours dominated
by rich damson fruits, but underpinned by some smoky oak flavours
too. Roast lamb would be the local
favourite.

*Andersons Food Hall & Café; Brechin Watchorn; The
Grapevine; Michael's Wines; Mitchell & Son*

Price **€15–€18**
Region **Castilla-León**
Grape **Tempranillo**
Alc/vol **14.5%**

Approach Trade

★ Mas d'en Pol Clua Terra Alta 2005

Smooth prunes, cool,
savoury, intense wild
herbal notes—funky but
classy, with very good
structure and closed
tannic length. This is
excellent.

Ballymaloe Shop

Price **€15–€18**
Region **Catalonia**
Grape **Garnacha/Syrah/**
         Merlot/Cab Sauv
Alc/vol **13.5%**

Smith & Whelan

Muga Rioja Reserva 2002

Relatively big, rounded Rioja with
some sweet coconut to go alongside
the soft cherry and raspberry fruits;
smooth and very seductive.

*Coolers, Clonee; Egans Food Hall, Drogheda; McHughs
Kilbarrack & Malahide Rd; Martins of Marino; Shiels, Dorset
St; Strand Off Licence, Fairview; Unwined, Swords*

Price **€15–€18**
Region **Rioja**
Grape **Tempranillo/**
         Garnacha/Mazuelo
Alc/vol **13.5%**

Comans

Negre Barbara Forés Terra Alta 2002

A big, cool, meaty, savoury wine with a very attractive herbiness; compact, full-bodied young wine.

Michael's Wines; Next Door @ Myles Creek

Price	€15–€18
Region	Catalonia
Grape	Garnacha/Cariñena Syrah/Carignan
Alc/vol	14%

Approach Trade

Ochoa Navarra Reserva 1999

Soft, rounded dark fruits on the palate, with good acidity and soft tannins. This one slips down easily enough to have with or without food.

Dunnes Stores; Kellys Wine Vault, Clontarf; SuperValu

Price	€15–€18
Region	Navarra
Grape	Tempranillo/ Cab Sauv
Alc/vol	14%

Kelly & Co.

★ Taurus Toro Crianza 2003

Very herbal, minty, swish aromas that carry on through an elegant herbal palate of damsons with good acidity and very nice length. Lots of chocolate—both dark and milk.

Price	€15–€18
Region	Castilla-León
Grape	Tempranillo
Alc/vol	14%

Smith & Whelan

Ballymaloe Shop

€18–€22

Agejas Tinto Roble VdlT de Castilla y Léon 2002

Smooth, smoochy wine with silky damsons and blackcurrant, overlain with cloves and vanilla; elegant, well-defined wine.

Andersons Food Hall & Café; Brechin Watchorn; Dicey Reillys; Harvest; McCambridges; Michael's Wines; Vanilla Grape

Price	€18–€22
Region	Castilla-León
Grape	Tempranillo
Alc/vol	13.5%

Approach Trade

Albet y Noya Col.leccio Penedès 1999   Organic

The nose shows some maturity; the palate has developed flavours of cloves and savoury fruits with grippy minerals on the finish. Living on the edge a little—drink over the next year.

Sweeneys, Fairview

Price	€18–€22
Region	Catalonia
Grape	Syrah
Alc/vol	13.5%

Mary Pawle

Artadi Viñas de Gain Rioja Cosecha 2003

Very elegant and smooth with some
tight tannins on a long, dry finish. A
good concentrated centre palate and a
strong mineral element on the finish.

Patrick Stewart Wines, Sligo

Price €18–€22
Region Rioja
Grape Tempranillo
Alc/vol 13.5%

Nicholson

Clos Mont-Blanc Masia Les Comes Conca de Barbera Reserva 2001

Fig and dried fruit aromas. Sensuous,
mature palate with notes of figs,
leather and cedar. An evolved wine,
but still with some fine-grained
tannins. It will deliver its best over the
next year or so.

Grape Escape; Vaughan Johnson

Price €18–€22
Region Catalonia
Grape Cab Sauv/Merlot
Alc/vol 13.5%

Papillon

★ Javier Asensio Cabernet Sauvignon Navarra Reserva 2000

Rich, deep, dark fruits
on the nose; classy,
smooth, velvety, ripe
fruit—supple, hedon-
istic, quite alcoholic,
but with a good spicy
finish.

Ballymaloe Shop

Price €18–€22
Region Navarra
Grape Cab Sauv
Alc/vol 13.5%

Smith & Whelan

Scala Dei Negre Priorat 2002

Intense cloves and liquorice, with a
firm edge—solid and savoury with
plenty of black pepper on a dry finish.

Price €18–€22
Region Catalonia
Grape Garnacha
Alc/vol 13.5%

Bacchus

★ Telmo Rodriguez Gago Toro 2003

Huge, punchy, muscular wine with
masses of ripe plum fruits, some
charred smoky oak and strapping
tannins. Perfect for a posh barbecue or
hearty casserole.

*Brechin Watchorn; The Corkscrew; Dicey Reillys; Egan's Too;
Gaffney's; Harvest*

Price €18–€22
Region Castilla-León
Grape Tempranillo
Alc/vol 14%

Approach Trade

€22–€30

★★ Allende Rioja Cosecha 2001

A beautiful, fragrant nose leads on to velvety smooth cherries and blackcurrants, underpinned by some cloves and vanilla, finishing with lovely ripeness and great length. Modern-style Rioja *par excellence*.

Berry Bros & Rudd

Price	€22–€30
Region	Rioja
Grape	Tempranillo
Alc/vol	13.5%

Berry Bros & Rudd

★ Contino Rioja Reserva 2000

Developed blackcurrants and plums with fine drying tannins and lovely length—elegant and restrained, with lovely mid-palate intensity. A very classy traditional style of Rioja.

Cheers Delgany; Chester Beatty OL, Ashford; Corkscrew, D2; Donnybrook Fair; Fallon & Byrne, D2; Grape Escape, Lucan; Jus de Vine, Portmarnock; Kellys, Clontarf; Macs, Limerick; Marthas Vineyard, Rathfarnham; McCabes; O'Donovans, Cork; On The Grapevine Dalkey & Booterstown; Red Island Wine Co., Skerries; Thomas Martins, Fairview; Thomas Woodberrys, Galway; World Wide Wines, Waterford

Price	€22–€30
Region	Rioja
Grape	Tempranillo/ Mazuelo/Graciano
Alc/vol	13%

Cassidys

Cune Imperial Rioja Reserva 1999

Developed nose and palate with some vegetal notes, good firm tannic structure throughout, with fine mature fruits.

Cheers Delgany; Chester Beatty OL, Ashford; Corkscrew, D2; Donnybrook Fair; Fallon & Byrne, D2; Grape Escape, Lucan; Jus de Vine, Portmarnock; Kellys, Clontarf; Macs, Limerick; Marthas Vineyard, Rathfarnham; McCabes; O'Donovans, Cork; On The Grapevine Dalkey & Booterstown; Red Island Wine Co., Skerries; Thomas Martins, Fairview; Thomas Woodberrys, Galway; World Wide Wines, Waterford

Price	€22–€30
Region	Rioja
Grape	Tempranillo
Alc/vol	13%

Cassidys

Emilio Moro Ribera del Duero 2003

Big, broad, meaty, baked damson and fig fruits; very good intensity of flavour, wrapped in a firm envelope of dry tannins. Needs food to soften it.

Brechin Watchorn; The Corkscrew; The Kingdom Food & Wine; Gibney's; Probus Wines; Harvest; Karwig; McCambridges; Michael's Wines; O'Brien's; Spanishwines.ie; The Wicklow Arms; The Wicklow Wine Co.

Price	€22–€30
Region	Castilla-León
Grape	Tempranillo
Alc/vol	14.5%

Approach Trade

Laurona Monsant 2001

Muscular and powerful, developing spicy, leathery fruit with solid, concentrated dark forest fruits; plenty of alcohol, but a very classy wine.

Brechin Watchorn; Spanishwines.ie

Price	€22–€30
Region	Catalonia
Grape	Garnacha/Cariñena/ Syrah/Merlot
Alc/vol	14%

Approach Trade

Les Terrasses Priorat 2003

Herb-scented aromas along with dark fruits. Very soft palate of creamy richness, crammed with juicy blackberries and plums. Edgy tannins and balanced alcohol. Definitely a food wine, and a great match for steak.

Andersons Food Hall & Café; Brechin Watchorn; The Corkscrew; Dicey-Reillys; Egan's Too; Harvest; Karwig; Listons; Mitchell & Son; O'Brien's; On The Grapevine; Probus; Vanilla Grape; The Wicklow Arms

Price	€22–€30
Region	Catalonia
Grape	Garnacha/Cariñena/ Cab Sauv
Alc/vol	14%

Approach Trade

Muga Selección Especial Rioja Reserva 2001

RED WINE OF THE YEAR

This has everything; elegance combined with real concentration in the developing blackcurrant and cherry fruits, hints of vanilla spice and a lovely long-drawn-out finish with some peppery dry tannins. Try it with plain roast lamb.

Price	€22–€30
Region	Rioja
Grape	Tempranillo/ Garnacha/Mazuelo/ Graciano
Alc/vol	13.5%

Comans

Callans Off Licence, Dundalk; Jus de Vine, Portmarnock; McHughs of Kilbarrack & Malahide Rd; Mill Wine Cellar, Maynooth; Next Door, Enfield; Terrys of Limerick

Pegaso Barrancos de Pizarra VdlT de Castilla y Léon 2001

Jammy, ripe strawberry aromas and rich, baked earth flavours—power plus, with the tannins to go with it; very tannic with ripe fruit; try it in a year or two.

The Corkscrew; Dicey Reillys; Mitchell & Son

Price	€22–€30
Region	Castilla-León
Grape	Garnacha
Alc/vol	15%

Approach Trade

★ Telmo Rodriguez M2 de Matallana Ribera del Duero 2003

Broad, earthy aromas. Huge, concentrated, ripe dark plums encased in a cloak of dry tannins; amazing concentration and amazing levels of tannin too. Now with red meat, or hold a year or two.

Price	€22–€30
Region	Castilla-León
Grape	Tempranillo
Alc/vol	14.5%

Approach Trade

Dicey Reillys; French Flair; Michael's Wines

€30–€40

★ Mas d'en Compte Priorat 2003

This has very seductive, smooth, complex blackcurrant fruit and some well-judged new oak; meaty, supple, big and very classy.

Price	€30–€40
Region	Catalonia
Grape	Tempranillo/ Cab Sauv
Alc/vol	14%

www.jnwine.com

Nicholson

Mas d'en Gil Coma Vella Priorat 2002

Powerful, rounded wine with a distinct note of clove and eucalyptus; behind that lurk some intense, dark, meaty fruits and a long, focused, clean, smooth finish.

Price	€30–€40
Region	Catalonia
Grape	Garnacha/Cariñena
Alc/vol	14%

Searsons

Patrick Stewart, Sligo; Power & Smullen Wine Merchants, Lucan; Searsons, Monkstown

---

★ Muga Prado Enea Rioja Gran Reserva 1996

Old-school Rioja at its best; developed vegetal aromas and flavours vie with soft mature raspberry fruit. It has a powerful, long, dry finish.

Price	€30–€40
Region	Rioja
Grape	Tempranillo/ Garnacha/Mazuelo
Alc/vol	13.5%

Comans

O'Donovans, Cork; O'Neills, SCR; Terrys of Limerick; Mitchells, Kildare St; The Swiss Cottage, Santry

---

★ San Román Toro 2001

Maturing aromas of prunes and vegetation. Massively structured wine with a huge concentration of dark, ripe plums, with an enjoyable fieriness and sheer power; very long too—a monster in every way.

Price	€30–€40
Region	Castilla-León
Grape	Tempranillo
Alc/vol	14%

Approach Trade

Egan's Too; Vanilla Grape

Rosé

Chivite Gran Feudo Rosado Navarra 2005

Special Value!

Light minerals with some racy raspberry and strawberry flavours, finishing dry. Lovely fresh wine.

Price	Under €9
Region	Navarra
Grape	Garnacha
Alc/vol	12.5%

Ampersand Wines

Parvus Privat Cabernet Rosé Alella 2005   Organic

A different but very enjoyable wine— fresh redcurrants with minerals, and a long, lightly textured finish. By itself or with salads.

Price	€12–€15
Region	Catalonia
Grape	Cab Sauv
Alc/vol	12.5%

Mannings Emporium, Co. Cork

Mary Pawle

Uruguay

Just one entry from a developing country that can offer some exciting wines. A trade mission earlier this year may increase their presence here. Uruguay can produce some excellent red wines with structure and balance. The local favourite happens to be one of mine too, the Tannat grape, a French variety that can make delicious, elegant, dry red wines.

Red

€9–€12

Dom. Monte de Luz Tannat 2005   **Special Value!**

Not very Tannat-like at all! Not a classic Tannat by any means, with its ripe, soft, sweet plum fruit and vanilla essence, but a very seductive, smooth wine that will certainly win friends for Uruguay.

Mitchells, Kildare Street; Mitchells, Glasthule

Price €9–€12
Region San José
Grape Tannat
Alc/vol 13.5%

Mitchell & Son

USA

A slightly better performance from the USA this year, with 11 entries, but this still does not reflect the quality of wine the country can produce. It would still appear that despite the favourable exchange rate, most US wine is too expensive for the Irish consumer. Leaving aside a number of very successful lower-priced brands, we see very little wine from California, the largest producer, or any of the smaller, but often interesting, states.

White

€15–€18

Fetzer Bonterra Vineyards Chardonnay 2004　　　　　　　**Organic**

Good crisp lemons and green fruits with a light spritz and a clean, dry finish.

Tesco; SuperValu, Greystones/Foxrock; Molloys; O'Briens, Sandymount; Nolans, Supermarket; O'Briens Stillorgan; McCabes, Blackrock/Foxrock

Price €15–€18
Region Mendocino, California
Grape Chardonnay
Alc/vol 13.5%

Dillons

€18–€22

Robert Mondavi Napa Valley Fumé Blanc 2003

Lemon sherbet nose with creamy oak influence. The creaminess continues on the palate, with lots of lemon zest and an evident layer of oak. A good example of oaked Sauvignon.

Price €18–€22
Region Napa Valley, California
Grape Sauv Blanc
Alc/vol 14%

Allied Drinks

€22–€30

Ch. Ste Michelle Dr Loosen Eroica Columbia Valley Riesling 2001

Germany meets the New World? Delicate honey and crisp red apples with a distinctive, maturing honey and mineral finish. Fascinating, delicious wine.

Comans, Rathgar; Dalys of Boyle; O'Briens Fine Wines, Limerick; SPAR, Rathcoole; Sweeneys, Harts Corner

Price €22–€30
Region Columbia Valley, Washington
Grape Riesling
Alc/vol 12%

Comans

Red

€12–€15

L de Lyeth 2004

Broad, maturing, ripe strawberries and tangy plums backed by a fair punch of power and an easy finish. An elegant wine underpinned by some lightly spicy new oak.

Donnybrook Fair; Fallon & Byrne; Le Caveau

Price	**€12–€15**
Region	**Sonoma, California**
Grape	**Merlot**
Alc/vol	**13.5%**

Liberty Wines

Ravenswood Vintners Blend Zinfandel 2003

Supple, ripe, rounded loganberries and dark cherries—very attractive wine with a nice tangy edge.

O'Brien's

Price	**€12–€15**
Region	**California**
Grape	**Zinfandel**
Alc/vol	**13.5%**

Allied Drinks

€15–€18

Ravenswood Lodi Old Vine Zinfandel 2003

Fine but intense dark fruits, with some nicely worked tannins coming through on the finish; big, with plenty of fruit and a good dry follow-through.

Next Door; O'Brien's; Selected independent retailers

Price	**€15–€18**
Region	**Sonoma, California**
Grape	**Zinfandel**
Alc/vol	**14.5%**

Allied Drinks

€22–€30

★ Au Bon Climat Pinot Noir 2003

Lovely Pinot Noir with a heady ripeness that is never excessive and a maturing barnyardy touch. Rounded, lush, sweet and beautifully fruity.

Berry Bros & Rudd

Price	**€22–€30**
Region	**Santa Maria Valley, California**
Grape	**Pinot Noir**
Alc/vol	**13.5%**

Berry Bros & Rudd

Where to buy the wine
If your local retailer does not stock a particular wine, contact the distributor named in italic after the tasting note who will be pleased to give you details of the nearest stockist.

★ Limerick Lane Collins Vineyard Zinfandel 2003

An outstanding wine, showing the power and heady heights of Zinfandel with rich, supple, voluptuous dark fruits, some developing earthiness and a soft and easy finish that lasts and lasts.

Price	€22–€30
Region	Russian River, California
Grape	Zinfandel
Alc/vol	14.8%

Karwigs

Eugene's, Kenmare; Karwigs; Redmonds, Ranelagh

★ Ridge Lytton Springs 2002

Wonderful, classy wine with intense, rich dark fruits, a herby edge and some ripe tannins kicking through on the long, tangy finish. Full-bodied and full of complex flavours.

Price	€22–€30
Region	Monte Bello, California
Grape	Zinfandel/Petite Sirah/Carignan
Alc/vol	14%

www.jnwine.com

Nicholson

★ Seghesio Sonoma Zinfandel 2004

A delicious Zinfandel combining the traditional power and alcohol of the grape with a real elegance—pure, fresh damsons and plums with subtle spice and excellent length. A quality wine, one to savour with red meats.

Price	€22–€30
Region	Sonoma, California
Grape	Zinfandel
Alc/vol	15%

Liberty Wines

Claudio's Wines; Fallon & Byrne; Hole in the Wall; McCabes; Redmonds

★ Zaca Mesa Z Cuvée 2003

Big, meaty wine with intensely ripe, silky sweet loganberries and plums; lush and dangerously easy to knock back!

Price	€22–€30
Region	Santa Ynez Valley, California
Grape	Mourvèdre/Grenache/Shiraz
Alc/vol	14.5%

Straffan

All of the wines in this book are ready to drink now (October 2006), and for the next 12 months. Some will improve further over time and this is mentioned in the tasting note.

Sparkling wines

The selection of beers and spirits on the shelves of our off-licences has changed dramatically with the arrival of thousands of east European workers on our shores. Apparently, they also have an insatiable thirst for sweet sparkling wines, hence the appearance of a range of fizzy Muscats from Latvia and Russia. Sadly, we did not get the opportunity to taste these wines this year, but we do have a great selection of sparkling wines and champagnes.

Our tastings included wines from New Zealand, Australia, Spain, Italy, South Africa, and even Argentina. Not all got through, but we list 20 champagnes, including the Joseph Perrier 1996, which wins our Sparkling Wine of the Year award for an unprecedented second time, and some 18 sparkling wines, including a few delicious thirst-quenching Proseccos.

Champagne

€22–€30

Oudinot Cuvée Brut Champagne nv

Light, elegant, classy wine with crisp lemon and biscuit flavours and snappy, clean length.

Price	**€22–€30**
Region	**Champagne**
Grape	**Chardonnay**
Alc/vol	**12%**

Marks & Spencer

Raymond Boulard Champagne nv

Warm bread aromas. Delicious, rich, nutty palate, with a creamy roundness backed by pleasant acidity. Good flavours on the finish.

Baily Wines, Howth; Sheridans

Price	**€22–€30**
Region	**Champagne**
Grape	**Pinot Meunier/ Pinot Noir/ Chardonnay**
Alc/vol	**12%**

Baily Wines

€30–€40

★ **Charles Heidsieck Brut Réserve Champagne nv**

Quite a deep colour. A fine nose of red apples and redcurrants with some honey and a lovely elegant biscuity touch. Rich palate of red fruits, very good length, and a nice honeyed touch on the finish.

Price	€30–€40
Region	Champagne
Grape	Pinot Noir/ Chardonnay/ Pinot Meunier
Alc/vol	12%

Barry Fitzwilliam Maxxium

Mangan Bros; Next Door

Charpentier Brut Prestige Champagne nv

Gentle, brioche, yeasty aromas. Subtle toasty flavours on the creamy palate, with subdued acidity and a touch of citrus on the soft finish.

Wines Direct

Price	€30–€40
Region	Champagne
Grape	Pinot Noir/ Pinot Meunier/ Chardonnay
Alc/vol	12%

Wines Direct

Pierre Paillard Champagne nv

Nutty, toasty aromas. Quite strong flavours on the palate—citrus, some nuts and baked apples, backed by smooth acidity. Toasty finish.

Wicklow Wine Co., Listons, Red Island Wine Co., The Corkscrew, Redmonds Wines & Spirits, Louis Albrouze, Bin No. 9, Clonskeagh, Jus de Vine, French Flair, Harvest Off-licences, Galway

Price	€30–€40
Region	Champagne
Grape	Pinot Noir/ Chardonnay
Alc/vol	12%

Wicklow Wines

Valéry Robert Cuvée Désirée Champagne nv

Very attractive rounded redcurrants and a honeyed touch on a nicely concentrated, stylish, lightly creamy champagne with very good length.

Firhouse Inn; Great Escape, Banna; Next Door, Enfield; The Wicklow Wine Co.; Wine Cluster, Moycullen

Price	€30–€40
Region	Champagne
Grape	Chardonnay/ Pinot Noir/ Pinot Meunier
Alc/vol	12%

Probus Wines

Where to buy the wine
If your local retailer does not stock a particular wine, contact the distributor named in italic after the tasting note who will be pleased to give you details of the nearest stockist.

★ Jacquart Champagne 1996

Classy developing nose; a complex palate with mushrooms, toasted brioche and rich honey, but underpinned by a firm backbone of acidity and good clean length.

Price	Over €40
Region	Champagne
Grape	Chardonnay/ Pinot Noir/ Pinot Meunier
Alc/vol	12.5%

Gleesons

Donnybrook Fair; McCabes; Selected independent retailers

Joseph Perrier Cuvée Royale Brut Champagne 1996

Delicately fruity and toasty nose. Serious power, however, on the palate, with a melange of honey, pears and apples. Lovely balance of acidity with fruit— the rich centre palate carries through to a finish that shows finesse and a creamy elegance.

Price	Over €40
Region	Champagne
Grape	Chardonnay/ Pinot Noir
Alc/vol	12%

Comans

Cheers, Bray; Corks, Terenure; O'Dwyers, Navan, O'Neills, SCR; Uncorked, Rathfarnham; Wine Deli, Waterford

SPARKLING WINE OF THE YEAR

★ Laurent-Perrier Ultra Brut Champagne nv

Big, rich, developed biscuit nose; lightly honeyed in the mouth, but with fine, crisp, well-integrated acidity; there is a light creaminess and good, very dry lemony length.

Price	Over €40
Region	Champagne
Grape	Chardonnay/ Pinot Noir
Alc/vol	12%

Gilbeys

Louis de Sacy Brut Grand Cru Champagne nv

Full, cool redcurrants and summer fruits with a long, dry finish. Will probably improve with a year, but good, well-made champagne.

Carvill's, Camden St; Celtic Wine Shop, Dawson St; Donnybrook Fair; Mill Wine Cellar, Maynooth; Mitchell & Son; Morton's

Price	Over €40
Region	Champagne
Grape	Pinot Noir/ Chardonnay/ Pinot Meunier
Alc/vol	12%

Champers

Louis de Sacy Grand Soir Champagne 1999

A very different style of champagne, but it works well—delicious redcurrants and raspberries in an elegant, refined wine with a lovely long finish.

Carvill's, Camden St; Celtic Wine Shop, Dawson St; Donnybrook Fair; Mill Wine Cellar, Maynooth; Morton's

Price	Over €40
Region	Champagne
Grape	Pinot Noir/ Chardonnay/ Pinot Meunier
Alc/vol	12%

Champers

★ 'R' de Ruinart Brut Champagne nv

Wonderful, rich, biscuity champagne with some complex brioche and grilled nuts on the palate; the finish is delicate, light and dry.

The Vintry, Rathgar; Jus de Vine, Portmarnock; McCabes, Blackrock; Bin No. 9, Goatstown; Uncorked, Rathfarnham; Lonergans, Clonmel; Terrys Wine Shop, Limerick; Fallon & Byrne D2

Price	Over €40
Region	Champagne
Grape	Chardonnay/ Pinot Noir
Alc/vol	12%

Taserra

Raymond Boulard Petraea Champagne nv

Attractive nose of hot buttered toast, baked apples and nuts. This is a gentle, subtle wine, with rich apple fruit and the merest touch of lemon. It lasts in the mouth and gives a rounded, satisfying finish.

Baily Wines, Howth; Sheridans

Price	Over €40
Region	Champagne
Grape	Pinot Noir/ Chardonnay
Alc/vol	12%

Baily Wines

Rosé

€22–€30

Lombard Rosé Champagne nv

Palest pink. Nutty, strawberry nose. Not overly dry, with fresh, zesty summer fruit flavours and nervy acidity.

Most branches Dunnes Stores

Price	€22–€30
Region	Champagne
Grape	Chardonnay/ Pinot Noir
Alc/vol	12%

Dunnes Stores

Marguet-Bonnerave Brut Rosé Champagne nv

Deep salmon pink. Rich flavours of summer fruits and nuts bound up in a palate of great flavour and depth. Beautiful balance and a great finish.

Berry Bros & Rudd

Price	€22–€30
Region	Champagne
Grape	Pinot Noir/ Chardonnay
Alc/vol	12%

Berry Bros & Rudd

€30–€40

Pierre Paillard Bouzy Grand Cru Rosé Champagne nv

Dry, crisp palate of baked red fruits with gentle acidity and a dry, layered finish.

Wicklow Wine Co., Listons, Red Island Wine Co., The Corkscrew, Redmonds Wines & Spirits, Louis Albrouze, Bin No. 9, Clonskeagh, Jus de Vine, French Flair, Harvest Off-licences, Galway

Price	€30–€40
Region	Champagne
Grape	Chardonnay/ Pinot Noir
Alc/vol	12%

Wicklow Wines

Over €40

★ Laurent-Perrier Cuvée Rosé Brut Champagne nv

Lovely rosy pink. Summery aromas of soft red fruits. Concentrated and structured palate of ripe strawberries with nutty overtones; crisp acidity. Superb, nuanced, long finish.

Price	Over €40
Region	Champagne
Grape	Pinot Noir
Alc/vol	12%

Gilbeys

★ Louis de Sacy Grand Cru Rosé Champagne nv

Juicy fruit on the nose with a hint of nuts. Full-flavoured baked strawberry palate, with great acidity and a lovely complexity.

Carvill's, Camden St; Celtic Wine Shop, Dawson St; Donnybrook Fair; Mill Wine Cellar, Maynooth; Morton's

Price	Over €40
Region	Champagne
Grape	Pinot Noir/ Pinot Meunier
Alc/vol	12%

Champers

Pol Roger Rosé Champagne 1998

Fresh strawberry fruit flavours with lively acidity and a toasty finish.

Superquinn; Vineyard, Leeson St, Dublin 2

Price	Over €40
Region	Champagne
Grape	Pinot Noir/ Chardonnay
Alc/vol	12%

Barry Fitzwilliam Maxxium

★ Ruinart Brut Rosé Champagne nv

Salmon pink. Delicious palate of very ripe strawberries and redcurrants backed by vivid acidity. Lovely dry finish.

Price	Over €40
Region	Champagne
Grape	Chardonnay/ Pinot Noir
Alc/vol	12.5%

Taserra

Sparkling

€9–€12

White

Alborada Cava nv

This is a very enjoyable glass of fizz with some lemon sherbet and a lovely, light, persistent mousse.

All branches Dunnes Stores

Price	€9–€12
Region	Catalonia
Grape	Xarel-lo/Macabeo/ Parellada
Alc/vol	11.5%

Dunnes Stores

€12–€15

Ca'Morlin Prosecco Frizzante nv

Good, lightly flavoured, crisp, dry Prosecco, with a nice pineapple flourish on the finish.

The Bottle Shop; Donnybrook Fair, Fallon & Byrne; Hole in the Wall

Price	€12–€15
Region	Veneto
Grape	Prosecco
Alc/vol	11%

Liberty Wines

Lindauer Brut nv

Nice lemon and lime fruit, light, fresh and zippy on the palate, with some fresh redcurrants—good stuff.

Selected independent retailers

Price	€12–€15
Region	Marlborough
Grape	Chardonnay/ Pinot Noir/ Chenin Blanc
Alc/vol	12%

Irish Distillers

Verdea IGT Collina del Milanese 2005

Frothy wine, lightly sparkling with delicate, very unusual fruits—minerals, some banana, even dried fruit peel. It is fresh and clean—certainly more *frizzante* than *spumante*, and definitely one for the thrill-seeker!

Mitchell & Son

Price	€12–€15
Region	Lombardy
Grape	Verdea
Alc/vol	11%

Select Wines from Italy

All of the wines in this book are ready to drink now (October 2006), and for the next 12 months. Some will improve further over time and this is mentioned in the tasting note.

Peter
LEHMANN
The Barossa

Grenache
A soft and smooth Australian red wine with flavours of soft ripe berry fruits. A fruit driven, easy drinking wine with a mellow finish.

Chenin Blanc
An Australian white wine with flavours of apple and tropical citrus fruits. A well balanced wine crisp, zesty and easy to drink with no oak flavours.

UNDURRAGA®
EXCELENCIA EN VINOS DESDE 1885

CABERNET SAUVIGNON
100% Cabernet Sauvignon from the Colchagua valley. An intense ruby red colour with ripe blackcurrant & vanilla flavours and softening tannins perfectly balanced.

SAUVIGNON BLANC
An excellent example of new world Sauvignon. A fresh crispy wine with zesty citrus fruit flavours and a long finish.

COMANS WHOLESALE LTD,
BELGARD ROAD, TALLAGHT, DUBLIN 24.
TEL: 01 - 451 9146. FAX: 01 - 451 9772.

Christmas titles from A. & A. Farmar

All in the Blood

Geraldine Plunkett Dillon
Edited by Honor O Brolchain

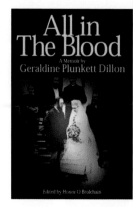

The absorbing story of the eccentric Plunkett family, including the strenuous days before the Rising and the tragic aftermath. Told by the sister of the executed 1916 leader, Joseph, *All in the Blood* puts the manoeuvres of the national struggle in the context of the life of a rich but unhappy family.

350 pages heavily illustrated HB €25

Bright Brilliant Days—

Douglas Gageby & The Irish Times Edited by Andrew Whittaker

A glittering array of writers celebrate (or dissect) the work and times of Ireland's most famous editor—with contributions from Bruce Arnold, Maeve Binchy, John Bowman, John Horgan, Conor Brady, Olivia O'Leary, Michael Viney and others. Plus—a selection of Douglas Gageby's *Irish Press* despatches from Germany in 1946.

200 pages PB €20

€15–€18

Conti d'Arco Prosecco Brut nv

A richer, more honeyed style with pear drops, a good persistent mousse, and a rounded finish.

Price	€15–€18
Region	Veneto
Grape	Prosecco
Alc/vol	11%

Drinkstore; Gibney's; Kelly's, Clontarf; Leopardstown Inn; McHugh's, Kilbarrack; Redmond's, Ranelagh; Thomas's, Vesey Arms, Village Stores, Ballyvaughan

Findlater Grants

La Riva dei Frati Vino Frizzante Prosecco di Valdobbiadene nv

Lovely, light, fresh pear drop fruit with plenty of lively acidity; a great aperitif to get your party going with a touch of style.

Price	€15–€18
Region	Veneto
Grape	Prosecco
Alc/vol	11%

Baily Wines, Howth; Cana Wines, Mullingar; Celtic Whiskey; Fallon & Byrne; Jus de Vine; Liston's, Camden Street; Nicola's Food Emporium, Westport; On the Grapevine, Booterstown and Dalkey; The Mill Wine Cellar, Maynooth; Wicklow Wine Co.; World Wide Wines, Waterford

WineKnows

Langlois Crémant de Loire nv

Plump, rounded, quite rich fruit—red apples and raspberries; fine, fairly lean finish. Lovely fruity fizz.

O'Briens

Price	€15–€18
Region	Loire Valley
Grape	Chenin Blanc/ Chardonnay/ Cabernet Franc
Alc/vol	12.5%

O'Briens

€18–€22

Bisol Desiderio Jeio Prosecco di Valdobbiadene Brut nv

This is absolutely delicious, thirst-quenching Prosecco with racy, crisp, clean fruit and a tart, dry finish. Light and beautifully balanced.

Price	€18–€22
Region	Veneto
Grape	Prosecco
Alc/vol	11.5%

Next Door; Power & Smullen Wine Merchants, Lucan; The Vintry, Rathgar

Searsons

De Faveri Vino Spumante Brut Prosecco di Valdobbiadene nv

Soft, light pears and raspberries with a delightful creamy texture. Delicate, classy fizz.

Claudio's; Fallon & Byrne; Kennedys

Price	€18–€22
Region	Veneto
Grape	Prosecco
Alc/vol	11%

Straffan

Dom. Henri Naudin-Ferrand Crémant de Bourgogne nv

A riper, fruitier style of fizz with lovely raspberries and pears, a lightly honeyed note and a rich finish.

Wines Direct

Price	€18–€22
Region	Burgundy
Grape	Chardonnay/ Pinot Noir/Aligoté
Alc/vol	12%

Wines Direct

Marco Oro Valdo Prosecco di Valdobbiadene nv

Relatively rich Prosecco, filled with canned pineapples and pears, with a nice creaminess, but still retaining a lovely freshness.

Wine OnLine

Price	€18–€22
Region	Veneto
Grape	Prosecco
Alc/vol	11%

Febvre

€22–€30

★ Green Point nv

Sweet, ripe raspberry aromas; rich, sweet, ripe red fruits, raspberries and strawberry shortcake. Characterful and full of flavour.

Price	€22–€30
Region	Victoria
Grape	Chardonnay/ Pinot Noir
Alc/vol	12.5%

Dillons

Sweeneys Wine Merchants, Glasnevin; Bin No.9, Goatstown; Jus de Vine, Portmarnock; Cheers, Palmerstown; Kellys Wine Vault, Clontarf; Joyces Supermarket, Knocknacara; Next Door, Blessington; Molloys; The Vintry, Rathgar

---

How to use this book
The wines are listed in order of country/region, colour (red or white), price band, then by name. There are separate chapters for sparkling (including Champagne) and dessert wines. If you can't find the wine you are looking for try the index. The price bands are guidelines only. All of the wines in this book are ready to drink now (October 2006), and for the next 12 months. Some will improve further over time and this is mentioned in the tasting note.

★ Green Point Vintage Brut 2002

Light, very classy
maturing wine with
ripe, seductively
honeyed fruit and
some brioche on the
centre palate, held together by very
well-integrated citrus acidity. A wine
of real style and finesse.

Price	€22–€30
Region	Victoria
Grape	Chardonnay/ Pinot Noir
Alc/vol	12.5%

Dillons

Next Door, Kilkee; Londis, Bettystown; Harvest Off Licence, Galway; Boggans Shop, Waterford

Rosé

€9–€12

Raboso Vino Spumante Brut Prosecco nv

A very faint pink colour; tasty, ripe
cherry fruit with some raspberries;
decent length and an off-dry finish.
Delicious simple drinking.

Price	€9–€12
Region	Veneto
Grape	Prosecco/Raboso
Alc/vol	11%

Marks & Spencer

€12–€15

Jacob's Creek Sparkling Rosé nv

Light strawberry aromas. Crushed
strawberry palate with nicely judged
acidity and a savoury finish.

Many branches of: Dunnes Stores; Londis; Mace; SPAR; SuperValu/Centra; Tesco

Price	€12–€15
Region	South Australia
Grape	Chardonnay/ Pinot Noir
Alc/vol	11.5%

Irish Distillers

€15–€18

Codorníu Pinot Noir Cava nv

Lightly toasted red fruit aromas.
Rounded palate with red fruits, toast
and excellent acidity. Savoury finish.

Deveneys, Dundrum; Dunnes Stores; Jus de Vine, Portmarnock; Martha's Vineyard; O'Donovans, Cork; Redmonds, Ranelagh; Sullivans, Clifden; Vintage Crop, Newbridge

Price	€15–€18
Region	Catalonia
Grape	Pinot Noir
Alc/vol	12%

Findlater Grants

€18–€22

Taltarni Brut Taché 2004

A very pale colour; deceptively light, fresh, clean raspberry and redcurrant fruit with lively minerality on a good dry finish. Different, and well worth a shot.

Macs, Limerick; Red Island, Skerries

Price	€18–€22
Region	Tasmania
Grape	Chardonnay/ Pinot Noir/ Pinot Meunier
Alc/vol	13%

Searsons

€22–€30

Banfi Rosa Regale Brachetto d'Acqui 2005

A most unusual sparkling wine; a deep rosé colour, lightly fizzy, with fresh raspberry and dark cherry fruits, ending on a sweet note but with a slightly bitter twist. The locals use it to celebrate, or drink it with dark choco-late desserts.

Price	€22–€30
Region	Piedmont
Grape	Brachetto
Alc/vol	6.5%

Febvre

Dessert wines

Many true wine-lovers are very partial to a glass of dessert wine at the end of a meal. Sadly, the rest of the population does not always share our enthusiasm—most wine shops report disappointing sales. As in previous years, I would urge you to give sweet wines a chance; they are very adaptable wines, good with some savoury dishes, excellent with fruit tarts and pies, or the ideal way to end a meal on its own.

For the most part, making sweet wine is a precarious business, working with far lower yields and harvesting later than with normal wines. Those willing to take the risk deserve our support. Given that most are available in half-bottles, you are hardly going to have any waste. This year we list some 19 wines, 11 of those in half bottles.

€9–€12

Maculan Dindarello Breganze 2005

Very sweet, pure grape juice with some tangy lemon zest; light, refreshing and honeyed.

Oddbins

Country	Italy
Price	€9–€12 (½ bottle)
Region	Veneto
Grape	Moscato
Alc/vol	11%

Oddbins

Peter Lehmann Botrytis Semillon 2002

Special Value!

A deep colour, with rich textured pears and barley sugar with a tangy lemon bite; lovely, light, refreshing dessert wine.

Martins of Marino; O'Donovans, Cork; Rowans of Rathfarnham; The Goose, Santry; The Vineyard, Galway

Country	Australia
Price	€9–€12 (½ bottle)
Region	Barossa Valley
Grape	Semillon
Alc/vol	11%

Comans

€12–€15

Mitchell's Gold Graves Supérieur 2004

A very nicely balanced wine featuring fresh orange peel, mandarin juice and a rich, honeyed centre palate. Finishes with a flourish—lovely refreshing sweet wine.

Andersons, Glasnevin; Coopers, Navan; Douglas Food, Donnybrook; Mitchells, Grape Escape, Navan; Kildare Street; Mitchells, Glasthule

Country	France
Price	€12–€15
Region	Bordeaux
Grape	Sémillon/Sauv Blanc
Alc/vol	13%

Mitchell & Son

€15–€18

Castaño Dulce Monastrell Yecla 2003

Deep, youthful purple colour. Sweet, intense primary loganberry and damson fruit with dry tannins and a long, sweetish finish; almost seems savoury given the levels of tannin. Try it with dark chocolate.

Country	Spain
Price	€15–€18 (½ bottle)
Region	Murcia
Grape	Monastrell
Alc/vol	16%

Comans

On the Grapevine, Dalkey & Booterstown; Bin No. 9, Goatstown; Redmonds, Ranelagh; The Vintry, Rathgar

DESSERT WINE OF THE YEAR

Ch. Court-les-Mûts Saussignac 2001

Rich marzipan and barley sugar aromas; intense barley sugar and almonds given real life by some tangy orange-peel acidity and a wonderfully clean finish. Beautifully balanced dessert wine. A superb, mature wine and a worthy winner of this year's award.

Country	France
Price	€15–€18 (½ bottle)
Region	South West
Grape	Sémillon
Alc/vol	12%

Wicklow Wine

Corkscrew, D2; Fallon & Byrne, D2; French Flair, Tralee; Hand Made Wines, Lismore, Co. Waterford; Harvest, Galway; Jus de Vine, Portmarnock; Listons, D2; Louis Albrouze, D2; Michael's Wines, Mount Merrion; Mitchells, Kildare Street & Glasthule; Morton's, Ranelagh; On the Grapevine, Dalkey; Power & Smullen, Lucan; Probus Wines, Oughterard; Red Island, Skerries; Redmonds, Ranelagh; Wicklow Wine Co.

Dom. des Schistes Muscat de Rivesaltes 2005

Delicious, fresh grapey fruit—exuberantly sweet and floral—drink well chilled with tropical fruit.

Country	France
Price	€15–€18
Region	Languedoc-Roussillon
Grape	Muscat
Alc/vol	15.5%

The Bottle Shop; Louis Albrouze Wine; World Wide Wine, Waterford

Louis Albrouze

> **Where to buy the wine**
> If your local retailer does not stock a particular wine, contact the distributor named in italic after the tasting note who will be pleased to give you details of the nearest stockist.

★ Grains Nobles de la Truffière Monbazillac 2003

Ginger and barley sugar aromas; a huge concentration of distinctive, very gingery, spicy vanilla; rich, sweet wine, with a slightly bitter smoky finish.

Country	France
Price	€15–€18 (½ bottle)
Region	South West
Grape	Sémillon/Sauv Blanc/Muscadelle
Alc/vol	13.5%

Wicklow Wine

Wicklow Wine Co., Harvest Off-licences, Galway, Michael's Food & Wine, The Corkscrew

Marchesi di Barolo Zagara Moscato d'Asti 2004

A lightly bubbly glass of pure elderflowers and freshly crushed grape juice. Light, sweet and refreshing—perfect on a summer's day.

Country	Italy
Price	€15–€18
Region	Piedmont
Grape	Moscato
Alc/vol	6%

Dunne & Crescenzi; Vanilla Grape

Select Wines from Italy

Paul Cluver Weisser Riesling Noble Late Harvest 2004

Rich but tangy, with a distinctive orange-peel, even marmalade, edge to the vibrant pear and pineapple fruit. Lovely clean length.

Country	South Africa
Price	€15–€18 (½ bottle)
Region	Elgin
Grape	Riesling
Alc/vol	13%

Greenacres; Jus de Vine; McHugh's; O'Donovan's; The Vintry

Findlater Grants

Telmo Rodriguez MR Mountain Wine Málaga 2004

Very complex, immensely sweet tangerines, melons and preserved ginger—rich, luscious, but with great concentration and length. You could only drink a glass, but what a glass!

Country	Spain
Price	€15–€18 (½ bottle)
Region	Andalucía
Grape	Moscatel
Alc/vol	13%

Brechin Watchorn; The Corkscrew; Mitchell & Son

Approach Trade

€18–€22

Ch. Laville Sauternes 2001

The rich, toasty, marzipan and honeyed element, with some real spice, is just balanced by some light lemon zest; finishes long with plenty of vanilla and pineapple.

Country	France
Price	€18–€22 (½ bottle)
Region	Bordeaux
Grape	Sémillon/Sauv Blanc/Muscadelle
Alc/vol	13.5%

Donnybrook Fair

Liberty Wines

Clos Uroulat Jurançon 2004

Fresh, tangy pineapples in a really lively, finely balanced wine; it hardly tastes sweet such is the refreshing acidity. Delicious wine—try it with blue cheese, foie gras or other savoury dishes.

Country	France
Price	€18–€22
Region	South West
Grape	Petit Manseng
Alc/vol	12.5%

Le Caveau

The Corkscrew; Fallon & Byrne; Le Caveau

Dom. des Jougla Viognier Vendange Passerillé VdP de l'Hérault 2005

Big, rich, tangy, ripe peaches and apricots with a bitter edge—interesting, well made with plenty of concentration.

Country	France
Price	€18–€22
Region	Languedoc-Roussillon
Grape	Viognier
Alc/vol	14%

Foodhall, Portlaoise; Gaffney's, Nenagh; Morton's, Galway; Patrick Stewart, Sligo

Inis Wines

★ Dom. Rotier Renaissance Gaillac Doux 2004

Here's something different—textured, rich orange and lanolin with a herby kick. It has a lovely liveliness despite the richness and a long, classy finish.

Country	France
Price	€18–€22 (½ bottle)
Region	South West
Grape	Len de l'El
Alc/vol	12.5%

Vanilla Grape, Kenmare

Tyrrell

★ Maculan Torcolato Breganze 2003

A previous award winner, and one that still impresses with its delicious orange and lemon peel, subtle, toasty grilled nuts, a touch of barley sugar, light body, and a seamless moreish finish that lasts and lasts.

Country	Italy
Price	€18–€22 (½ bottle)
Region	Veneto
Grape	Vespaiola/Tocai Friulano
Alc/vol	13%

Oddbins

Oddbins

★ Rietvallei Muscadel 2004

A pale tawny colour. The palate is a fascinating mix of delicate red fruits—raspberries and cherries—with caramel, chocolate and toffee; a complex young wine that will undoubtedly age well. Lovely tanginess and excellent length.

Country	South Africa
Price	€18–€22
Region	Robertson
Grape	Muscadel (Muscat)
Alc/vol	17%

Rushdale Wines

€22–€30

★ Dom. des Schistes Solera Rivesaltes nv

Complex aromas and flavours of raisins, caramel and butterscotch in a rich but tangy wine that improves still further with every sip.

Country	France
Price	€22–€30
Region	Languedoc-Roussillon
Grape	Grenache Gris/Macabeu
Alc/vol	16%

Louis Albrouze

The Bottle Shop; Louis Albrouze Wine; World Wide Wine, Waterford

---

★ Rietvallei Muscadel 1908 2003

Hugely concentrated and very sweet, with wonderfully defined tangy raspberry and raisin fruit overlain with some caramel. Still very young, it will certainly improve, but it's delicious already.

Country	South Africa
Price	€22–€30 (½ bottle)
Region	Robertson
Grape	Muscadel (Muscat)
Alc/vol	15%

Rushdale Wines

€30–€40

★ Dom. des Baumard Clos de Ste Catherine Coteaux du Layon 2004

A very finely balanced blend of light pineapples and pears with barley sugar and honey; charming primary fruits at present, which will certainly evolve, but a lovely glass of wine now.

Tyrrell (045) 870 882

Country	France
Price	€30–€40
Region	Loire Valley
Grape	Chenin Blanc
Alc/vol	13%

Tyrrell

Royal Tokaji Aszú 5 Puttonyos 2000

Wonderfully fresh, piercing lemon acidity counters the maturing barley sugar and orange-peel notes. Lovely piquant, refreshing finish.

Greenacres, O'Brien's, The Vintry, Wine Cellars in Phibsborough

Country	Hungary
Price	€30–€40 (½ litre)
Region	Tokaj
Grape	Hárslevelü/Furmint
Alc/vol	12%

Findlater Grants

Reference section

'the odour of Burgundy,
and the smell of French
sauces, and the sight of
clean napkins and long
loaves, knocked as a very
welcome visitor at the door
of our inner man.'

Jerome K. Jerome
Three Men in a Boat

The tasting panel

All the members of the tasting panel are professionally qualified, holding the WSET Diploma or equivalent, with many years' experience of tasting.

Niamh L. Boylan is a food and wine consultant. She lectures for the Wine Development Board and the Restaurants Association of Ireland.

Brian Brady is catering manager at a leading private club in Dublin.

Pat Carroll is an editor specialising in wine and food. Recent work includes *Tom Stevenson's Wine Report*. Pat also works part-time in Gibney's Off-Licence.

Tony Cleary is wine consultant to Galvins Wines and Spirits and a number of producers in Europe and South America.

Helen Coburn is a wine writer, contributing to *Wine Ireland*, the *Farmers' Journal* and other outlets.

Willie Dardis is National Off Licence Manager for Ampersand Wines.

Laurence Faller is winemaker for Domaine Weinbach, her family's winery in Alsace.

Catherine Griffith is wine consultant to Molloy's Liquor Stores.

Cathal McHugh is the proprietor of McHugh's Off Licence.

Anne Mullin is a wine consultant with Wineonline.ie, the virtual wine warehouse.

Monica Murphy is Research and Development Manager with Febvre and Co.

Claire O'Boyle is account manager with Le Caveau, a specialist French wine importer.

Mary O'Callaghan is Lecturer, Culinary Arts Degree, Dublin Institute of Technology; Lecturer, Wine Development Board of Ireland; Wine Consultant, Cheers Take Home, LVA.

Eileen O'Driscoll is author of *The Best of Irish Soups*.

Colette Scullion is a lecturer with the Wine Development Board.

Kevin Summons-Walsh is Wines Manager for Sweeney's Wine Merchants.

David Whelehan is marketing manager of the O'Briens Wine Off-Licence Group.

John Wilson is Editor of *The Best of Wine in Ireland*, author of *101 Great Wines for under €10* and wine columnist for *The Sunday Tribune*.

How the wines were assessed

How did we select the wines included in this book?
Firstly, John Wilson discussed the most likely candidates for *The Best of Wine in Ireland* with over 70 different wine importers, and together they made an initial selection. Over the summer of 2006 some 2,000 samples of the wines were tasted and reduced to 750 for inclusion in the book. A small number of these were ultimately excluded because vintage change meant that the wine actually tasted was no longer available on the market.

Of this 750, some 200 were presented to an expert tasting panel for further assessment. These were the *crème de la crème*, all potential stars and candidates for the coveted Wines of the Year Awards.

How were the wines tasted by the panel?
Each of the 200 wines was tasted separately by two professionally qualified tasters (see page 202 for details of this year's tasting panel). Each tasting was blind—the taster knew neither the identity nor the price of the wine. The session began at 11 in the morning and each taster was asked to assess 20 wines. Since this was a quality assessment, not a quiz, they were told the region, the grape and the vintage, and, as far as possible, like was tasted with like.

After separate tasting the two tasters compared their scores and comments. Remarkably, demonstrating the objectivity of this process, in about 85 per cent of cases the two tasters spontaneously agreed their marks to within 1 point out of 20. If they could not agree, the editor was asked to adjudicate.

How were the wines scored?

Less than 12	thin, dull or faulty
12	perfectly well-made, drinkable, but without much character
13	satisfactory wines but not good enough to be included in The Best of Wine in Ireland
14	high quality, with a touch of flair and complexity, finesse or flavour
15	exceptional by any standard, amongst the best of their style, and well worth seeking out
16 ★	excellent, with an extra dimension, showing character and style, very appealing
17 ★★	wonderful, highly desirable, with elegance, character and complexity, true to their origin, balanced and subtle
Award winners	outstanding in their categories—the winners

How were the Wines of the Year judged?

During the panel tasting certain very distinctive wines emerged as clearly scoring 17 or more out of 20. These were then tasted blind a third time by the editor and his colleagues and finally were confirmed as Wines of the Year.

How were the SPECIAL VALUE! wines chosen?

Since the tasters were not told the prices of the wines, they judged the value quite independently of cost. We were therefore able to calculate a statistically valid quality/price ratio. The 100 wines scoring the highest quality/price ratio are identified as our value wines with the *SPECIAL VALUE!* mark—they are well worth seeking out.

Where can I buy the wines?

Like other products, the most distinctive wines can sometimes be difficult to track down. This year we have asked the importers to provide us with a list of the outlets in which each wines can typically be found. We believe that this will be a significant aid in using the book. However, some wines are very new to the market, and so in case of difficulty readers are urged to contact the listed importer. To that end a directory of distributors is included before the index of wines—see page 246.

Vintages *Pat Carroll*

Do vintages matter? The short answer is yes—but they matter more in some places than others. In the charts below we have not included 'New World' countries (Australia, New Zealand, South Africa, North and South America), because there is less variation in the climate in those countries, so the quality of the wines is more consistent.

In Europe, vintage is hugely important, especially for fine wines. In a cool, wet year, grapes will not ripen properly and can suffer from rot, which ruins the flavour. A warm, sunny year with just the right amount of rain will produce ripe grapes in good health. Take an example. If you order a 1990 Sauternes to finish off a great meal in a restaurant, and you are given the 1991 instead, the wine will be dull and disappointing instead of ethereal and sublime. All the elements combined in 1990 to produce a superb Sauternes vintage; in 1991, rain throughout September diluted the crop, so the two wines are completely different in character. Prices for different vintages will reflect variations in quality. It should be acknowledged, however, that careful grape selection and modern winemaking techniques help producers to make good wine in difficult years.

The figures below are necessarily generalisations, but they will give you an idea of what to look out for and what to avoid. And remember that, even in poor years, good producers can make excellent wine. There can also be vintage variation within regions. The northern Rhône Valley, for example, was dryer than the south in 2002, producing an average vintage that was marginally better than the washed-out vintage in the south.

Vintage chart

1 = Poor   2 = Fair/average   3 = Good   4 = Very good   5 = Excellent

Region	1989	1990	1991	1992	1993	1994	1995	1996	1997	1998	1999	2000	2001	2002	2003	2004
Bordeaux red	5	5	1	1	2	3	5	5	3	3	4	5	4	4	4	4
Burgundy red	5	5	3	3	4	2	4	5	4	4	5	3	3	5	4	4
Burgundy white	5	5	3	4	3	3	5	5	4	4	4	4	3	5	2	4
Rhône Valley	5	5	4	3	2	3	4	4	4	5	5	4	4	1	4	4
Loire Valley	5	5	1	2	3	2	4	5	5	4	3	4	4	5	5	4
Alsace white	5	5	2	3	4	3	4	4	5	4	3	3	4	4	2	4
Sauternes	5	5	1	1	1	2	4	5	4	4	4	3	5	4	4	3
Germany	4	5	2	3	4	4	3	4	4	4	4	2	5	4	4	4
Italy Piedmont	5	5	2	1	2	3	4	5	5	3	5	4	5	2	3	4
Italy Tuscany	2	5	2	2	3	4	4	4	5	3	4	3	4	2	4	5
Spain Rioja	3	4	4	3	3	5	5	4	2	4	4	3	5	2	4	4
Port	2	3	4	4	1	5	3	3	4	3	3	5	3	2	5	4
Champagne	5	5	2	3	3	1	4	5	4	4	4	4	1	4	3	4

Food and wine matching

Pat Carroll

These tables are designed to give general guidelines on matching food and wine. The guidelines shouldn't be taken too seriously—drinking Sauvignon Blanc with grilled steak won't result in a visit from the style police. However, some wine/food matches are happier than others. A good general guideline is to match the weight of the food with the weight of the wine: simply cooked seafood goes well with a light-bodied Sancerre, while a rich game casserole requires something altogether more substantial, such as a mature red Rhône or even an Amarone. Weight, or 'body', is not the only factor, however. Other elements in wine that affect food are tannin and acidity. Tannin in red wine overpowers the delicate flavour of white fish, which is much better served with a crisp white such as Chablis. When red wine is drunk with hearty meat dishes, the tannin is much less noticeable. Acidity, the element in wine that gives it crispness and bite, counteracts richness, so higher-acidity whites, such as Rieslings and Sauvignon Blancs, go well with creamy sauces or cheeses. Remember too that it is not just the prime ingredient that you are matching; the sauce can be an equally important consideration.

We have given suggestions for matching wine with a range of different foods, but they are only suggestions. There are many more combinations that would work just as well and finding your own favourites is the enjoyable part!

Note: *New World* = Australia, New Zealand, South Africa, North America and South America.

Matching food with wine

Food	Wine
Almonds, salted	Fino, manzanilla
Anchovy dishes	Fino, Provence rosé
Antipasti	Barbera
Aperitif	Cabernet d'Anjou rosé, Cava, Blanc de Blancs Champagne, non-vintage brut Champagne, Prosecco, dry German Riesling
Apple desserts	Vin Santo
Apple tart	Coteaux du Layon, Eiswein, Vin Santo, sweet Vouvray

Food (Continued)	Wine
Arrabiata, pasta	Red Côtes du Rhône, Salice Salentino, South African Shiraz
Asian dishes	Gewürztraminer, Marsanne, Torrontés; see also Chinese, curries, fusion, Indian, Japanese, Thai
Asparagus	New World Sauvignon Blanc
Aubergine dishes	Portuguese reds, Salice Salentino
Avocado	French Sauvignon Blanc (especially Sancerre)
Bacon dishes	Pinot Gris/Pinot Grigio
Bean dishes	Southern French reds (especially Bandol and Fitou), Malbec, red Valdepeñas, red Zinfandel
Beef, barbecued	New World Cabernet Sauvignon, Malbec, Pinotage, Australian Shiraz, red Zinfandel
Beef casseroles	Bairrada, Australian Cabernet Sauvignon, Chianti, southern Italian reds (especially Salice Salentino), Madiran, Malbec, Rhône reds (especially Châteauneuf-du-Pape, Côtes du Rhône, Gigondas), Syrah/Shiraz
Beef hamburgers	Chilean Cabernet Sauvignon, Chianti, Montepulciano d'Abruzzo, Tempranillo
Beef, peppered	Barolo
Beef, roast	Amarone, Barolo, red Bordeaux, New World Cabernet Sauvignon, Carmenère, red Châteauneuf-du-Pape, Chianti, red Rioja, St Émilion, Syrah/Shiraz, red Zinfandel
Bolognese sauce	Barbera, Chianti, Dolcetto, Chilean Merlot, Valpolicella
Bouillabaisse	Bordeaux rosé
Bread and butter pudding	Monbazillac, Sauternes, sweet Sémillon
Bresaola	Valpolicella
Cake	Demi-sec Champagne; see also chocolate cake, Christmas cake, fruit cake
Cantucci biscuits	Vin Santo
Carbonara, pasta	Frascati
Cassoulet	Madiran
Cheese, blue	Classics: Roquefort with Sauternes; Stilton and port; dry amontillado, Banyuls, dry madeira, Monbazillac, dry oloroso, Tokaji
Cheese dishes	Cabernet Franc, unoaked Chardonnay, French Pinot Noir (gratins), Vermentino
Cheese fondue	Bourgogne Aligoté, Dolcetto, Jura whites, Jurançon, white Rioja, Savoie whites
Cheese, fresh rindless, e.g. cream cheese, Ricotta	Unoaked Chardonnay (especially Chablis), Pinot Gris/Pinot Grigio, dry Riesling, French Sauvignon Blanc

Food (Continued)	Wine
Cheese, goats'	White Bordeaux, Chenin Blanc (especially dry Vouvray), French Sauvignon Blanc (especially Pouilly-Fumé, Sancerre)
Cheese, hard, e.g. Cheddar, Gruyère, Parmesan	Classic: Parmesan with Barolo; Barbera, Cabernet Sauvignon/Shiraz blends, oaked Chardonnay, Côtes de Bourg, madeira (strong cheese), New World Pinot Noir, Pomerol, port, dry Sémillon, Syrah/Shiraz
Cheese, hard, mature	Barbera, Cabernet Sauvignon, Cabernet Sauvignon/Shiraz blends, Gigondas, dry madeira, Madiran, dry oloroso, Rhône whites
Cheese, smoked	Alsace Gewurztraminer, Pinotage
Cheese, washed-rind, e.g. Gubbeen, Pont l'Évêque	A difficult match: try Beaujolais, fruity Alsace Gewurztraminer or older Pinot Noir
Cheese, white-mould, e.g. Brie, Camembert	Aged Bandol, Beaujolais cru, Bordeaux reds (especially St Émilion), French oaked Chardonnay, Pinot Noir
Cheesecake	Asti, sweet Muscat
Chicken in cream sauce, e.g. chicken Véronique	Chenin Blanc, Torrontés, red Valdepeñas
Chicken, grilled/roast	Red Bergerac, white Bordeaux, Cabernet Franc, rosé Champagne, Chardonnay (especially from Burgundy), red Châteauneuf-du-Pape, Côtes de Bourg, Fumé Blanc, Gamay, Marsanne, Pinot Noir, red Rioja, Viognier
Chicken, light dishes	Fitou, Montepulciano d'Abruzzo, Soave
Chicken liver pâté	Dry amontillado
Chicken noodles	Frascati
Chicken wings, spicy	Merlot, Provence rosé
Chilli dishes	Corbières (chilli con carne), Shiraz
Chinese dishes	Meaty soy dishes—reds: Beaujolais, Côtes du Rhône, New World Pinot Noir, Zinfandel
	Light dishes—whites: Cava, Blanc de Blancs Champagne, Alsace Gewurztraminer, Marsanne, dry Muscat, French Sauvignon Blanc, Torrontés
	see also Asian, fusion
Chocolate cake	Banyuls, Málaga Moscatel, Maury, sweet Muscat, Sauternes
Chocolate desserts	Málaga Moscatel, Maury, sweet Muscat
Chorizo	Portuguese reds
Christmas cake	Sweet madeira
Christmas pudding	Asti, sweet Muscat, cream sherry, Tokaji, Vin Santo

Food (Continued)	Wine
Cod	White Bordeaux (roast cod), white Mâcon or other white Burgundy, Sémillon, Vermentino, Viognier
Confit	Malbec, red Zinfandel
Consommé	Dry amontillado
Cottage pie	Merlot
Couscous	Bianco di Custoza, Grenache/Garnacha, Pinot Blanc, Tavel
Crab	White Bordeaux (especially Entre Deux Mers), Rueda, New World Sauvignon Blanc, Viognier
Crème brûlée	Sweet Muscat, Sauternes, cream sherry, Tokaji
Crème caramel	Sweet Muscat, Sauternes, Tokaji
Crèpes Suzette	Orange Muscat
Curries	New World oaked Chardonnay (coconut curry), white Rhône wines (creamy curries), off-dry Riesling, Viognier (mild curries); see also Asian, Indian
Custard-based desserts	Monbazillac, Sauternes, sweet Sémillon
Desserts	Demi-sec Champagne; see also apple desserts, chocolate desserts, custard-based desserts, fruit desserts, nutty desserts
Dim sum	Off-dry Riesling
Duck	Red Bordeaux, Cahors, vintage Champagne (smoked duck), oaked Chardonnay, Gigondas, Madiran, Malbec, Navarra, Pinot Noir, Ribera del Duero, St Émilion, Shiraz
Fish	Unoaked Chardonnay, Chenin Blanc, Fumé Blanc (chargrilled fish), Grüner Veltliner, Jurançon, manzanilla (fried fish), Orvieto, Pinot Blanc, Pinot Gris/Pinot Grigio, dry Riesling (grilled fish), Rueda (grilled fish), Sauvignon Blanc, dry Sémillon, Soave, New World sparkling wine, Verdicchio, Vermentino, Vernaccia
Fish and chips	White Bergerac, Cava, Blanc de Blancs Champagne, non-vintage brut Champagne, New World oaked Chardonnay, unoaked Chardonnay, white Graves, Sauvignon Blanc
Fish, oily	Albariño/Alvarinho
Fish pie	New World oaked Chardonnay
Fish in rich sauce	White Graves
Fish, smoked	Albariño/Alvarinho, Cava, Blanc de Blancs Champagne, Crémant (smoked trout), Fumé Blanc, Muscadet (smoked mackerel), off-dry Riesling, French Sauvignon Blanc (especially Pouilly-Fumé and Sancerre), Spanish rosé (smoked fish pâté)

Food (Continued)	Wine
Foie gras	Alsace Gewurztraminer Vendange Tardive, Monbazillac, Sauternes
Fruit cake, rich	Sweet oloroso
Fruit desserts	Bonnezeaux, Coteaux du Layon, Eiswein, Canadian Icewine, Monbazillac, Muscat de Beaumes de Venise (crumbles), sweet Riesling, sweet Vouvray (baked fruit desserts)
Fruit salad	Asti, sweet Muscat, sweet Riesling
Fusion food	Gewürztraminer, off-dry Riesling; *see also* Asian
Game	Amarone, red Châteauneuf-du-Pape, Pinot Noir (light game), French Syrah
Goose	Barolo, Bordeaux reds, Cabernet Sauvignon, Cabernet Sauvignon/Shiraz blends, red Châteauneuf-du-Pape, Merlot, Pinot Noir, dry Riesling, Shiraz
Guacamole	Cava
Guinea fowl	Fine red Burgundy, white Graves, New World Pinot Noir, Tempranillo (especially Navarro, Ribera del Duero, red Rioja)
Hake	French oaked Chardonnay (especially Mâcon), New World oaked Chardonnay, Chenin Blanc, Soave, Verdicchio
Ham	Barbera, manzanilla (cured ham), Pinot Noir, dry Riesling, white Rioja, Valpolicella; Prosecco or New World sparkling wine for Parma ham and melon
Herb and olive oil dishes	Greek reds
Ice cream	Sweet Muscat, cream sherry (vanilla ice cream)
Indian dishes	Rosé Champagne, New World oaked Chardonnay, Grenache/Garnacha, dry Muscat, dry German Riesling, Verdelho; *see also* Asian, curries
Irish stew	Southern Italian reds (especially Salice Salentino)
Japanese dishes	Blanc de Blancs Champagne, fino, dry Riesling, French Sauvignon Blanc (especially Sancerre), New World sparkling wine; *see also* Asian
Kedgeree	Sekt
Kidneys	French Pinot Noir
Lamb casseroles	Red Châteauneuf-du-Pape, Corbières, Gigondas, southern Italian reds (especially Salice Salentino), Malbec, Mourvèdre, Syrah/Shiraz
Lamb with garlic or rosemary	Tempranillo

Food (Continued)	Wine
Lamb, grilled/roast	Bandol, red Bergerac, Bordeaux reds (especially Pomerol, St Émilion), Cabernet Franc, Cabernet Sauvignon, red Châteauneuf-du-Pape, Gigondas, Californian Merlot, Minervois, Navarra, Ribera del Duero, red Rioja
Lamb kebabs	Greek reds, Grenache/Garnacha, Portuguese reds
Lasagne	Barbera, Chianti, Montepulciano d'Abruzzo
Liver	Southern French reds (especially Bandol), Merlot (lambs' liver)
Lobster	Meursault, Puligny-Montrachet, Viognier
Macaroni cheese	Malbec
Mackerel, smoked	Muscadet
Marzipan	Bonnezeaux, cream sherry (marzipan desserts)
Meat dishes	Amarone (rich dishes), Cabernet Franc (lighter dishes); *see also* beef, lamb, pork
Meatballs	Corbières, Merlot, red Valdepeñas
Meats, cold	Gamay, dry Riesling
Melon and Parma ham	Prosecco, New World sparkling wine
Meringue	Asti, sweet Muscat, Vin Santo
Mince pies	Asti, sweet madeira, sweet Muscat, port, cream sherry
Monkfish	Oaked Chardonnay, especially from Burgundy (Meursault, Puligny-Montrachet) or California
Moussaka	Greek reds, Salice Salentino
Mullet, red	Cabernet Franc, French Pinot Noir, Sauvignon Blanc
Mushroom dishes	Dry amontillado, red Châteauneuf-du-Pape, Fumé Blanc, Gamay, Pinot Noir, Pomerol (wild mushrooms), Sardinian reds
Mussels	Bianco di Custoza, Chablis, Blanc de Blancs Champagne, Chenin Blanc, fino, Muscadet
Niçoise salade	Provence rosé
Noodles	Dry Muscat
Nut dishes	French oaked Chardonnay (especially Meursault, Puligny-Montrachet)
Nuts	Fino, manzanilla, port, Vin Santo
Nutty desserts	Maury, sweet Muscat
Olive oil/herb dishes	Greek reds
Olives	Fino, manzanilla
Omelettes, herb	Muscadet

Food (Continued)	Wine
Oysters	Blanc de Blancs Champagne, non-vintage brut Champagne, unoaked Chardonnay (especially Chablis), Muscadet
Panforte	Vin Santo
Parma ham and melon	Prosecco, New World sparkling wine
Pasta	Creamy: French oaked Chardonnay (especially Mâcon and Pouilly-Fuissé), New World oaked Chardonnay, Orvieto, Verdicchio Rich: Chianti, Dolcetto, Merlot, Valpolicella Spicy: Salice Salentino see also Bolognese, carbonara, lasagne, pesto, primavera
Pâté	Dry amontillado (chicken liver pâté), Crémant, Gewürztraminer (rich pâtés), Spanish rosé (smoked fish pâtés)
Peaches	Eiswein, Canadian Icewine
Pecan pie	Sweet Muscat, sweet Sémillon
Peppers, baked	Dolcetto
Pesto, pasta	Lugana, Pinot Blanc, Soave
Pheasant	Red Bordeaux, red Châteauneuf-du-Pape, Merlot (especially Californian)
Picnics	Crémant
Pigeon	Red Bordeaux, Cabernet Franc, Chianti Classico, Montepulciano d'Abruzzo
Pineapple	Sauternes
Pissaladière	Provence rosé
Pizza	Cabernet d'Anjou, Dolcetto, Montepulciano d'Abruzzo, Provence rosé
Plaice	Unoaked Chardonnay, Orvieto, Pinot Gris/Pinot Grigio, Rueda
Polenta	Gavi
Pork casseroles	Red Châteauneuf-du-Pape, southern French reds, Gigondas, Greek reds, southern Italian reds (especially Salice Salentino), Malbec, Pinot Gris/ Pinot Grigio (lighter dishes), Pinotage, Portuguese reds, Rhône whites (lighter dishes), Syrah/Shiraz
Pork, grilled/roast	Beaujolais, Cabernet Franc, Chianti, Dolcetto, Gamay, Minervois, Portuguese reds, Rhône whites, Viognier
Pork ribs	Red Châteauneuf-du-Pape, Pinotage, Shiraz
Prawns	Albariño/Alvarinho, rosé Champagne, Chenin Blanc (especially dry Vouvray), fino, Gavi, manzanilla, dry Muscat, Soave

Food (Continued)	Wine
Primavera, pasta	White Bordeaux
Provençale vegetables	Bandol, Cabernet Sauvignon, Corbières, Provence rosé
Pudding, Christmas	Asti, sweet Muscat, cream sherry, Tokaji, Vin Santo
Pudding, sticky toffee	Tojaki
Quiches	Chenin Blanc (vegetarian quiche), Pinot Blanc (Quiche Lorraine), Pinot Gris/Pinot Grigio, Vermentino
Ratatouille	Mourvèdre/Monastrell
Risottos	Barbaresco, Bianco di Custoza, Bordeaux rosés (seafood risotto), Cabernet Franc (mushroom risotto), Chenin Blanc, Grenache/Garnacha, Pinot Blanc, Pinot Noir, Soave
Rosemary-based dishes	Viognier
Salads	White Bergerac, Cabernet d'Anjou (summer salads), Cabernet Franc (cheese salad), Dolcetto, Entre Deux Mers, Gamay (summer salads), white Graves, Jurançon, manzanilla (rocket and Parmesan salad), Pinot Gris/Pinot Grigio, Provence rosé (salade Niçoise), dry Riesling, Rueda
Salami	Barbera, Cabernet Franc, red Côtes du Rhône, Gamay, Grenache/Garnacha
Salmon, barbecued	New World oaked Chardonnay
Salmon, fresh	Cabernet Franc, French oaked Chardonnay, Pinot Noir, Spanish rosé
Salmon, smoked	Blanc de Blancs Champagne, non-vintage brut Champagne, vintage Champagne, New World oaked Chardonnay, dry German Riesling, Sauvignon Blanc (especially Pouilly-Fumé, Sancerre)
Sardines, grilled	Chilean rosé
Sausages	Red Côtes du Rhône, Fitou, Merlot; for spicy sausages Minervois, Mourvèdre/Monastrell, Syrah
Scallops	Vintage Champagne, unoaked Chardonnay (especially Chablis), Chenin Blanc (especially dry Vouvray), Grüner Veltliner
Sea bass	Unoaked Chardonnay, dry Riesling, Tavel
Seafood	Albariño/Alvarinho, Bianco di Custoza, Bordeaux rosé (seafood risotto), non-vintage brut Champagne, oaked Chardonnay (Mâcon, Pouilly-Fuissé for light seafood, Meursault, Puligny-Montrachet for rich seafood), unoaked Chardonnay, Chenin Blanc, Entre Deux Mers, Frascati, Gavi, white Graves, Marsanne, Muscadet, Sauvignon Blanc, dry Sémillon, Verdelho, Viognier
Seafood chowder	New World oaked Chardonnay

Food (Continued)	Wine
Shellfish	see seafood
Shepherd's pie	Malbec
Snapper, red	Alsace Pinot Noir
Sole	Chenin Blanc (especially dry Vouvray), Soave
Soufflé, crab	Entre Deux Mers, Rueda
Soufflé, savoury	White Bergerac (vegetable soufflés), Entre Deux Mers, white Graves (vegetable soufflés)
Spaghetti	see Bolognese, carbonara, pesto, primavera, pasta
Spicy food	Red Côtes du Rhône, Gewürztraminer, New World sparkling wine, Verdelho
Spicy pasta dishes	Salice Salentino
Squid	Grenache/Garnacha, Provence rosé
Steak	Amarone, Barolo, red Bordeaux, New World Cabernet Sauvignon, Carmenère, red Châteauneuf-du-Pape, Chianti, red Rioja, St Émilion, Syrah/Shiraz, red Zinfandel
Steak and kidney pie	Carmenère, Côtes de Bourg, Malbec
Stew, Irish	Southern Italian reds (especially Salice Salentino)
Sticky toffee pudding	Tokaji
Stir-fries	Marsanne, dry Sémillon (chicken stir-fries), Valpolicella
Strawberries	Bonnezeaux, Sauternes
Swordfish	Chilean rosé, Rhône whites, dry Sémillon, Vernaccia
Tapas	Fino, manzanilla
Tarts, fruit	Coteaux du Layon
Thai dishes	Beaujolais cru, non-vintage brut Champagne, Fumé Blanc, Pinot Blanc, Alsace Riesling, Sauvignon Blanc, Vermentino; see also Asian
Tiramisu	Sweet Muscat, Sauternes
Tomato-based dishes	Barbera, southern Italian reds (especially Salice Salentino)
Tomato sauces	Pinot Gris/Pinot Grigio, Sauvignon Blanc
Trifle	Bonnezeaux, sweet sherry, Tokaji
Trout, river	Pinot Gris/Pinot Grigio, French Sauvignon Blanc (especially Pouilly-Fumé, Sancerre)
Trout, sea	Spanish rosé
Trout, smoked	Crémant
Truffles	Cahors, mature French Pinot Noir, red Rioja, St Émilion
Tuna	Cabernet Franc (especially Chinon and Saumur-Champigny), New World Merlot, light-bodied Pinot Noir, dry Sémillon

Food (Continued)	Wine
Turbot	Oaked Chardonnay (especially Meursault, Napa Valley), Viognier (especially Condrieu)
Turkey, roast	Dry amontillado (cold turkey), Barbaresco, Barbera, Cabernet Franc, oaked Chardonnay (especially Meursault, Puligny-Montrachet), Chianti, white Graves, Pinot Noir, French Syrah (especially Crozes-Hermitage), red Zinfandel
Veal	Barbaresco, Barbera, oaked Chardonnay, Chianti, Gavi, Pinot Gris/Pinot Grigio, Pinot Noir
Vegetable dishes	Grenache/Garnacha, Lugana (roasted vegetables), Sardinian reds (vegetable stews), Valpolicella (roasted vegetables)
Vegetarian dishes	Red Côtes du Rhône, Fumé Blanc, Grüner Veltliner, New World Pinot Noir (vegetable gratins), Syrah (vegetable gratins), Viognier (root vegetable dishes)
Venison	Barbaresco, Barolo, red Châteauneuf-du-Pape, French Syrah (especially Hermitage), Shiraz (especially Barossa Valley)
Whitebait	Dry Muscat

Matching wine with food

White	
Albariño/Alvarinho	*Oily or smoked fish, seafood (especially prawns)*
Aligoté, Bourgogne	*Cheese fondue*
Bergerac	*Fish and chips, salads, vegetable soufflés*
Bianco di Custoza	*Couscous, risottos, light seafood (especially mussels)*
Bordeaux	*Goats' cheese, grilled/roast chicken, roast cod, crab, pasta primavera*
Burgundy *see* Chardonnay, French	
Chablis *see* Chardonnay, unoaked	
Chardonnay, oaked, French (Burgundy), e.g. Mâcon, Meursault, Pouilly-Fuissé, Puligny-Montrachet	*Hard cheese, white-mould cheese, grilled/roast chicken (Mâcon, Pouilly-Fuissé), cod (Mâcon), duck, hake (Mâcon), lobster (Meursault), monkfish (Meursault), nut dishes (Meursault, Puligny-Montrachet), creamy pasta dishes (Mâcon, Pouilly-Fuissé), fresh salmon, light seafood (Mâcon, Pouilly-Fuissé), rich seafood (Puligny-Montrachet), turbot, roast turkey (Meursault, Puligny-Montrachet), veal*
Chardonnay, oaked, New World	*Hard cheese, grilled/roast chicken, coconut curry, duck, fish and chips, fish pie, hake, Indian dishes, monkfish, creamy pasta dishes, barbecued or smoked salmon, seafood, seafood chowder, turbot, roast turkey, veal*
Chardonnay, unoaked, e.g. Chablis	*Cream cheese (Chablis), cheese dishes, grilled/roast chicken, simply cooked fish (especially plaice and sea bass), fish and chips, seafood (especially mussels, oysters and scallops) (Chablis)*
Chenin Blanc	*Goats' cheese dishes, chicken in cream sauce, fish (especially hake, sole), risottos, seafood (especially mussels, prawns, scallops), vegetarian quiche*
Condrieu *see* Viognier	
Entre-Deux-Mers	*Crab (especially soufflés), salads, simple seafood, savoury soufflés*
Frascati	*Chicken noodles, pasta carbonara, seafood*
Fumé Blanc	*Grilled/roast chicken, chargrilled or smoked fish, mushroom dishes, Thai dishes, vegetarian dishes*
Gavi	*Polenta, seafood (especially prawns), veal*

White (Continued)

Gewürztraminer	*Asian dishes (especially light Chinese), smoked cheese, washed-rind cheese, foie gras (Alsace Vendange Tardive), fusion food, rich pâtés, spicy food*
Graves	*Fish and chips, fish in rich sauces, guinea fowl, salads, simple seafood, vegetable soufflés, roast turkey*
Grüner Veltliner	*Fish, scallops, vegetarian dishes*
Jura whites	*Cheese fondue*
Jurançon	*Cheese fondue, fish, salads*
Lugana	*Pasta pesto, roasted vegetables*
Mâcon *see* Chardonnay, French oaked	
Marsanne	*Asian dishes (especially light Chinese), grilled/roast chicken, seafood, stir-fries*
Meursault *see* Chardonnay, French oaked	
Muscadet	*Smoked mackerel, herb omelettes, seafood (especially mussels, oysters)*
Muscat	*Light Chinese dishes, Indian dishes, noodles, prawns, whitebait*
Orvieto	*Fish (especially plaice), creamy pasta dishes*
Pinot Blanc	*Couscous, fish, pesto sauce, Quiche Lorraine, risottos, Thai dishes*
Pinot Gris/Pinot Grigio	*Fresh cheese, fish (especially plaice), light pork and bacon dishes, quiches, salads, tomato sauces, river trout, veal*
Pouilly-Fuissé *see* Chardonnay, French oaked	
Pouilly-Fumé *see* Sauvignon Blanc, French	
Puligny-Montrachet *see* Chardonnay, French oaked	
Rhône whites	*Mature hard cheese, creamy curries, grilled/roast pork, light pork dishes, swordfish*
Riesling, dry	*Aperitifs, fresh cheese, grilled fish, goose, ham, Indian dishes (German wines), Japanese dishes, cold meats, salads, smoked salmon, sea bass, Thai dishes (Alsace wines)*
Riesling, off-dry	*Curries, dim sum, smoked fish, fusion food*
Rioja	*Cheese fondue, ham*
Rueda	*Crab (especially soufflés), grilled fish, plaice, salads*
Sancerre *see* Sauvignon Blanc, French	

White (Continued)

Sauvignon Blanc, French, e.g. Pouilly-Fumé, Sancerre	*Avocado, fresh cheese, goats' cheese, light Chinese dishes, fish (especially fish and chips, smoked fish, red mullet, river trout), Japanese dishes, seafood, Thai dishes, tomato sauces*
Sauvignon Blanc, New World	*Asparagus, crab, fish (especially fish and chips, red mullet), seafood, Thai dishes, tomato sauces*
Savennières *see* Chenin Blanc	
Savoie whites	*Cheese fondue*
Sémillon	*Hard cheese (especially Gruyère), chicken stir-fry, fish (especially cod, swordfish, tuna), seafood*
Soave	*Light chicken dishes, fish (especially hake, sole), pesto sauce, prawns, risottos*
Torrontés	*Asian dishes (especially light Chinese), chicken in cream sauces (especially chicken Véronique)*
Verdelho	*Indian dishes, seafood, spicy food*
Verdicchio	*Fish (especially hake), creamy pasta dishes*
Vermentino	*Cheese dishes, fish (especially cod), quiches, Thai dishes*
Vernaccia	*Fish (especially swordfish)*
Viognier	*Grilled/roast chicken, cod, crab, mild curries, lobster, grilled/roast pork, dishes cooked with rosemary, seafood, turbot, root vegetable dishes*
Vouvray *see* Chenin Blanc	

Red

Amarone	*Roast beef, game, rich meat dishes, steak*
Bairrada	*Beef casseroles*
Bandol	*Bean dishes, white-mould cheese, grilled/ roast lamb, liver, Provençal vegetables*
Barbaresco	*Risottos, roast turkey, veal, venison*
Barbera	*Antipasti, Bolognese sauce, hard cheese (especially mature), ham, lasagne, salami, tomato-based dishes, roast turkey, veal*
Barolo	*Peppered beef, roast beef, goose, Parmesan, steak, venison*
Beaujolais *see* Gamay	
Bergerac	*Grilled/roast chicken, grilled/roast lamb*

Red (Continued)

Bordeaux (claret)	*Roast beef, white-mould cheese, duck, goose, grilled/roast lamb, pheasant, pigeon, steak*
Burgundy *see* Pinot Noir, French	
Cabernet Franc	*Cheese dishes (especially gratins), cheese salad, grilled/roast chicken, grilled/roast lamb, light meat dishes, red mullet, mushroom risottos, pigeon, grilled/roast pork, salami, fresh salmon, tuna, roast turkey*
Cabernet Sauvignon	*Barbecued beef, beef casseroles, roast beef, mature hard cheese, goose, hamburgers, grilled/roast lamb, steak, Provençale vegetables*
Cabernet Sauvignon/Shiraz blends	*Mature hard cheese, goose*
Cahors *see* Malbec	
Carmenère	*Roast beef, steak, steak and kidney pie*
Châteauneuf-du-Pape	*Roast beef, grilled/roast chicken, game (especially pheasant), goose, grilled/roast lamb, meat casseroles, mushroom dishes, pork ribs, steak, venison*
Chianti *see* Sangiovese	
Chinon *see* Cabernet Franc	
Corbières	*Chilli con carne, lamb casseroles, meatballs, Provençale vegetables*
Côte-Rôtie *see* Syrah, French	
Côtes de Bourg	*Hard cheese, grilled/roast chicken, steak and kidney pie*
Côtes du Rhône	*Arrabiata sauce, beef casseroles, soy-based Chinese dishes, salami, sausages, spicy food, vegetarian dishes*
Crozes-Hermitage *see* Syrah, French	
Dolcetto	*Cheese fondue, rich pasta dishes (especially Bolognese sauce), baked peppers, pizza, grilled/roast pork, salads*
Fitou	*Bean dishes, light chicken dishes, sausages*
Fleurie *see* Gamay	
French reds (south of France)	*Bean dishes, liver, pork casseroles*
Gamay	*Washed-rind cheese, white-mould cheese, grilled/roast chicken, soy-based Chinese dishes, cold meats (especially salami), mushroom dishes, grilled/roast pork, summer salads, Thai dishes*

Red (Continued)

Gigondas	*Mature hard cheese, duck, grilled/roast lamb, meat casseroles*
Greek reds	*Lamb kebabs, moussaka, olive oil/herb dishes, pork casseroles*
Grenache/Garnacha	*Couscous, Indian dishes, lamb kebabs, risottos, salami, squid, vegetable dishes*
Hermitage *see* Syrah, French	
Italian reds (south of Italy)	*Meat casseroles, Irish stew, tomato-based dishes*
Loire reds *see* Cabernet Franc	
Madiran	*Beef casseroles, cassoulet, strong cheeses, duck*
Malbec	*Bean dishes, barbecued beef, confit, duck, macaroni cheese, meat casseroles, shepherd's pie, steak and kidney pie, truffles*
Merlot	*Spicy chicken wings, cottage pie, goose, grilled/roast lamb (Californian Merlot), lambs' liver, meatballs, rich pasta dishes (especially Bolognese sauce), pheasant, sausages, tuna*
Minervois	*Grilled/roast lamb, grilled/roast pork, spicy sausages*
Monastrell *see* Mourvèdre	
Montepulciano d'Abruzzo	*Light chicken dishes, hamburgers, lasagne, pigeon, pizza*
Mourvèdre/Monastrell	*Lamb casseroles, ratatouille, spicy sausages*
Navarra	*Duck, guinea fowl, grilled/roast lamb*
Pinot Noir, French	*Washed-rind cheese, white-mould cheese, grilled/roast chicken, duck, light game, goose, gratins, guinea fowl, ham, kidneys, red mullet, mushroom dishes, fresh salmon, red snapper (Alsace Pinot Noir), truffles, tuna, roast turkey, veal, vegetable risottos*
Pinot Noir, New World	*Hard cheese, washed-rind cheese, white-mould cheese, grilled/roast chicken, soy-based Chinese dishes, duck, light game, goose, guinea fowl, ham, mushroom dishes, risottos, fresh salmon, tuna, roast turkey, veal, vegetable gratins*
Pinotage	*Barbecued beef, smoked cheese, pork casseroles, pork ribs*
Pomerol	*Hard cheese, grilled/roast lamb, wild mushroom dishes*

Red (Continued)

Portuguese reds	*Aubergine dishes, chorizo, lamb kebabs, pork casseroles, grilled/roast pork*
Rhône reds	*Beef casseroles*
Ribera del Duero	*Duck, guinea fowl, grilled/roast lamb*
Rioja *see* Tempranillo	
St Émilion	*Roast beef, white-mould cheese, duck, grilled/roast lamb, steak, truffles*
Salice Salentino	*Aubergine dishes, meat casseroles, moussaka, spicy pasta dishes (especially pasta arrabiata), Irish stew, tomato-based dishes*
Sangiovese	*Beef casseroles, roast beef, hamburgers, lasagne, rich pasta dishes (especially Bolognese sauce), pigeon, grilled/roast pork, steak, roast turkey, veal*
Sardinian reds	*Mushroom dishes, vegetable stews*
Saumur-Champigny *see* Cabernet Franc	
Shiraz, New World *see also* Syrah, French	*Barbecued beef, roast beef, hard cheese, chilli dishes, duck, goose, meat casseroles, pasta arrabiata, pork ribs, steak, venison*
Shiraz/Cabernet Sauvignon blends	*Mature hard cheese, goose*
Syrah, French *see also* Shiraz, New World	*Roast beef, hard cheese, game (especially venison), meat casseroles, spicy sausages, steak, roast turkey, vegetable gratins*
Tempranillo	*Roast beef, grilled/roast chicken, guinea fowl, hamburgers, lamb (especially with garlic or rosemary), steak, truffles*
Valdepeñas	*Bean dishes, chicken in cream sauce, meatballs*
Valpolicella	*Bresaola, ham, rich pasta dishes (especially Bolognese sauce), stir-fries, roasted vegetables*
Zinfandel	*Bean dishes, barbecued beef, roast beef, soy-based Chinese dishes, confit, steak, roast turkey*

Rosé

Bordeaux	*Bouillabaisse, seafood risotto*
Cabernet d'Anjou	*Aperitifs, pizza, summer salads*
Chilean	*Grilled sardines, swordfish*
Provence	*Anchovy dishes, spicy chicken wings, pissaladière, pizza, Provençale vegetables, salade Niçoise, squid*

Rosé (Continued)	
Spanish	*Smoked fish pâté, fresh salmon, sea trout*
Tavel	*Couscous, sea bass*

Sparkling	
Asti	*Cheesecake, fruit salad, meringue, mince pies, Christmas pudding*
Cava	*Aperitifs, light Chinese dishes, fish and chips, smoked fish, guacamole*
Champagne, Blanc de Blancs	*Aperitifs, light Chinese dishes, fish and chips, smoked fish (especially smoked salmon), Japanese dishes, mussels, oysters*
Champagne, demi-sec	*Cake, desserts*
Champagne, non-vintage Brut	*Aperitifs, fish and chips, fresh salmon, seafood (especially oysters), Thai dishes*
Champagne, rosé	*Grilled/roast chicken, Indian dishes, prawns*
Champagne, vintage	*Smoked duck, fresh salmon, scallops*
Crémant	*Pâté, picnics, smoked trout*
New World	*Fish, Parma ham and melon, Japanese dishes, spicy food*
Prosecco	*Aperitifs, Parma ham and melon*
Sekt	*Kedgeree*

Fortified/sweet	
Amontillado, dry	*Blue cheese, chicken liver pâté, consommé, mushroom dishes, cold roast turkey*
Amontillado, sweet	*Trifle*
Banyuls	*Blue cheese, chocolate cake*
Bonnezeaux	*Fruit desserts, marzipan, strawberries, trifle*
Coteaux du Layon	*Fruit desserts, fruit tarts (especially apple)*
Eiswein	*Fruit desserts (especially apple), peaches*
Fino	*Tapas, e.g. salted almonds, anchovies, olives; Japanese dishes, mussels, nuts, prawns*
Icewine, Canadian	*Fruit desserts, peaches*
Madeira, dry	*Blue cheese, strong hard cheese*
Madeira, sweet	*Christmas cake, mince pies*
Málaga Moscatel	*Chocolate cake, chocolate desserts*

Fortified/sweet (Continued)

Manzanilla	Tapas, e.g. salted almonds, cured ham, olives, rocket and Parmesan salad; fried fish, nuts, prawns
Maury	Chocolate cakes and desserts, nutty desserts
Monbazillac	Blue cheese, custard-based desserts, foie gras, fruit desserts
Muscat	Cheesecake, chocolate cakes and desserts, crème brûlée, crème caramel, fruit salad, ice cream, meringue, mince pies, nutty desserts, pecan pie, Christmas pudding, tiramisu
Muscat de Beaumes de Venise	Fruit crumbles
Oloroso, dry	Blue cheese, mature hard cheese
Oloroso, sweet	Rich fruit cake, trifle
Orange Muscat	Crêpes Suzette
Port	Blue cheese (especially Stilton), hard cheese (especially Cheddar), mince pies, nuts
Riesling	Fruit desserts, fruit salad
Sauternes	Blue cheese (especially Roquefort), chocolate cake, custard-based desserts (especially crème brûlée, crème caramel), foie gras, pineapple, strawberries, tiramisu
Sémillon	Custard-based desserts, pecan pie
Sherry, cream	Crème brûlée, vanilla ice cream, mince pies, marzipan desserts, Christmas pudding, trifle
Tokaji	Blue cheese, crème brûlée, crème caramel, Christmas pudding, sticky toffee pudding, trifle
Vin Santo	Apple desserts/tarts, cantucci biscuits, meringue, nuts, panforte, Christmas pudding
Vouvray	Baked fruit desserts (especially apple tart)

Grape varieties *Pat Carroll*

The market in Ireland is dominated by the Big Six—Cabernet Sauvignon, Chardonnay, Merlot, Syrah/Shiraz, Sauvignon Blanc and Pinot Noir. Undoubtedly these are great grapes that make great wines, but there are so many other varieties worth trying. Listed below is a selection of grape varieties from all over the world. Some are grown only in their local environment, while others have taken on another life elsewhere, mainly in the New World. The white grape Verdelho, for example, is now grown successfully in Australia, a long way from its Iberian roots. Experimentation in growing grapes continues all the time—don't be surprised to see Italian varieties such as Sangiovese being grown in Chile or (a New World–New World transplant) the South African variety Pinotage in New Zealand.

Some transplants work better than others. Carmenère grows much more successfully in Chile than in its native Bordeaux, where it has practically ceased to exist due to poor fruit set causing low yields. Malbec in Argentina is another example of a French grape happily putting its roots down in foreign soil. But it doesn't always work that way. Experimental plantings of the Italian grape Nebbiolo in Chile have not been successful and will be discontinued by Errázuriz.

This section gives basic information on over seventy grape varieties and lists the principal wines where the grapes are found. Whether it is indigenous or imported from elsewhere, each grape has something to offer.

White

Albariño/Alvarinho (Galicia, Spain; N Portugal)	
Dry, aromatic, lemon/peach aromas, full flavours of citrus and peaches, firm backbone of acidity; can become honeyed with age but usually drunk young	*Rías Baixas, Vinho Verde*

Catarratto (Sicily)	
Dry or sweet, three clones: *normale*, *lucido* and *extra lucido*: the high-quality *extra lucido* makes wine with grapefruit/apricot flavours and firm acidity	*Marsala, IGT Sicilia*

Chardonnay (originally from Burgundy but now grown everywhere)

Chameleon—ranges from very dry, light, minerally, high-acid, citrus-dominated wines from cooler climates to dryish oaked heavyweights full of butterscotch, peaches, melons and pineapples from hotter regions; affinity with oak-cask ageing	*Champagne, white Burgundy, including Chablis, Mâcon, Marsannay, Meursault, Montagny, Montrachet, Pouilly-Fuissé and Rully; varietal from Argentina, Australia, Bulgaria, California, Chile, New Zealand, South Africa*

Chenin Blanc/Pineau/Steen (Loire; South Africa; California)

Dry to sweet, pale lemon in youth maturing to pale gold in older sweet wines, honey, wet wool and damp straw flavours, possibly nuts and marmalade in mature sweet wines; high acidity ensures that Loire sweet wines will age for decades	*Dry: Savennières; South African varietals; mass-produced Californian blends* *Dry/medium dry/sweet: Vouvray* *Sweet: Bonnezeaux, Coteaux du Layon, Montlouis, Quarts de Chaume* *Sparkling: Saumur Mousseux*

Colombard/Colombar (SW France, California, South Africa, Australia)

Originally used in Armagnac and Cognac, Colombard's high yields, crisp acidity, floral aromas and peachy fruit flavours made it ideal for jug wines in California's Central Valley; now enjoying success as a Vin de Pays in SW France	*Vin de Pays des Côtes de Gascogne, Vin de Pays des Charentais; varietal or blended in New World*

Cortese (Piedmont, NW Italy)

Dry, crisp wines with fresh acidity, slightly floral, lemony aromas and steely lemon fruit	*Gavi*

Fiano (Campania, Puglia, Sicily)

Dry, full-bodied, peachy, spicy wine with flowery overtones; can take some oak and can age well	*Fiano di Avellino, Cilento, Puglia DOCs, IGT Sicilia*

Furmint/Mosler/Zapfner (Hungary, mainly Tokaji region; Burgenland, Austria)

Dry or sweet, very high in acidity, high in alcohol, long lived, rich, fiery flavours—smoke, pears and citrus for dry wines, apricots, marzipan, citrus and spice for sweet wines	*Principal ingredient of Tokaji, Hungary's ancient sweet wine; Hungarian dry wines; Ausbruch (sweet) wines from Austria*

Garganega (Veneto, NE Italy)

Dry, aromas of lemon and almonds in the best wines, fresh and fruity; drink very young	*Soave (with Trebbiano—dry), Recioto di Soave (sweet)*

Gewurztraminer/Gewürztraminer (Alsace; Germany; Austria; Chile; New Zealand; Australia)

Medium dry to sweet, colour can be deep; very characteristic perfumed aromas of lychees, roses and spice, flowery flavour but lacking the acidity of Riesling; classic accompaniment to spicy food	*Varietal from Alsace, Germany, Austria, Chile, New Zealand, Australia*

Greco Bianco (Calabria, Campania, Puglia, Tuscany)

Dry or sweet, crisp, fresh wine with a hint of minerals and apples	*Greco di Tufo, Calabria and Campania DOCs; a sweet Greco di Bianco is also produced in Calabria*

Grillo (Sicily)

Dry or sweet, lemony fruit with some earthiness, full-bodied with good structure	*Marsala, IGT Sicilia*

Gros Manseng (SW France)

Dry but occasionally sweet, high acidity, floral, apricots and spice; character changes depending on soil	*Béarn, Irouléguy, Jurançon, Pacherenc du Vic Bilh*

Grüner Veltliner (Austria)

Dry, occasionally sweet, not much aroma in youth, complex, grapefruit, peppery, spicy flavours, ages well, taking on honey tones	*Grüner Veltliner varietals*

Inzolia/Ansonica/Anzonica (Sicily, Tuscany)

Dry or sweet, low-yielding grape, making delicate, nutty wines with firm acidity	*Marsala, IGT Sicilia, blended in some Tuscan whites*

Macabeo/Maccabéo/Viura (Spain; S France)

Nearly always dry, floral character, lowish acidity, resists oxidation well, sometimes blended into red wines	*In Spain whites from Alella, Bullas, Campo de Borja, Penedès, Rioja, Rueda, Utiel-Requena, part of Cava blends; in France white Corbières, rosé Coteaux du Languedoc, white Côtes du Roussillon, Fitou, white Minervois, vins doux naturels*

Malvasia/Malmsey (Friuli, NE Italy; central Italy; Sardinia; Madeira)

Ancient grape, making dry to sweet styles, pale lemon (dry) to deep amber (sweet), nuts, cream and apricots, slightly spicy; early drinking or long ageing	*Collio, Isonzo, blended with Trebbiano in Frascati and central Italian whites; sweet wines in Sardinia; Madeira*

Marsanne (Rhône; Australia)

Dry, deep coloured, full bodied, peach, honeysuckle and almond aromas (melons and mangos in Australia), quite heavy, usually matured in oak, often blended with Roussanne	*White Coteaux du Tricastin, white Côtes du Rhône, white Crozes-Hermitage, white Hermitage, white St Joseph, St Péray; varietal in Australia, e.g. Ch. Tahbilk*

Melon de Bourgogne/Muscadet (Loire)

Very dry, light, fresh, crisp, some green apple flavours but often fairly neutral; best examples are 'sur lie' (matured in barrels containing yeast sediment); classic seafood wine	*In ascending order of quality— Muscadet, Muscadet de Sèvre et Maine, Muscadet de Sèvre et Maine Sur Lie*

Müller-Thurgau/Rivaner (Germany)

Usually off-dry to medium-sweet wines, light in colour, not much aroma or acidity; not a quality grape; drink young	*Liebfraumilch blends and some varietals*

Muscat (Alsace; Rhône; Italy; Australia; Greece)

Dry to very sweet, pale lemon (dry) to deep amber (sweet), marked grape and musk aromas, scented fruity flavours, touch of spice, moderate acidity	*Dry: Muscat d'Alsace*
	Sparkling medium sweet: Asti Spumante
	Sweet: vins doux naturels from France, e.g. Muscat de Beaumes de Venise; liqueur Muscats from Australia and Greece

Palomino (Jerez, Spain; South Africa; Australia; California)

Low acidity, low sugar levels and its tendency to oxidise make Palomino the perfect grape for dry, medium or sweet sherry	*All styles of sherry—manzanilla, fino, amontillado, oloroso, palo cortado*

Parellada (Spain)

Dry, lemon and flower aromas, zesty acidity, apple fruit; drink very young	*Blended in Spanish sparkling wine Cava and white Costers del Segre; 100% in Torres' Viña Sol*

Pinot Blanc/Pinot Bianco/Weissburgunder (Alsace; Italy; Germany; Austria)

Mostly dry, some apple aromas, almonds in Austria, soft, quite full bodied, moderate/high acidity; usually for early drinking	*Alsace varietal; Italian varietal or blend, e.g. Colli Orientale del Friuli, Collio; Italian sparkling wine; dry wines from Pfalz and Baden; sweet and dry wines from Austria*

Pinot Gris (formerly Tokay d'Alsace)/Pinot Grigio/Ruländer/ Grauburgunder (Alsace; NE Italy; Germany; Austria; Australia; New Zealand; Oregon)

In Alsace styles range from dry to sweet, with fairly deep colour and quite full body, slightly spicy, floral, perfumed aromas, peach fruit that develops buttery flavours with age; rich and spicy wine; drier, lighter, crisper and not so aromatic in Italy	*Varietal in Alsace; varietal in Italy or part of the blend in Collio; varietal elsewhere*

Prosecco (NE Italy)

Dry or off-dry sparkling wine, fresh, appley, moderate acidity; drink young	*Prosecco, mainly sparkling, but some semi-sparkling and a little still wine*

Riesling (Germany; Alsace; Austria; Australia; New Zealand; USA; South Africa)

Dry to sweet, pale straw with green hints to deep gold in older sweet wines, floral and honey aromas when young, developing petrol-like notes on ageing; apple or peach flavours in Europe (depending on sweetness), limes in New World, piercing acidity, rich fruit on the palate; can age for decades	*Made usually as a 100% varietal, from dry to sweet, in Germany (Mosel-Saar-Ruwer, Rheingau, Pfalz, Nahe), Alsace, Austria, Australia, New Zealand (Marlborough and Central Otago), California, Oregon, Washington State, South Africa*

Roussanne (Rhône; Languedoc-Roussillon)

Dry, aromatic, herbal aromas, elegant, good acidity, flowery, becoming nutty with age; often blended with Marsanne	*White Châteauneuf-du-Pape, white Coteaux du Tricastin, white Côtes du Rhône, white Crozes-Hermitage, white Hermitage, white St Joseph, St Péray, whites from S France*

Sauvignon Blanc (Loire; Bordeaux; New Zealand; Chile; California; South Africa; Australia)

Dry or sweet, grassy, herbaceous, gooseberries, green apples, even cat's pee aromas, with citrus and green apple flavours, steely acidity; mostly for early drinking	*Sancerre, Pouilly-Fumé, part of the blend in white Bordeaux and Sauternes; varietal from New Zealand (especially Marlborough), Chile, California (oaked), South Africa, Australia (often blended)*

Sauvignon Gris/Sauvignon Rosé (France; Chile)

Dry or sweet, pink skin, more power and aroma than Sauvignon Blanc; more floral than citrus/grassy aromas	*Favoured by some Pessac-Léognan and Graves producers, who find that it adds weight to their whites; Chilean producer Cousiño Macul makes a 100% Sauvignon Gris*

Sauvignon Vert/Sauvignonasse (Chile)

Dry or sweet, green apple aromas; loses acidity with high alcohol, so can be flabby; still blended with Sauvignon Blanc in many Chilean wines	*Thought to be Sauvignon Blanc in Chile until the 1990s, but lacks its intensity of flavour; thought to be the same grape as Tocai Friulano*

Sémillon/Semillon (Bordeaux; Australia; South Africa)

Dry to sweet, light in colour to deep gold, not much aroma when young, perhaps some toast or wax, lowish acidity, but matures to nutty, waxy, honeyed aromas in Australia and honey and marmalade In Sauternes and Barsac; citrus and nuts on the palate in drier wines, marmalade and honey in sweet wines; very long-lived wines	*Most important grape in Sauternes, Barsac and white Bordeaux; varietal in the Hunter Valley and Barossa Valley; often blended with Chardonnay or Sauvignon Blanc in Australian wines; blended or varietal in South Africa*

Tocai Friulano (Friuli-Venezia Giulia, NE Italy; New York State)

Dry, light colour, floral/apple aromas, good acidity, full-bodied but not strongly flavoured (the way the Italians like it); drink young	*Colli Orientali, Grave del Friuli, Isonzo, New York State; no connection with Tokay d'Alsace (Pinot Gris) or the Hungarian dessert wine Tokaj; thought to be the same grape as Sauvignon Vert/Sauvignonasse*

Torrontés (Argentina; Spain)

Dry, with distinctive flowery, Muscat-like fragrant nose, zesty acidity, rich, peachy fruit, some citrus; early drinking	*Blended or varietal*

Trebbiano/Ugni Blanc (Italy; SW France)

Dry, light, high acidity, quite neutral flavour, medium body, workaday grape; early drinking	*Found in Trebbiano d'Abruzzo, Trebbiano di Romagna, Orvieto, Frascati, Soave, Lugana, Galestro, Vin de Pays des Côtes de Gascogne; base wine for French Cognac and Armagnac*

Verdejo (Spain)

Dry, aromatic, slightly grassy character, pear flavours, good body; most drunk young but can age well, developing slightly nutty, honeyed nuances	*Rueda (blended with Viura or Sauvignon Blanc), Toro, Cigales*

Verdelho/Godello/Gouveio (Portugal; Spain; Australia; Madeira)

Dry, fresh, lively, lemony wines of good quality; good ageing potential	*Dry whites from the Douro Valley, Spain and Australia; Madeira*

Verdicchio (Marches, central Italy)

Dry, pale straw with green tinge, crisp, lemony acidity, nutty flavour with a mineral, salty edge, slight bitter almonds finish; drink young, though best can age for five years; good with seafood; semi-sweet and sweet wines also made	*Verdicchio dei Castelli di Jesi, Verdicchio di Matelica (white and sparkling)*

Vernaccia (Italy, especially Tuscany)

Dry, crisp acidity, steely, citrus flavour, good body	*Several different Vernaccia wines in Italy, but the best is Vernaccia di San Gimignano*

Viognier (Rhône; Languedoc-Roussillon; Australia; California; South Africa)

Dry, pale straw developing to pale gold, apricot, peach and spring blossom aromas becoming honeyed with maturity, deep, rich palate with apricot and peach flavours, quite high alcohol; drink young, less than eight years old; moderate to low acidity	*Condrieu (vast majority dry, but a few producers make demi-sec wines), Ch. Grillet; can appear in Côte Rôtie; increasingly used in white Côtes du Rhône; vins de pays from Languedoc-Roussillon; varietal elsewhere*

Xarel-lo/Pansá Blanca (Spain, especially Penedès)

Dry, aromatic, fairly high acidity, vegetal, strong, earthy flavours	*Part of the blend in white Alella, Cava, white Costers del Segre, white Penedès, white Tarragona*

Red

Aghiorghitiko/St George (Greece, mainly on the Peloponnese in Nemea)

Versatile grape, rich colour, very fruity, with spice, plums, blueberries, lowish acidity, soft tannins, full bodied, blends well with Cabernet Sauvignon; best wines from higher altitudes, as acidity retained	*Sole constituent of Nemea, ranging from fruity, early-drinking wines to meaty wines with longevity; also makes good rosés*

Aglianico (S Italy, particularly Campania and Basilicata)

Deep colour, aromatic, concentrated smoky berry fruit, tobacco tones, good acidity, very tannic in youth	*Taurasi, Aglianico del Vulture, Aglianico del Taburno*

Baga/Poerininha/Tinta Bairrada/Tinta de Baga/Tinta Fina (Portugal, particularly Bairrada, Dão, Ribatejo)

A thick-skinned and tannic grape; formerly wines had to be aged for 10–15 years before the tannins softened, but modern vinification techniques produce a softer, rounder, fruitier wine; most widely planted variety in Portugal	*Bairrada, Dão, Ribatejo wines*

Barbera (Piedmont, NW Italy; Argentina; Australia; California)

Deep ruby, fruity, full bodied, high acidity, not very tannic; for early drinking	*Barbera d'Alba, Barbera d'Asti, Barbera del Monferrato; varietal elsewhere*

Blaufränkisch/Lemberger/Limberger/Kékfrankos (Austria; Germany; Hungary; Washington State)

Similar characteristics to Gamay, with which it has been confused; good colour, tannin, high acidity, earthy, cherry/redcurrant flavours	*Varietal or blended in Austria and Germany; part of Bull's Blood from Hungary; varietal in Washington State*

Bonarda (Argentina; N Italy)

Dense, fruity, plummy, full-bodied, soft wines	*Rising star in Argentina; Oltrepò Pavese in Italy*

Brunello (Tuscany, central Italy)

Relative of Sangiovese, but with more flavour and body; plums, prunes and spice, fair bit of tannin, ages well	*Brunello di Montalcino*

Cabernet Franc (Bordeaux; Loire; Australia; California; Washington State)

Fragrant, lighter in colour and less tannic than its relative, Cabernet Sauvignon; redcurrant fruit, medium body	*Blended in Bordeaux, playing a more important role on the right bank of the Gironde in the St Émilion/Pomerol area; on its own or blended in Loire reds—Saumur-Champigny, Bourgueil, Chinon, Anjou-Villages; blended or varietal in New World*

Cabernet Sauvignon (originally from Bordeaux but now planted world wide)

Deep ruby with a purple tinge, blackcurrants, chocolate, violets, green peppers, cigar-box aromas when mature, firm tannins; capable of very long ageing; good affinity with oak-cask maturing	*Blended in Bordeaux clarets, ranging in quality from AC Bordeaux through crus bourgeois to crus classés; on its own or blended in Australia (with Shiraz), California (with Merlot etc.); Chile, Italy (Supertuscans), South Africa, Spain, Romania, Bulgaria—everywhere*

Carignan/Cariñena/Mazuelo (S France; Sardinia; Rioja, Priorat, Tarragona in Spain)

Lots of colour, tannin, alcohol and bitterness, but little fruit or aroma; some good examples from old vines in S France, but mostly blended with Cinsault and Grenache	*Part of the blend in many Languedoc-Roussillon wines such as Corbières, Costières de Nîmes, Coteaux du Languedoc, Côtes du Roussillon, Faugères, Fitou, Minervois, St Chinian; Carignano del Sulcis from Sardinia; can be part of blend in Rioja, Priorat and Tarragona*

Carmenère/Grande Vidure (Chile; Bordeaux)

Deep ruby, red berry fruit aromas, soft red fruit flavours, mulberries, hint of chocolate, grilled meat, full bodied, similar to Merlot but less ageing potential	*Grown and bottled with Merlot in Chile for years, Carmenère is now produced as a varietal in its own right; rarely grown in Bordeaux*

Castelão/Periquita/Castelão Francês (S Portugal)

Medium colour, raspberry fruit, lowish acidity, mellow tannins, good for early drinking	*Often blended in Portuguese reds, especially in the south; J M da Fonseca's Periquita is one of Portugal's best-known wines*

Cinsault/Cinsaut/Hermitage (S France; Lebanon; South Africa)

Pale, soft, light, quite perfumed and fruity; used a lot for rosé in France	*Blended in Languedoc-Roussillon wines such as Corbières, Costières de Nîmes, Côtes du Roussillon, Faugères, St Chinian; blended with Cabernet Sauvignon and Syrah in Ch. Musar (Lebanon); crossed with Pinot Noir in South Africa to produce the Pinotage grape*

Corvina (Veneto, NE Italy)

Light in colour, cherry and floral aromas, fruity wines with a hint of almond, lively acidity, low tannin; thick skins make it suitable for drying	*Up to 70% of the blend in Valpolicella, Recioto and Amarone Valpolicellas, Bardolino*

Dolcetto (Piedmont, NW Italy)

Deep purple-ruby colour, soft, gentle wine with a touch of liquorice; drink young	*Dolcetto varietals, e.g. Dolcetto d'Alba*

Dornfelder (Germany; UK)

Good colour, juicy, red berry flavours, can age for two to three years; variety developed for the German climate	*Dornfelder varietals*

Gamay (Beaujolais; Loire)

Pale in colour with a bluish tinge, light wine with juicy red fruit aromas; some people find bananas and boiled sweets; drink very young	*Beaujolais, Beaujolais crus (Brouilly, Chénas, Chiroubles, Côte de Brouilly, Fleurie, Juliénas, Morgon, Moulin-à-Vent, Regnié, St Amour), Cheverny, St Pourçain*

Grenache/Garnacha/Cannonau (Rhône; S France; Spain; Sardinia; Australia; California)

Fairly light colour, fruity, juicy, slightly sweet raspberry fruit, lowish tannin and acidity, high alcohol; can be spicy if not overcropped; huge variation in quality	*One of the ingredients in Châteauneuf-du-Pape; S France reds and rosés, vins doux naturels such as Rivesaltes and Banyuls (great with chocolate desserts); Spanish Priorato and Rioja; Cannonau di Sardegna; blended or varietal wines in Australia and California*

Malbec/Cot (Argentina; Cahors, SW France)

Dark-coloured, ripe, tannic wines with good concentration and blackberry flavour; can be austere, peppery, spicy; wines age well	*Argentinian varietal; part of the blend in Cahors and other wines from SW France*

Marselan (S France)

Tiny berries; deep colour, soft, plummy flavours with a spicy edge; retains some of the structure and tannin of its Cabernet Sauvignon parent, but with the juiciness and spice of Grenache	*A 1961 cross of Grenache and Cabernet Sauvignon but registered as an official variety only in 1990, Marselan was authorised as a vin de pays grape in 2005. Also being grown experimentally in Argentina*

Merlot (Bordeaux; S/SW France; Italy; California; Washington State; South America; Bulgaria; Romania; Australia; New Zealand)

Deep ruby, smooth, plummy, maturing to rich fruit cake flavours—velvety texture, with less colour, tannin and acidity than Cabernet Sauvignon; softer and earlier maturing	*Generic Bordeaux, St Émilion, Pomerol, Buzet, Cahors, vins de pays from S France, N Italian varietal, US varietal or Meritage (a blend of Cabernet Sauvignon, Merlot, Cabernet Franc, Malbec and Petit Verdot); varietal elsewhere*

Molinara (Veneto, NE Italy)

Pale colour, high acidity, juicy, easy drinking	*With Rondinella, up to 30% of the blend in Valpolicella, Recioto and Amarone Valpolicellas, Bardolino*

Montepulciano (central Italy, mainly Abruzzo)

Deeply coloured, rich, brambles, cherries, pepper, spice, zesty acidity, firm tannins, best can age well	*Montepulciano d'Abruzzo, Rosso Conero, Biferno, Rosso Piceno (NB: Vino Nobile di Montepulciano is made with Sangiovese, not Montepulciano)*

Mourvèdre/Monastrell/Mataro (Provence; S Rhône; Languedoc-Roussillon; Spain; Barossa Valley, Australia; California; Chile)

Lots of blackberry fruit, fleshy, high in alcohol and tannin, slightly meaty flavour in youth; blends well with Grenache or Cinsault, giving structure	*Blended in Bandol, Côtes du Rhône, Côtes du Ventoux, Vacqueyras, Costières de Nîmes, Côtes du Roussillon, Faugères, Fitou, Minervois, St Chinian; used in many Spanish DOs, e.g. Alicante, Almansa, Jumilla, Valencia, Yecla; varietal or blend elsewhere*

Nebbiolo (Piedmont, NW Italy; Argentina; Australia; California; South Africa)

Not very deep colour, but powerful truffle, raspberry, liquorice, chocolate and prune aromas—even violets; high acidity, very firm tannins; usually needs long ageing	*Barolo, Barbaresco, Gattinara, Nebbiolo d'Alba, Valtellina; varietal elsewhere*

Negroamaro (Puglia, S Italy)

Deep colour, high alcohol, rich, robust red wines, some of which can age well	*Salice Salentino, Rosso di Cerignola*

Nero d'Avola (Sicily)

Dark colour, soft fruit, rich texture, responds well to barrel maturation and oak ageing	*Nero d'Avola*

Petit Verdot (Bordeaux; California)

Rich colour, hint of violets on the nose, concentrated tannic wines with a touch of spice	*Used as a small part of the blend in Bordeaux clarets and Californian Meritage wines*

Petite Sirah (California; South America)

Inky, quite tannic, firm, robust, full-bodied wines	*Unrelated to the Syrah of the Rhône; traditionally blended with Zinfandel in California, now offered as a varietal as well; varietal in South America*

Pinot Meunier (Champagne; Australia; California)

Gives freshness, fruitiness and crisp acidity to sparkling wines	*Champagne; sparkling wines from Australia and California*

Pinot Noir/Pinot Nero/Spätburgunder (Burgundy; Champagne; Loire; Alsace; Austria; Germany; Italy; California; Oregon; Australia; New Zealand; South Africa; Romania; Chile)

Light in colour and low in tannin, quite high acidity, magical sweet aromas of strawberries or cherries, turning to mushrooms, truffles and even farmyards as it ages; velvety texture; long ageing; used in sparkling wines to give body and fruit; best in cool, marginal climates	*Red Burgundy from basic Bourgogne to Grand Cru; blended in Champagne; used in sparkling wines from the New World; red Menetou-Salon, red Sancerre; varietal elsewhere*

Pinotage (South Africa; New Zealand)

South African crossing of Pinot Noir and Cinsault, deep colour, strong tannins; best have good body and juicy berry fruit	*South African varietal and Cape blends; New Zealand varietal*

Primitivo (Puglia, S Italy)

Deep colour, early maturing, berries, liquorice, spicy fruit, good body, making full-bodied wines high in alcohol; related to California's Zinfandel	*Primitivo di Manduria, Primitivo di Gioia, IGT Puglia, IGT Salento*

Rondinella (Veneto, NE Italy)

Robust grower, yields well, but a fairly bland variety, with less aroma and flavour than Corvina	*With Molinara, up to 30% of the blend in Valpolicella, Recioto and Amarone Valpolicellas, Bardolino*

Ruby Cabernet (USA; South Africa; Australia)

Crossing of Cabernet Sauvignon and Carignan; makes deep-coloured, soft wines with black fruit flavour; gives bulk to blended wines	*Originated in California but losing ground there; blended in cheaper wines in South Africa and Australia*

Sangiovese/Morellino/Prugnolo/Brunello (central Italy, especially Tuscany; Australia; Argentina; California)

Slightly pale colour, very dry, cherry and possibly farmyard aromas, cherry and plum flavours, high acidity, robust tannins, slightly bitter finish; good for ageing, can be austere in youth	*Part of the blend in Chianti, Carmignano, Vino Nobile di Montepulciano, Torgiano and the Supertuscan Tignanello; varietal elsewhere*

Syrah/Shiraz (Rhône; Languedoc-Roussillon; Australia; South Africa; California; Washington State; Chile; Argentina)

Deep colour, aromas of black fruits, becoming gamy and leathery with age; intense blackberry, raspberry, earthy, spicy, pepper, burnt rubber flavours, more black cherries and chocolate in Australia; tannic, rich, needs time to soften	*Hermitage, Crozes-Hermitage, St Joseph, Châteauneuf-du-Pape, vins de pays from Languedoc-Roussillon; on its own or blended with Cabernet Sauvignon in Australia; varietal in South Africa; varietal or blend in the US; varietal in Chile and Argentina*

Tannat (SW France; Uruguay)

Very dark, very tannic, raspberry aromas, needs time in bottle; can age well	*Part of the blend in Madiran and Cahors; varietal in Uruguay*

Tempranillo/Tinta Roriz/Aragonez (Spain; Portugal)

Deep colour, strawberry and tobacco aromas, low acidity and tannin, good for early drinking or ageing	*Blended or varietal in Rioja, Costers del Segre, Navarra, Penedès, Ribera del Duero, Somontano, Valdepeñas; Portuguese red wines; part of the blend in port*

Teroldego/Teroldego Rotaliano (Trentino, NE Italy)

Dark colour, smoky, spicy fragrance, black cherry fruit, lively acidity, moderate tannins and great structure	*Teroldego Rotaliano*

Touriga Nacional/Touriga (N Portugal; Australia; Priorat, N Spain)

Tiny berries and low yields; makes dark-coloured wine with blackberry and mulberry aromas; tannic but with fruit to match	*The most important variety for port, but also makes superb monovarietals; Douro, Dão; used to make 'port'-style wine in Australia; has even found its way to Priorat*

Trincadeira Preta/Tinta Amarela (Portugal, mainly Alentejo and Ribatejo regions)

Deep colour, strong tannin, good body, sturdy structure, plum and blackberry fruit, pepper and herbs	*Borba, Douro, Redondo, Reguengos, many IPR wines*

Zinfandel (California; South Africa; Chile; Australia; New Zealand)

Varies in style from very dark, alcoholic, bramble-flavoured reds to mass-produced sweetish 'blush' wines; can make excellent dry reds in the right hands	*Zinfandels in all shades from palest pink to deepest red in California; dry red wines elsewhere*

Glossary *Katherine Farmar*

AC: Appellation Contrôlée, a French wine classification system that certifies a wine as coming from a particular area.
The geographical area may be as large as a region (e.g. AC
Bordeaux) or as small as a vineyard (e.g. AC Montrachet).
Rules of inclusion differ from AC to AC, but they may
prescribe any or all of the following over and above the
wine's place of origin—grape varieties, density of planting, yield, alcohol level. AC wines are analysed and tasted
annually before being admitted to the AC.

accessible/approachable: tasting term meaning that the
wine's flavours and texture are familiar or friendly, easily
recognised and appreciated; ready to drink.

acidification: The addition of tartaric acid, citric acid or
malic acid during fermentation to raise the acidity levels
of wine made from very ripe grapes. A common practice
in hot climates. See also *chaptalisation*.

acidity: all wines contain acids of various kinds, including
malic, lactic, tartaric, citric (fixed acids) and acetic (the
acid found in vinegar). The fixed acids give wines a crispness to the taste and contribute to the ageing process.

aftertaste: the flavours left in the mouth after the wine is
swallowed or (in a tasting) spat out.

American oak: see *oak*.

Amarone: Amarone wines are made by fermenting grapes
that have been dried for a prolonged period in a special
drying house. This drying process increases the sugars,
and therefore the alcohol content of the wine, and results
in rich, concentrated, sometimes raisined, flavours.

aroma: a somewhat imprecise term, sometimes applied to
the entire *nose*, sometimes only to specific easily distin-
guishable smells.

austere: unforthcoming, sometimes harsh, but not necessarily in a derogatory sense; may indicate immaturity.

balance: a term of praise when applied to a wine, indicating
that the wine's *tannins*, *acidity* and alcohol blend well
and complement each other, without any individual element dominating.

barrel-fermented: Wine fermented in wooden barrels (see
oak). These can be new or old, large or small. Small new
barrels impart flavours to the wine; large old barrels do not
affect it.

barrique: an *oak* barrel with a capacity of 225 litres.

bâtonnage: 'Stirring' the wine in its barrel to mix through the *lees* to give extra flavour to the wine.

big wine: a full-bodied wine with an exceptionally rich flavour.

biodynamics: Method of viticulture that focuses on the health and balance of the soil, rejecting the use of chemical pesticides and artificial fertilisers. Lunar cycles determine whether the time is right for the development of leaves, roots, flowers or fruit. Compost plays an important role in promoting the health of the soil and vines are treated with preparations made from plants such as yarrow, dandelion, camomile and nettles.

black fruits: tasters' term used to refer to dark berry *fruits* such as blackberries, blackcurrants, black cherries, blueberries, etc.

blend: a wine made from more than one grape variety, as opposed to a *varietal*.

blind tasting: a tasting in which the identities of the wines are unknown to the taster until after tasting notes have been made and scores assigned. All competitive tastings are blind, as are all tastings for this guide.

body: the combination of *fruit* extract and alcoholic strength that gives the impression of weight in the mouth.

Botrytis: properly *Botrytis cinerea* (noble rot), a fungus that attacks grapes on vines. Depending on weather conditions and the ripeness of the grapes, it will either spoil the harvest completely (in which case it is known as grey rot) or concentrate the sugars in the *fruit* to produce a high-quality, sweet, very long-lived wine.

bottle: the standard bottle size is 75 centilitres. A magnum contains two bottles or 1.5 litres. See also *maturation*.

bouquet: strictly speaking, this refers only to those mature aromas that develop as the wine ages in the *bottle*, but it is often used to refer to all characteristics of the grape variety on the *nose*.

buttery: a rich, fat and delicious character found in some barrel-fermented or barrel-aged Chardonnay wines.

Cap Classique: South African sparkling wine.

carbonic maceration: see *maceration*.

chaptalisation: The addition of sugar or grape must before or during fermentation to raise the potential alcohol level of wine; the procedure does not make the wine sweet, since the sugar will have been converted to alcohol. Used in cooler-climate areas when grapes are not fully ripe. See also *acidification*.

chewy: tasting term referring to the texture imparted to wine by high tannins.

claret: an English term for a red Bordeaux wine. It comes from the French *clairet*, a wine between a dark rosé and a light red.

classic: word used by wine tasters to indicate that a wine is of high quality, showing the correct characteristics for its type and origin, and possesses great style.

closed: tasting term which is generally applied to wines which give out very little smell; sometimes referred to as being dumb. Common in very good but youthful wines.

complex: a wine with lots of different layers of flavours, often resulting from age or maturation.

corked: a wine is corked when it has been spoiled by contact with a contaminated cork. This is the most common cause of wine spoilage and can be identified by the wine's stale, woody, mouldy smell.

crémant: French ***méthode traditionnelle*** sparkling wine from areas other than Champagne. The term is also used for Luxembourg sparkling wines.

crianza: Term for Spanish wine that has been aged for two years with at least six in *oak* (red) or 12 months with at least six in *oak* (white).

cru: literally means 'growth', but on a French wine label refers to the status of the vineyard in which the vines were cultivated; the cru classification is in addition to the *AC*. The system is rather complicated and varies from region to region. In the Médoc region of Bordeaux, there are five *grand cru classé* divisions, beginning with *premier cru* (1st growth), *deuxième cru* (2nd growth), and so on down to the *cinquième cru* (5th growth). In St Émilion, there are three levels—*premier grand cru classé* at the top, then *grand cru classé* and *grand cru*. In Burgundy the top vineyards are *grands crus*; *premiers crus* come below them. *Grand cru* is also used in Alsace and Champagne to distinguish particularly good vineyard sites.

crust: *sediment* that forms in bottle-aged port.

cuvée: Batch of wine; 'bin' in the New World.

Deutscher Tafelwein: lowest level of wine classification in Germany.

DO: Denominación de Origen (designation of origin) is the main quality classification in Spain, similar to the *AC* category in France.

DOC: (1) Denominazione di Origine Controllata (controlled denomination of origin) is the main Italian quality category and is broadly similar to the French *AC*. (2) In Portugal Denominação de Origem Controlada (demarcated region) is the highest quality category. (3) Denominación de Origen Calificada (qualified designation of origin) (sometimes DOCa) is the highest quality category in Spain, currently awarded only to Rioja.

DOCG: Denominazione di Origine Controllata e Garantita (controlled and guaranteed denomination of origin) is the highest Italian quality category.

fermentation: the chemical process whereby the sugar in grapes is converted into alcohol.

fining: the process of adding substances such as egg whites, gelatine or clay to a wine, which causes microscopic suspended solids to fall to the bottom, so that after being racked (transferred to another barrel) or bottled, there will be a minimum of *sediment* or cloudiness in the wine.

finish: the last flavours a wine leaves in the mouth, especially after being swallowed or (in a tasting) spat out.

French oak: see *oak*.

fruit: the fruity flavour of a wine.

GI: Geographical Indication: term used in Australia to define the boundaries of recognised wine regions.

grand cru: see *cru*

gran reserva: Spanish wine that has been aged for five years with at least 18 months in *oak* (red) or four years with at least six in *oak* (white).

grapey: though all wine is made from grapes, this tasting term refers to a distinctive smell and flavour of grapes usually associated with wines made from the Muscat variety.

grip: word applied to describe red wines with firm tannins, which are felt on the teeth and gums.

hard: refers to wines with too much tannin and possibly also acidity; ageing with time usually has a mellowing effect.

IGT: Indicazione Geografica Tipica (indication of regional typicity) is an Italian quality category similar to the French *VdP*.

IPR: Indicação de Proveniência Regulamentada (indication of origin) (also known as *VQPRD*) is a Portuguese category similar to the French *VDQS* and the Italian *IGT*.

large oak: see *oak*.

lees: sediment that falls to the bottom of a vat of wine after *fermentation* and *maturation*. Most wines are transferred to another container when the lees form; others, especially Muscadet and sparkling wines, are aged on the lees (*sur lie*).

length: the length of time a wine's flavours linger in the mouth after sipping. Long length is one of the markers of a quality wine.

lively: fresh and full of vitality, bursting with fruit and flavour, often due to some carbon dioxide that may have been intentionally left in the wine on bottling.

maceration: the period of *fermentation* of a red wine during which the *must* has contact with grape skins. It is during this process that red wines derive their colour and *tannin*. Rosé wines undergo a very short maceration period of one or two days. Red wines intended to be drunk young sometimes undergo carbonic maceration, in which uncrushed grapes are fermented under a layer of carbon dioxide. This results in a wine light in colour and low in tannin, but high in *fruit* and *aroma*.

malolactic fermentation: the conversion of malic into lactic acids as part of *fermentation*. This is a normal process which reduces the *acidity* of a wine. All red wines undergo malolactic fermentation whereas some white wines may not.

maturation: the ageing process by which wines develop character and complexity. Maturation is good only up to a point, beyond which the wine will start to decline, but that point differs for each type of wine. A Beaujolais Nouveau will spend only a few months maturing, while tawny port may be a blend of wines aged in *oak* for as long as forty years. The larger the *bottle*, the slower the maturation—half-bottles of wine mature and decline more quickly than whole bottles.

méthode traditionnelle: The 'traditional' or 'Champagne' method of making sparkling wine. Still wine is given a small *dosage* of sugar and yeast and fermented for a second time in bottle. This makes better sparkling wine than using a tank for the second fermentation.

mousse: the bubbles in a sparkling wine. Ideally these should be very small and long lasting.

mouthfeel: specifically refers to the texture of a wine, as opposed to the *palate*, which also refers to the flavour.

must: unfermented grape juice.

noble rot: see *botrytis*.

nose: the combined smells of a wine's grape varieties' *aromas* and *bottle*-matured *bouquet*.

New World/Old World: originally used to distinguish wines made in Europe from those made in Australia, New Zealand and the Americas, but now often applied to wines of any geographical origin as an indication of style. 'New World' style wines are approachable, fruity, bold and have more obvious oak influence; 'Old World' style wines are complex, subtle and refined.

nv: non-vintage; a blend of wines harvested in different years.

oak: maturation in new oak adds flavours to wine—the smaller the barrel, the greater the effect. Old oak does not have this effect, but it does allow for controlled *oxidation*. Other oak treatments include adding oak chips or oak staves. See also *barrique*.

off-dry: containing some residual sugar, but dry enough to be drunk before or during a meal.

organic: there is no one accepted definition of 'organic' in relation to wine, as different certifying organisations have different standards. It certainly involves using less chemicals and herbicides in the vineyard as well as the use of alternative and natural measures to control weeds and pests. Full organic viticulture forbids the use of any industrially made compounds.

oxidation: a chemical reaction that takes place when wine is exposed to air. Barrel *maturation* allows for slow, controlled oxidation, improving the flavour of the wine. However, if this happens too fast or if the process is allowed to go too far, it transforms the alcohol into acetic acid. Wine that is too oxidised tastes unpleasant and may look brown and smell of vinegar.

palate: the flavour and texture of the wine in the mouth; see also *mouthfeel*.

QbA: Qualitätswein bestimmter Anbaugebiete (quality wine from a specified region) is the second-highest quality category in Germany.

QmP: Qualitätswein mit Prädikat (quality wine with special attributes) is the highest classification for German wines. The classifications, which depend on the sugar levels in the grapes, are Kabinett, Spätlese, Auslese, Beerenauslese, Trockenbeerenauslese and Eiswein.

Reserve: in Italy, Portugal, Spain and Bulgaria, a wine labelled 'Riserva' or 'Reserva' must by law be of very high quality and, in the case of Italy and Spain, have undergone a certain minimum ageing, with at least some of it in *oak* barrels. Anywhere else, the word 'Reserve' or 'Réserve' just means that the winemakers think it is one of their best.

Ripassa/Ripasso: a wine made by re-fermenting Valpolicalla wine on the skins of grapes used to make Amarone wines. This takes place in the spring following the vintage, and adds extra richness and alcohol to the wine.

secondary fermentation: Process of fermenting wine for a second time with yeast and sugar to make a sparkling wine.

sediment: solid debris that falls to the bottom of a wine barrel or, in the case of an unfiltered wine, the *bottle*. Wines undergo *fining* or filtration to reduce the amount of sediment left after bottling.

small oak: see *oak*.

soft: tasting term generally applicable to red wines with very low or not noticeable tannins.

stainless steel vats: vessels used in *fermentation*. The use of stainless steel vats, rather than wood or concrete, makes it easier to control the wine's fermentation temperature.

steely: tasting term used to describe white wines with lots of *acidity* and very cool refreshing flavours; may be attributed in some cases to stainless steel fermentation or to a minerally character derived from the soil.

Stelvin: a form of screwcap specifically designed for bottled wine. An increasing number of producers in Australia and New Zealand have adopted these with the aim of keeping their wines as fresh and clean as possible and avoiding the possibility of the wines becoming *corked*.

structure: the sum of the component parts that shape a wine, including *fruit*, *alcohol* and *acidity*, and, in reds, *tannin*.

Supertuscan: refers to a wine made in Tuscany, from non-traditional grape varieties, and often by more modern methods. Although labelled with the inferior designation IGT, or Vino da Tavola, they are often of very high quality, and can be very expensive.

supple: a texture which is easier to sense than to define; generally applied to wines with generous appealing fruit and not too much tannin.

sur lie: see *lees*.

tannin: a chemical substance found in grape skins and hence in red wines but not whites. The ability of a red wine to improve as it matures depends very much on its tannins, but a wine that is too tannic will taste dry and hard; red wines intended to be drunk young will sometimes be put through a process called carbonic *maceration*, which minimises tannin. Tannins can also be derived from *oak*, stalks and pips. Tannin from pips is the harshest of all.

terroir: the complete growing environment of soil, aspect, altitude, climate and any other factor that may affect the vine.

vanilla: often used to describe the *nose* and sometimes the *palate* of an *oak*-aged wine, especially a Rioja.

varietal: a wine made entirely, or almost entirely, from a single grape variety, as opposed to a *blend*.

VCIG: Vino de Calidad con Indicación Geográfica: new Spanish category equivalent to the French *VDQS*.

VdlT: Vino de la Tierra (wine of the land) is a Spanish classification for country wines similar to the *VdP* category in France.

VdM: (1) Vino de Mesa (table wine) is the lowest quality category in Spain. Wines are basic and are often a blend of wines from different regions. This category is also used by progressive producers to make wines that don't conform to *DO* rules. (2) Vinho de Mesa (table wine) is the lowest quality category in Portugal.

VdP: Vin de Pays (country wine) is the third-highest quality classification of French wine.

VDQS: Vin Délimité de Qualité Supérieure (delimited wine of superior quality) is the second-highest classification for French wines, just below *AC*.

VdT: (1) Vin de Table (table wine) is the lowest quality category in France. No region or vintage may be stated on the label and the wine is likely to be of basic quality. (2) Vino da Tavola (table wine) is the basic table wine classification in Italy, but is also used by makers of fine wines that do not conform to *DOC* regulations.

vegetal: reminiscent of vegetative matter or a vegetable patch.

vintage: the year the grapes were harvested. Wines differ from year to year, depending on weather conditions during the vine's growing seasons. Champagnes and sparkling wines, unlike still reds and whites, are more often than not made from *blends* of grapes harvested in different years ('non-vintage'). A vintage Champagne—one made from grapes harvested in a single season—is rare and expensive.

VQPRD: see *IPR*.

VR: Vinho Regional (regional wine) is the Portuguese equivalent of French *VdP*.

WO: Wine of Origin: South African appellation classification. WO wines must be 100% from the designated region.

yeasty: bread or bakery aromas often evident in barrel fermented white wines but especially in Champagnes and sparkling wines where yeasts stay in contact with the wine after fermentation.

Distributors of listed wines

Aldi Stores (Ireland Ltd)
- Newbridge Road, Naas, Co. Kildare

Allied Drinks
- JFK Road, J. F. Kennedy Industrial Estate, Naas Road, Dublin 12
  Tel (01) 450 9777 Fax (01) 450 9699
  Email info@allieddrinks.ie

Amp&rsand Wines
- Naas Road, Clondalkin, Dublin 22
  Tel (01) 413 0100 Fax (01) 413 0123
  Email tdl@tdl.ie

Approach Trade Wine Merchants
- Mill River Business Park, Carrick-on-Suir, Co. Tipperary
  Tel (051) 640 164 Fax (051) 641 580
  Email info@approachwines.com

Bacchus Wine & Spirit Merchants
- 10 Western Parkway Business Park, Lr Ballymount Road, Dublin 12
  Tel (01) 294 1466 Fax (01) 295 7375
  Email Dublin mail@bacchus.ie Cork bacchuswines@eircom.net

Baily Wines
- Baily Court Hotel, Main Street, Howth, Co. Dublin
  Tel (01) 832 2394 Fax (01) 832 3730
  Email info@bailywines.com

Barry Fitzwilliam Maxxium
- Ballycurreen Industrial Estate, Airport Road, Cork
  Tel (021) 432 0900 Fax (021) 432 0910
  Email info@bfmws.ie
- 50 Dartmouth Square, Dublin 6
  Tel (01) 667 1755 Fax (01) 660 0479

Berry Bros & Rudd
- Harry Street, Dublin 2
  Tel (01) 677 3444 Fax (01) 677 3440

Bowes & Co. Wines
- 3 Upper Ely Place, Dublin 2
  Tel (01) 642 5609 Fax (01) 642 5748
  Email info@boweswines.com

Cassidy Wines
- Unit 18, Magna Drive, City West Business Campus, Dublin 24
  Tel (01) 466 8900 Fax (01) 466 8932
  Email contact@cassidywines.com

Celtic Whiskey Shop
- Dawson Street, Dublin 2
  Tel (01) 575 9744 Fax (01) 675 9768
  Email ally@celticwhiskeyshop.com

Champers
■ 4 The Oaks, Castletown, Celbridge, Co. Kildare
  Tel (01) 627 1373 Fax (01) 627 1373
  Email contact@champers.ie

Classic Drinks
■ GHS Classic Drinks, Unit 5, OC Commercial Park, Little Island,
  Cork
  Tel (021) 451 Fax (021) 435 5504
  Email sales@classicdrinks.ie

Comans Wines
■ Belgard Road, Tallaght, Dublin 24
  Tel (01) 451 9146 Fax (01) 451 9772
  Email sales@comans.ie

Dillons *see* **Edward Dillon & Co.**

Dunnes Stores
■ Head Office, Beaux Lane House, Mercer Street Lower, Dublin 2
  Tel (01) 475 1111 Fax (01) 611 2932

Edward Dillon & Co.
■ 25 Mountjoy Sq. East, Dublin 1
  Tel (01) 819 3300 Fax (01) 819 3390

Epicurean Fine Food & Wine
■ 30 Glen Drive, The Park, Cabinteely, Dublin 18
  Tel 086 837 1857 (01) 235 1748

Febvre & Co.
■ Highfield House, Burton Hall Road, Sandyford Industrial Estate,
  Dublin 18
  Tel (01) 216 1400 Fax (01) 295 9036
  Email info@febvre.ie

Findlater Grants
■ Kilcarberry Park, Nangor Road, Clondalkin, Dublin 22
  Tel (01) 630 4100 Fax (01) 630 4123
  Email customercare@candcgroup.ie

Galvins Wines & Spirits
■ Bessboro Road, Blackrock, Cork
  Tel (021) 431 6098 Fax (021) 431 4209
  Email sales@galvinswines.com

Gilbeys United Beverages
■ Nangor House, Nangor Road, Dublin 12
  Tel (01) 429 2200 Fax (01) 429 2230

Gleeson Group
■ 15 Cherry Orchard Estate, Ballyfermot, Dublin 10
  Tel (01) 623 9158 Fax (01) 623 9558
  Email michaelmaher@gleesongroup.ie

Grace Campbell of Dublin
■ 2 Grange Manor Avenue, Rathfarnham, Dublin 18
  Tel (01) 494 1203 Fax (01) 494 1203
  Email: kevinohara@eircom.net

Greenhills Wines & Spirits
- c/o Primeline Logistics, Rath Business Park, Ashbourne, Co. Meath
  Tel (01) 842 2188 Fax (01) 835 8298
  Email gomeara@bwg.ie

Inis Wines
- Inis Duirn, Lackenagh, Burtonport, Co Donegal
  Tel (074) 954 2940 Fax (074) 954 2941
  Email iniswines@eircom.net

Irish Distillers
- Bow Street Distillery, Smithfield, Dublin 7
  Tel (01) 872 5566 Fax (01 872 3109
  Email info@idl.ie, sales@idl.ie

James Nicholson Wine Merchant
- 27 Killyleagh Street, Crossgar, Co. Down BT30 9DQ
  Tel (048 44) 830 091 Fax (048 44) 830 028
  Email info@jnwine.com

J. Donohoe Beverages Ltd
- Templeshannon, Enniscorthy, Co. Wexford
  Tel (053 92) 42400 Fax (053 92) 33186
  Email drinks@jdonohoe.com

Karwig Wines
- Kilnagleary, Carrigaline, Co. Cork
  Tel (021) 437 2864 Fax (021) 437 4159
  Email info@karwigwines.ie

Kelly & Co.
- Unit 5, Park West Industrial Estate, Nangor Road, Dublin 12
  Tel (01) 623 4001 Fax (01) 623 4155
  Email info@kellywines.com

Koala Wines
- 25 Seatown, Dundalk, Co. Louth
  Tel (048) 417 52804 Fax (048) 417 52943
  Email rhode@koalawines.com

Le Caveau
- Market Yard, Kilkenny
  Tel (056) 775 2166 Fax (056) 775 2101
  Email lecaveau@eircom.net

Liberty Wines
- Unit D18, The Food Market, New Covent Garden,
  London SW8 5LL
  Tel 087 796 6222 Tel and Fax (01) 473 5173
  Email peter.roycroft@libertywine.co.uk

Louis Albrouze
- 127 Upper Leeson Street, Dublin 2
  Tel (01) 667 4455 Fax (01) 667 4454
  Email leesonstreet@louisalbrouze.com

Marks & Spencer
- 24-9 Mary Street, Dublin 1
  Tel (01) 872 8833 Fax (01) 872 8995

Mary Pawle Wines
- Gortamullen, Kenmare, Co. Kerry
  Tel (064) 41443 Fax (064) 41443
  Email info@marypawlewines.com

McCambridges Galway
- Ballybane Industrial Estate, Galway
  Tel (091) 750 134 Fax (091) 561 802
  Email wholesale@mccambridges.co

Mitchell & Son Wine Merchants
- 21 Kildare Street, Dublin 2
  Tel (01) 676 0766 Fax (01) 661 1509
  Email kildarestreet@mitchellandson.com
- 54 Glasthule Road, Sandycove, Co Dublin
  Tel (01) 230 2301 Fax (01) 230 2305

Molloys Group
- Head Office, Block 2 Village Green, Tallaght, Dublin 24
  Tel (01) 451 5544 Fax (01) 451 5658
  Email mainreception@molloys.com

Musgraves
- Tramore Road, Cork
  Tel (021) 480 3000 Fax (021) 431 3621
  Email msvc@musgrave.ie

Nectar Wines Ltd
- Unit 1, 3 Sandyford Village, Dublin 18
  Tel (01) 294 4067 Fax (01) 294 4068
  Email sales@nectarwines.com

Newgate Wines
- Unit 35B, Boyne Business Park, Greenhills Road, Drogheda,
  Co. Louth
  Tel (041) 984 3532 Fax (041) 984 7238
  Email newgate@indigo.ie

New Zealand Boutique Wines
- 120 Allum Street, Kohimarama, Auckland, New Zealand
  joyceaustin@xtra.co.nz

Nicholson's *see* James Nicholson

O'Briens Wine Offlicence
- Unit 33, Spruce Avenue, Stillorgan Industrial Park, Co. Dublin
  Tel (01) 269 3139 Fax (01) 269 7480
  Email info@obriensgroup.ie

Oddbins
- 6B West End Retail Park, Blanchardstown, Dublin 15
  Tel 1800 509 727 Fax (01) 824 3506
  Email oddbinsdirectireland@oddbinsmail.com

Papillon Wines
- 15 Harcourt Street, Dublin 2
  Tel (01) 479 4314 Fax (01) 479 4396

Probus Wines
- Main Street, Oughterard, Co. Galway
  Tel (091) 552 084 Fax (091) 552 066
  Email probuswines@eircom.net

PubVia
- 31 Wellington House, Wellington Road, Dublin 4
  Tel/Fax (01) 660 9968
  Email pubvia@yahoo.com
  Tel 086 842 8201 Fax (01) 660 9968

River Wines
- Jesmond, 140 Blackrock Road, Cork
  Tel 087 207 5970 Tel and Fax (021) 429 3393

Rushdale Wines
- 7 Woodlands, Cappagh, Kinsale, Co. Cork
  Tel 086 104 9879 (021) 477 4857
  Email info@rushdalewine.ie

Searsons Wine Merchants
- Monkstown Crescent, Blackrock, Co. Dublin
  Tel (01) 280 0405 Fax (01) 280 4771
  Email sales@searsons.com

Select Wines from Italy
- Waverly House, Church Road, Greystones, Co. Wicklow
  Tel (01) 201 7669 Fax (01) 201 7670
  Email mcglynn@select.ie

Smith and Whelan Wines Ltd
- Ballycotton, Co. Cork
  Tel 087 261 8754/086 353 1250 Fax (021) 465 2021

Straffan Wines
- Turnings, Straffan, Co. Kildare
  Tel and Fax (01) 627 6287
  Email info@straffanwines.ie

Taserra Wine Merchants
- 17 Rathfarnham Road, Terenure, Dublin 6W
  Tel (01) 490 4047 Fax (01) 490 4052
  Email wine@iol.ie

Tesco
- Gresham House, Dun Laoghaire, Co. Dublin
  Tel (01) 280 8441 Fax (01) 280 0136

Tindal Wine Merchants
- Unit B4 Centrepoint, Rosemount Business Park, Ballycoolin,
  Blanchardstown, Dublin 11
  Tel (01) 885 3240 Fax (01) 885 3242
  Email sales@tindalwine.com

Tyrrell & Co.
- Rathernan, Kilmeague, Naas, Co. Kildare
  Tel (045) 870 882 Fax (045) 890 503
  Email sales@tyrrellandcompany.com

Vendemia Wines
- Unit 24, Hebron Road Industrial Estate, Kilkenny
  Tel (056) 777 0225 Fax (056) 778 6989
  Email info@vendemiawines.com

Vineyard (Galway) Ltd
- Unit 1B Oldenway Industrial Estate, Ballybane, Galway
  Teland Fax (091) 771707
  Email frankk@iol.ie

Vinitalia Ireland Ltd
- 82 Belgrove Park, Mount Prospect Lawns, Clontarf, Dublin 3
  Tel 087 634 4784 Fax (01) 853 5246
  Email vinitalia@vinitaliaireland.com

Wicklow Wine Co.
- Main Street, Wicklow
  Tel (0404) 66767 Fax (0404) 66769
  Email wicklowwineco@eircom.net

WineKnows
- 10 Castle Yard, St Patrick's Road, Dalkey, Co. Dublin
  Tel (01) 284 9624 Fax (01) 235 1690
  Email info@wineknows.com

WineOnline
- Unit 4B Santry Hall Industrial Estate, Santry, Dublin 9
  Tel (01) 886 7732 Fax (01) 886 7747

Wines Direct
- Ashe Road, Mullingar, Co. Westmeath
  Tel 1890 579 579 Fax (044) 40015
  Email sales@winesdirect.ie

Wine Obsessed
- 15 John Street, Kilkenny
  Tel (056) 772 2034 Fax (056) 772 2466

Wine Select Ireland
- 5 Bramley Heath, Castleknock, Dublin 15
  Tel (01) 820 6407 087 261 8681
  Email chrisharrison@Ireland.com

Woodford Bourne
- 79 Broomhill Road, Tallaght, Dublin 24
  Tel (01) 404 7300 Fax (01) 404 7311
  Email wine@woodfordbourne.com

Index of advertisers

Index of wines

Wines of the year are indicated in **bold** *type.*